Dedication

To those who are waiting at home:

This book is dedicated to everyone who is waiting, or has waited, for someone to be released from prison.

I am full of admiration, appreciation and respect for you. The support and strength of spouses, children, parents, family and friends is what keeps people in prison going through the darkest of days.

Apart from the 70 prisoners that are serving all of their natural life, the other 82,000+ will one day become eligible for release on licence.

Prisons must therefore be considered as part of our communities.

The people they house are just passing through.

Being in prison is a temporary situation.

For most prisoners, returning to the loving arms of their family is the light at the end of the tunnel.

Sometimes the light is very distant and the tunnel is dark, dismal and dirty, but by looking ahead and focusing on the future, prisoners can keep moving forwards and eventually get through it.

Personally, I would like to take this opportunity to express my appreciation, love and affection for my wife Wendy.

Wendy, the road has been rocky these last few years but your determination to keep our family united has inspired me (and others).

When I met you on my 22nd birthday, I did not know that 25 years later we would still feel as strongly for each other as we did then. I look forward to each day of the next 25 years. You are my dream come true, my inspiration and my hope.

Phil x

Contents

Foreword by Faith Spear FRSA..7

Supporting Children Heard and Seen Charity (For families affected by imprisonment))..11

Introduction 13

Chapter 1 - The People in Prison 16

    Quotes - If I hadn't come to prison… 50

Chapter 2 - The Potential for Prison to be a Catalyst of Change..................55

    Quotes - The things that would help me to never come back to prison....99

Chapter 3 - The Vital Role of Pastoral Care and Faith Provision in Prison 105

    Quotes - I could have coped better with My Prison Sentence if..............115

Chapter 4 - Mind-set Milestones; The 5 R's of Change..............................119

Chapter 5 - WHY I went to PRISON (By 150 people who are determined never to return) 125

    Quotes - The BEST ADVICE I can give to someone coming to prison ..201

Chapter 6 - Institutionalisation and Recovery 205

    Recovering from the Detrimental Effects of Closed Conditions and Improving Wellbeing 208

GLOSSARY 239

Quotes, Memory-aids and Acronyms 257

    Books by the Author 268

    About the Author...273

97% of offenders say that they don't want to re-offend.
(Source: Making prisons work: skills for rehabilitation - MOJ)

The People in Prison and their Potential
Foreword

My general take on prisons are that they are warehouses for the vulnerable. We pack them in and stack them high and overcrowding is prevalent.

Punishment has become a mental torture. Lack of purposeful activity has stripped many of any hope for the future. Short sightedness on behalf of the Government is bringing the whole prison estate to its knees. Recent years has seen Benchmarking, loss of experienced staff, under-investment, resulting in volatile prisons where safety and security for staff and inmates alike is compromised. It is like a ticking time bomb.

Incidents in prisons are now almost commonplace, but are lessons being learnt?

Do we really believe the Government when they say that the loss of liberty is the punishment?

There needs to be more programmes in prison that are designed to provide a guide for re-integration alongside elements for rehabilitation.

Rehabilitation can be described as restoring, rebuilding, or repairing and in the context of those that have spent time in prison a means of re-joining society and hopefully being accepted, but that is not always the case.

I often question why would people who have been released from prison want to be integrated back into a society that thinks it's okay for them to be locked up for 23 hours a day, with little nutritious food, lack of education, virtually no purposeful activity, squalid living conditions, unsafe, rife with drugs and violence, where staff struggle to maintain order, where corruption, suicides, self-harm and unrest are all increasing, where budgets are cut and staff numbers reduced.

It is society that puts people in prison and expects them to reintegrate after their sentence and not reoffend. But recidivism is high because often the root cause of offending is not addressed.

Whatever happens in society is transferred to prisons, so if there is a problem with drugs on the outside there will certainly be a drug problem in prison. High walls, barbed wire and security is no real barrier. Bullying through debt is rife and so is corruption.

You see, prisons create homeless individuals; poverty and mental health issues and they breed criminality.

Sentencing removes many from society and places them in Prison.

But what happens when they are released back?

With their belongings in a bag and a small grant off they go back to the society that removed them in the first place.

Due to the nature of the crime or the often-complex background many face the prospect of no real home and no job.

I speak at every opportunity of my frustration that many skills acquired in prison are seemingly just worthless on release. The skills need to match the work available. However, I have seen some excellent examples of tutors training those in prison and encouraging them to reach standards that they never thought possible. I have read letters and cards sent to these tutors in thanks for believing in them and helping to achieve qualifications that have led to decent jobs on release.

Unfortunately, this does not happen enough.

What about those with existing skills that have had to lay dormant whilst they serve their sentence?

How can they re-join the workplace?

Should they be able to go back into their old job or field?

For some picking up where they left off is not an option due to the nature of the crime, family circumstances or health.

But if we build a barrier to those who pose no threat to society which prevents them from re-joining their work sector then are we continuing to punish?

I find I continue to have many questions when looking at the Criminal Justice System

Is there a better way?

Reading a draft manuscript of 'The People in Prison and Their Potential', I remember telling Phil that it is as though you have read what is in my head. We appear to be on the same wavelength here.

Those with convictions do have potential, deserve to be given opportunities and can be valuable members of society. Many are willing to change but are we willing to accept them?

Faith Spear FRSA

Writer. Criminologist. Commentator on Prisons.

The Criminal Justice Blog: www.faithspear.wordpress.com

Twitter: @fmspear

Prisons that help and support

Criminals that change for good

Society that forgives and accepts

With Thanks from Children Heard and Seen

In July 2014, I set up the charity 'Children Heard and Seen' to support children and families impacted by parental imprisonment. This was a result of my concern that a significant number of children with a parent on prison were entering the criminal justice system due to a lack of adequate support.

Children Heard and Seen is the only UK charity dedicated to supporting this isolated and stigmatised group of young people, providing support to 262 children this year alone. We strive to support their needs, listen to their concerns and ensure that their voices are heard. We offer family support work, 1-1 support, a volunteer mentor for 12 months, Drawing and Talking therapy sessions in school, music projects and holiday activities. In 2019, Children Heard and Seen were delighted to be awarded the Queen's Award for Voluntary Service.

We are very grateful to all who have supported this book and its overall ethos of supporting prisoners and families humanely, and giving due respect to rehabilitation and the rebuilding of social bonds. Too often, when a parent is punished with a prison sentence, a child suffers greatly for a crime of which they are wholly innocent. The loss of a parent to a prison sentence has the potential to destabilise all corners of a child's life, as the severing of parental bonds detrimentally impacts the young person's mental and physical wellbeing.

Children with a parent in prison are at a much greater risk of experiencing mental health problems, often manifesting as depression, anxiety, insomnia, and/or eating disorders. Negative school experiences such as bullying, persistent truanting, and a failure to achieve in educational settings are also common in this demographic, alongside an increased likelihood of committing criminal offences. Our one to one mentoring support seeks to ensure that a child is able to access resources, and develop resilience, coping strategies and life skills to help them make sense of their situation. This provides them with the tools to make positive life choices and maximise their potential, breaking the cycle of intergenerational offending.

This year, the COVID–19 pandemic has significantly increased the hardships faced by children with a parent in prison. Lack of contact with a parent(s) and the damaging impact this has on the child/parent bond cannot be underestimated.

In a recent online consultation with the children and families that we work with, all respondents commented on increasing manifestations of stress, anxiety and worry. Those caring for children described them as having *"lost their sparkle"*, or *"being withdrawn and emotional"*.

When lockdown began, we moved our support online, providing a range of new and modified services, including online support and activity groups, alongside one - one online sessions, where we find creative ways to explore complex and difficult feelings with children, allowing them to discuss these in a confidential and secure environment with an experienced professional, away from the potential stress of a group setting.

We'd like to thank Phil Martin for his generosity in donating a portion of the proceeds of this book to Children Heard and Seen to allow us to support even more children suffering with a parent in prison during this difficult time.

We are always overwhelmed by the amount of support and encouragement given to us by families that we support and by members of the public at large. If you would like to further support the work we do with children and families impacted by parental imprisonment, please visit our website and find out how you can get involved. Alternatively, feel free to email us at info@childrenheardandseen.co.uk call us on 07557339258, or send us a direct message to our Facebook page.

Sarah Burrows

Director and Founder

Children Heard and Seen

Registered Charity no: 1157879

Website: www.childrenheardandseen.co.uk

Introduction

Have you ever felt like your whole life was over?

I felt like this when I was sent to prison for business offences.

I went into shock; I curled into a ball in the corner of a dirty room in the downstairs of the court. I cried like an infant, and didn't stop for hours. I continued on and off for days.

The thought that I had failed so badly, that I warranted being taken away from my wife and children who had been my life.

Is your whole life actually over though?

Perhaps we write ourselves off a bit too quickly. Even if you feel that you have no value. You have so much left to give, you have so much potential…

If you went mountaineering and got lost, *mountain rescue* would pull out all the stops to try and find you. They would spend £1.6m and not think it too much. Helicopters, dog teams, volunteers, publicity, the works. They wouldn't say "oh hold up, stop, and let's just check if this person has been to prison before".

If you were washed out to sea, the lifeboats and sea rescue teams would do whatever it takes to locate and rescue you. They wouldn't ask "does this person have a criminal record?" They wouldn't care, it would be irrelevant, they want to save your life, BECAUSE YOUR LIFE HAS A VALUE.

If you wanted to donate blood to save someone's life, the donor team do not say "Quick! Check google first and find out whether this donor has any past misdemeanours or mistakes, we don't want criminal blood!"

If you were on the organ waiting list for a heart, your life would be given the same value as anyone else's. This was evidenced to me in open conditions when a life sentenced prisoner received the ultimate gift, a heart transplant.

Your life has a value and you still have more to give.

We do not change TV channel if Stephen Fry comes on thinking "He is an ex-offender, I better not listen to him or look at him in case crime is contagious and I somehow I get infected!" Of course not, we admire and respect the man for his positive qualities of humour, humanity and leadership.

We do not boycott 'Reggae Reggae' sauce because Levi Roots the creator was once a criminal who spent plenty of time in prison. Of course not, we pick up the sauce, enjoy the taste and hum his theme tune.

You have no idea of the good that you can still bring to the world - you still have more to give.

We all make mistakes.

As I type this, there are delete and back space buttons on the keyboard. I probably hit delete almost as much as I write. Why would they be there if people didn't make mistakes, or if they didn't do the wrong thing by accident?

Even the best people do not make all the right decisions.

Recently, I was helping my daughter with her homework and the pencil had an eraser on the end of it. We rubbed out mistakes and started again. If people didn't make mistakes there wouldn't be erasers on the ends of pencils.

What matters is the ability to leave our mistakes in the past to move forwards.

A fresh start, from today - Determined not to make the same mistakes again, to understand where we went wrong, why we did what we did, to learn from it and help others not to do the same.

I was helped during my prison sentence by a Supervising Officer called Dave Waddleton. Dave told me that he "helps people change their lives" and I saw him on the wings doing exactly that. He helped me to get a prison job in the segregation unit of HMP Woodhill, a trusted position which I later discovered, involved working in difficult and distressing situations.

Many residents who were located in the Seg (aka Care and Separation Unit) suffered mental illness and required a lot of understanding as well as practical help. I witnessed self-harm and mutilation beyond what I could have imagined. There were occasions where my brain could not believe my eyes and my heart would break for those people.

I began to question "why?" and talked to the people in the seg about their lives; most were passing through but some stayed longer term. Dave and I would often talk about the pathways that led people to prison. This was an A Cat with a remand facility (Woodhill is now a B Cat), so a wide range of people were imprisoned there.

I met some of the most extreme 1% of prisoners that made the news, that would be described as "evil" but it is a fallacy that our prisons house the very worst people in society. In fact, our prisons are full of Damaged, Disadvantaged & Disillusioned people, some of the most vulnerable.

I decided that rather than counting the days, I would make the days count.

It is almost impossible to imagine getting to the end of a prison sentence like this, but with the right support, you do, a day at a time.

I focused on fighting with myself constantly to maintain my positive attitude and on helping and supporting other people. I took myself out of my prison cell and got to know everyone, I refused to be scared to talk to anyone & my light-hearted easy-going manner broke down barriers.

Starting with the simple word "hi" I achieved my goal of helping a thousand people in prison through personal mentoring and practical help around the areas of sentence progression, restoring relationships, personal and career development and future life planning.

As I got to know the people in prison & understand their backgrounds and stories, I realised that more people in society & in our justice system NEED to hear these stories too. It was also apparent that with the right help & support people would be able to turn their lives around.

Getting through a prison sentence is hard for anyone, as well as for those left at home. My wife developed anorexia caused by our separation, the knock-on effects of this anxiety-based illness are long term & severe. My middle daughter, Joy, struggled to cope with me being away.

I talk about the effects of imprisonment a lot because I want people to know that I am a real person, who loves and is loved. Someone who messed up in a big way, paid a big price and is rebuilding his life. I am back in the loving arms of my family and every day is a blessing, but.... I can't help thinking about the people in prison and how tough it really is. I am a resilient person who grew up in a challenging environment, but it nearly broke me - it was my biggest test.

During Covid19 lockdown in 2020 #PrisonersArePeople #PrisonersPeopleToo were common tags on twitter; they were reminders that the people in prison deserve consideration as human beings and that they should be treated humanely.

Considering historically low staffing levels and 23+hr bang-up, both prisoners & prison officers need our compassion, understanding and support more than ever. There are going to be some very hurt and damaged people after this lockdown, across the UK inside & out.

"This book proves that prisons (and the people therein) can create positive change and be a force for good." AV, Prison Officer, Unlocked Graduate

Thank you for taking the time to read this book. I welcome any comments or questions; please let me know if I can help you in anyway.

Phil Martin

PS: This book contains numerous quotes and statements; in order to differentiate my opinions and quotes from those of other contributors, I include the initials 'PM' after mine.

Chapter 1 - The People in Prison

"Every shift shows me people repeatedly failed by society. I would have more belief in the system if we caught people when they fell and HELPED THEM GET BACK UP AGAIN." GR Prison Custodial Manager - 18 years' service

The People in Prison

Who are the people that comprise the prison population?

The media asserts that people in prison are "lags" or "cons", or they use their crime as a label, he's a "fraudster" or a "murderer".

These labels are not entirely accurate because they lead to stereotyping, closed mindedness and disinterest. Labels perpetuate the idea that the people in prison are less than human - they dehumanise.

The people in prison are imagined to be a sub-species, distinct from the normal population. The media would have us believe that they should all be locked away, out of sight and out of mind, lest they cause society even more harm.

The truth is somewhat harder to swallow - the people in prison are primarily 'normal' people; in the main they are not dissimilar to the people you interact with every day, they are people, just like me and you.

75% of people, who come to prison for the first time, are employed.
(Source: MOJ the impact of employment on re-offending)

Considering the jobs that people had before they came to prison is just one way that we can understand how apparently 'normal' most of their lives were. Here are 100 job roles that were held by people who I interviewed and which they were performing immediately before they came to prison:

Accountant, Accountant's assistant, Advertising executive, Advertising installation person, Advertising salesperson, Aerospace engineer, Air-con installation draftsman, Aircraft engineer (trainee), Alloy wheel restorer, Architect, Asbestos removal supervisor, Bank manager, Barber, Barista, Barrister (Human rights), Bartender, Bookkeeper, Bicycle mechanic, Biohazard waste disposal, General builder, Builder's mate/ Contractor's assistant, Bus driver, Butcher, Cable puller, Cable jointer's mate, Call centre team-leader, Car delivery manager, Carpenter, Carpet fitter and floor layer, Car sales person, Car valet, Car wash manager, Catering manager, Charity fundraiser, Chauffeur (VIP), Chimney sweep, Classroom assistant, Cleaning supervisor, Coach driver (school), Coach driver (tours), Commodities dealer, Company Director (various), Core driller, Customer service assistant, Delivery driver, Demolition engineer, Dental Hygienist, Detainee custody officer, Document shredder, Dog handler, Domestic goods exporter, Door supervisor, Dry cleaner, Ductwork engineer, Drainage worker, Dry lining specialist, Electrician, Estate agent, Events promoter, Fencing contractor, Financial director, Fire and flood emergency services, Fire-proofing specialist, Fitness instructor,

Forklift truck driver, Fresh produce manager, Garage owner, Golf club grounds man, Ground worker, Hairdresser (salon), Hairdresser (mobile), Highways maintenance and street-works operative (Ganger man), Hod carrier, Hotel receptionist, House clearance and general dealer, Household removals, HR Manager, Ice cream salesperson, Insulation installer, Interior designer, IT network support technician, IT systems coordinator, IT systems support team leader, IT technician, General labourer, Skilled labourer, Hard landscaper, Landscape gardener, Letting Agent, Life guard, Loft conversion specialist, Lorry driver (HGV1 articulated), Magazine circulation manager, Maintenance manager, Marketing manager, Trainee vehicle mechanic, Vehicle body work repairer, Vehicle mechanic, Ordained minister, Mobile food operator, Mobile phone technician, Multimedia installation specialist, NHS theatre assistant, NHS donor carer, Online retail, Online sales support manager, Painter and decorator, Paint sprayer, Pallet yard workman, Paneller, Panel maker, PC repairer, Personal trainer, Personnel coordinator, Plant operator, Plasterer, Apprentice plumber, Plumbing and Heating Engineer, Porter manager, Post-person, Postal worker, Printer, Product distributor, Production manager, Property developer, Property development consultant, Property maintenance operative, Pub owner and landlord, Quantity surveyor, Records management officer, Recruitment consultant, Renderer, Retail salesperson, Road haulier (proprietary business), Roofer, Sales director, Sales and marketing manager, Sales representative (door-to-door), Sales representative (in-homes), Sales representative (regional), Scrap metal merchant, Scuba diving instructor, Security and courier driver, Security manager, Security Officer (In Store), Shop Fitter, Shop Manager, Superstore Manager, Skip Yard foreman, British Army infantryman soldier, British Army avionics engineer soldier, Sound technician and music engineer, Steel fitter, Tailor, Taxi driver (Hackney carriage), Taxi driver (private hire), Teacher, Telesales person, Telephone engineer, Tennis coach, Tiler, Tool hire manager, Tool hire repairer, Track worker, Transport manager, Tree surgeon, Tyre fitter, Upholsterer, Vehicle inspector and tester, Volunteer co-ordinator, Waiter and kitchen porter, Warehouse operative, Warehouse supervisor, Waste management operative (dustman), Waste Management Operative (refuse site), Waste management operator (Proprietary business), Website developer, Welder, Window cleaner, Window installer, Window manufacturer, Youth worker.

This long and varied list of job titles serves to highlight the capacity which the people in prison had to maintain stable everyday employment.

It is important to mention that very few crimes were linked to employment; almost all were to do with other circumstances and events in their lives.

A lot of research has been done into the causes of crime and the ways to prevent it.

Poverty, **Abuse** (29% of prisoners experienced abuse as a child and 41% observed violence in the home) and **Neglect** (27% of prisoners have been in care) are three well-known indicators from a person's childhood which increase the likelihood of them committing criminal offences as an adult:

Children who experience 2 or 3 of these indicators over a prolonged period of time are substantially more likely to become rule-breakers (and eventually law-breakers) as adults, than those children who have happy and stable homes, where they are nurtured, educated and shown love and affection.

Although it is helpful to be aware of these childhood indicators, they do not however show the full picture of circumstances and situations that can cause adults to break the law.

"It is a fallacy that our prisons house the very worst people in society. In fact, our prisons are full of Damaged, Disadvantaged and Disillusioned people. These 'D's are kept alongside a small minority of the worst people we hear so much about." PM

People are sent to prison for many different reasons, often unexpectedly and sometimes unpredictably.

Having interacted with many thousands of people in prison, I believe that the types of people can be can be explained using the coincidental acronym -

D.A.M.A.G.E.D.

Desperate, Addicted, Mentally ill, Accident, Greedy, Evil, Disillusioned

Some of the people in prison may have more than one reason why they committed crime, there are some overlaps; for example, someone may:

- Suffer from psychosis (a mental illness) caused by NPS Spice (addiction).
- Need money urgently (desperate) and also feel excluded from society (disillusioned) so that they justify committing crime instead of resisting the temptation.

The more of these circumstances and reasons that people have or feel that they have, the more likely they are to commit crime.

I elaborate on each of these types of people and circumstances as follows:

D = Desperate

When people become desperate, they are in unfamiliar territory and tested outside of their comfort zone.

Desperate people make hasty decisions, they struggle to think objectively and often panic. The worst cases of desperation are when people disregard their usual moral boundaries, thinking that they have "no choice".

- "A man grabbed my girlfriend around the throat." SH
- "I acted instinctively and with fury, in order to protect my son." BE
- "My family was threatened with harm. The police did not take the threats seriously, so I took matters into my own hands." JM
- "I saw a man outside my house I got very scared. He was on the phone and I thought he was calling for people to come to attack me and my brother. I violently hurt that man and he sadly died a month later." FS

It is usually only with the benefit of hindsight that people see what they should have done differently.

"Act in haste, repent at leisure" is the old adage and prison sadly gives a lot of thinking time for repenting after the event.

A = Addicted to drugs, alcohol or gambling

Many people come to prison as a result of the flawed thinking and behaviour caused by drug use and/or addiction.

Drugs can create a desire so strong that everything else becomes irrelevant. Even eating and personal health come secondary to the intense need for the next fix or hit.

64% of prisoners reported using drugs in the 4 weeks prior to custody. (Source: MOJ Substance Misuse and Mental Health)

Some drugs are so powerful that Problematic Drug Users must take it no matter what. To put things into perspective, I once met a homeless man in Milton Keynes and when I approached him because I like to help, there was an overwhelming smell of rotting flesh. I couldn't help myself; my body took over; I heaved and retched. After recovering I spoke to him and he told me that he was addicted to a drug from Eastern Europe called "Crocodyl". This drug gives a powerful high but it literally rots the flesh from the bones.

I realised then that if a Drug User is willing to rot their own body for the drug then literally nothing is beyond limits. Nothing is more powerful than the urge to take the drug again.

"I was convicted of burglary and aggravated burglary and sentenced to 9 years. I would like to share some background, not to justify what I did, but to explain a little. I was working in an exceptional job installing wiring and cabling under the Thames tunnels. I was so well paid that when I hit a few months of upset and turmoil in my personal life and in a time of personal weakness, I started a cocaine and alcohol habit. This habit spiralled out of control to where I was spending £100 most days on drugs. Cocaine took over my life and I began not showing up for work on Fridays and Mondays - before I knew it, I had let my employer down so much that I was dismissed. My drug habit was an addiction, even though some people believe that cocaine is not addictive, I disagree; that drug controlled my life and dominated every decision I made. After losing my job I spiralled out of control into a circle of other problematic drug users and into crime. Looking back, I am ashamed of how far I fell and feel so horrible for what I did. I have been clean of drugs since 2016 and have resisted all temptations or desires to relapse. I hate drugs for what they did (or rather what I did to myself and others under their influence)." WP

Addiction is however, a treatable condition and recovery is possible.

The prison system and its service partners in this area have the ability to help users' detox, to support recovery and teach people to be aware of their triggers - what makes them turn to drugs, (relapse prevention).

"I was ready to commit suicide and would have done so. In prison I got the help I needed to recover from my addiction and the time and space to clear my head. Coming to prison saved my life." AV

The re-offending rate amongst drug users is substantially higher than the general prison population.

It is important that prisons:

- Provide purposeful and engaging activity
- Increase drug detection and disruption of supply
- Educate people on drug risks and long-term effects
- Support drug users and addicts with detox services and relapse prevention including helping people to understand their triggers

"I was sent to prison for supplying drugs. I had been working full time in a decent job but unfortunately, I was struggling with a secret addiction. My addiction was gambling and it has been really tough for me to admit to this and own it. It crept up on me over a number of years and got worse due to technology evolving and making it easier. I was gambling all the time and money from my involvement in the drug trade went straight to those gambling businesses and web sites. I pleaded guilty to my crimes because I had to accept full responsibility. Prison has been my opportunity to reinvent myself; I have been determined to change for the better. I have sought help to overcome my addiction and I have begun to fill that void in my life with better social connections and positive goals for the future. I have seen first-hand the problems that drug supply creates and how it messes people up and destroys lives. I really regret my involvement in the 'disease' that I now realise that drugs are." PL

The problem is that without purposeful activity, boredom becomes a trigger in itself and people turn to drugs as a holiday and a temporary escape.

In this manner, some prisons actually create new first-time drug users particularly where the focus is less on rehabilitation and more on warehousing (merely keeping people in prison securely).

> "It is apparent that drug addiction or alcohol misuse is the root cause of, or a contributing factor in at least 2/3rd of the crimes which lead to imprisonment." PM

Frequently it is not even addiction but the overuse of alcohol, which creates a sequence of events leading to something unjustifiable, completely out of character and criminal. Alcohol is so prevalent in our society and considered so normal that every Saturday night our children and young people go through 'inebriation initiations' exposing themselves to the very real risk of becoming criminals or of becoming victims of crime, all under the guise of 'having fun'.

Alcohol should be treated with great care - it is proven to do two things:

1) Make the drinker crave more of it; even the most well-intentioned people who start out thinking they will just have one drink can end up having five or six or more.

2) Reduce all inhibitions and increase basic, primitive urges. People end up doing things that they wouldn't normally do (typically violence and sex) and which are completely out of character. Very often things said and done under the influence of alcohol become a source of great regret for years afterwards. Alcohol is the most dangerous drug available in our society; although it is legal, many of the after-affects and consequences are illegal.

Someone who commits for example the crime of Grievous Bodily Harm S18 (deliberately wounding someone) after seeking out a person and without the influence of alcohol (or any other disinhibitors) must surely be deserving of a harsher punishment/ longer sentence, than someone who gets into a fight after drinking heavily on a night out.

"I was an alcoholic and got kicked out of home. I had a hostel place where I stayed for 5 weeks but after this I had to leave without any further accommodation. I lived on the streets, homeless for almost a year. I returned home in desperation and got into a drunken fight with my brother. I was convicted of GBH with deliberate intent and sentenced to 4 years' imprisonment. Since coming to prison, my Mum sadly died and I was unable to attend the funeral because of the arguments between myself and my brother. Alcohol and my crime have caused so many huge problems in my life for me and my family. I came to this realisation and I have been determined to change. I have detoxed from alcohol abuse and completed an intensive "Inclusion" course which helped me to become aware of triggers and handle cravings. I also graduated from Building Better Relationships course and Thinking Skills Programme." CF

I think that at the point of their arrest everyone should be tested for the presence and level of drugs and alcohol in their systems. This would at least provide accurate statistics and an evidential basis for any background explanations. Nevertheless, alcohol is rarely accepted as mitigation for crimes despite it being a major causative factor in a huge percentage of them.

We need to dramatically increase awareness of the impacts of alcohol on society until problem drinking and binge drinking become as socially unacceptable as drink driving.

M = Mentally ill

Mental illness impacts on all aspects of a person's life and has a significant effect on their thinking and behaviour.

At the most serious end of the scale some people suffer from severe and diagnosed mental health problems such as Schizophrenia, Paranoia and Psychosis and less severely, others struggle with temporary anxieties, erratic behaviours and problems coping. Many of us suffer from depression or obsessive thoughts and emotionally driven or unpredictable behaviour at some point in our lives.

49% of prisoners suffer from anxiety and/or depression.
(Source: House of Commons, Work and Pensions Committee)

Often Mental Illness can start as a result of stress, trauma or abuse, but it can be extremely difficult to shift or manage without major life changes, medication, or by developing personal coping mechanisms, usually over a long period of time. More compassion and understanding are needed for people with mental health problems.

There needs to be more joined-up thinking around continuity of care and supply of medication when prisoners are transferred between establishments because disruption of these demonstrably worsens symptoms. Prison is by its very nature, damaging to the mental health of people kept there. Recent restrictions of regimes due to staffing shortages in prisons have resulted in increasing the amount of time that people in prison spend banged up (locked up behind cell doors). This means that they have less purposeful activity and reduced ability to contact family or plan their resettlement.

"I had a panic attack whilst locked up with an aggressive offender. I had pressed my cell bell when I first felt bad and it was ignored for 30 minutes. The fear and anxiety of this episode sent my thoughts and my emotions in meltdown." JE

A prisoner's mental health is severely tested by excessive bang up. Humans are not meant to be kept in small enclosed spaces for long periods of time. This is worsened by the fact that many cells which were built to house one person are now being used to house two people. Even the Victorian prisons such as Lincoln were built to house one man per cell, but now accommodate two. It is illegal to keep zoo animals in such small spaces.

"You put an animal in a small cage with no purpose to its life, he's gonna get worse, he'll go mad! That's was me, day after day, my head went, it is taking me a long time to get over it." LI

On 21st October 2020 a man was sentenced to be held in HMP Bristol "for his own safety" because there was no mental health provision.

There has been a 28% reduction in funding of mental health treatment services since 2015. (Source BBC News: 15/08/2019)

Our prisons shouldn't be places where we hide people who are simply too challenging to manage in the community; these people just become even more traumatised and are eventually released with poorer mental health or new mental illness.

Prisons have, for far too long, been used as hidden dumping grounds for mentally ill & most vulnerable in society. They are absolutely not "places of safety" but places of pain, trauma & further deterioration of physical & mental health.

A = Accident - mistakes and unintentional crimes

It is particularly sad when people come to prison because they have broken laws by accident or where they are subsequently proven to be innocent.

Most crimes require two elements for someone to be convicted and held liable, these are the:

- Crime itself, called by the Latin "Actus Reus" (the guilty act)
- Deliberate intention, knowledge or recklessness behind the crime, called by the Latin "Mens Rea" (the guilty mind)

In other words, the accused person doesn't just have to have committed the crime but they also had to have done it deliberately or recklessly. Many laws however are known as "strict liability" so that even if the accused person did it by accident, with neither intent, nor negligence, they are still liable.

An example of legislation that catches accidental law breakers is the most recent incarnation of fraud legislation known as the Fraud Act. This can be used to convict those who make a statement which they **should have known** might be false or misleading.

This catches people who rely on employees for due diligence or who cut financial or procedural corners in haste without considering the seriousness of such an oversight or what the unintended consequences could be.

"Fraud by false representation essentially criminalises lying and one of the most significant dangers of the Fraud Act is the blurring of the boundary between criminal and private law. Conduct which might be regarded as commercially acceptable, might be criminalised." D.Ormerod, "The Fraud Act 2006: Criminalising Lying?" 2007 Criminal Law Review 193

A PA or office manager who fobs a supplier off with the rote phrase that 'the cheque is in the post' (if it's not) in order to secure an urgent delivery of goods needed, would now cause the employer themselves to be caught by the Fraud Act, if no cheque is subsequently forthcoming.

Causing death by careless or dangerous driving is an example of an accidental crime which anyone and everyone could be convicted of.

"I was approaching a roundabout at 32mph in a 40mph zone, a cyclist suddenly veered from the far left to the right straight into my car. He sadly died at the scene. I was convicted of causing death by dangerous driving. I have replayed the moment hundreds of time since that day and to this day I am not sure what I could have done differently." LW

Every time someone speeds to an important meeting, looks down at their radio, shouts at their children to stop arguing or turns their head in a moment of distraction, they are at risk of coming to prison for a long time, yet they had **no intention** of causing harm or death to another person.

"Upon learning of the death of my Grandad and in my haste to get home to my family I drove above the speed limit and also went through a traffic light that had just changed to red." PS

"I was the owner of a restaurant and was convicted of manslaughter when a man with a peanut allergy sadly died from eating food in my restaurant. We had been informed that he had a severe allergy and we assured him that the dish was safe. My staff and I made a terrible mistake." HL

Some laws are deliberately worded to remove possible defences from people falsely claiming that their crime was accidental, but in so doing they do catch the genuinely accidental law breakers.

It should be mentioned that where intention is not deliberate, it does usually result in a lesser sentence than where deliberate intent is clear. An example of this mitigation in action is that accidental manslaughter results in a lesser sentence than murder. Nevertheless, accidental criminals are treated the same as deliberate criminals by the prison system.

"I was involved in a car crash in which a person tragically died. I was convicted of causing death by dangerous driving despite it being proven in court that there was nothing I could have done to prevent the accident. I have been required to do gruelling 'Offending Behaviour' programmes in prison and have been told that I will have to complete a lengthy course after my release in the community. Prior to my accident, I have never been an offender, I have never committed a crime in my life, so it is bizarre how I have to complete victim awareness, getting it right and other courses to help me overcome my so-called criminogenic triggers/ needs." JD

The easiest thing in the world to do is judge. Can we ever be sure that we would behave differently from the person who is in prison as a result of an accident, or that our luck would be different; that the dice would fall differently in our case?

The impact of prison should never be underestimated:

- A third of all prisoners lose their homes (Source: Grayling 2012).
- 90% of prisoners lose their jobs (Source: Gerrard Lemos, the Good Prison).
- Many ex-offenders suffer from Post-Traumatic Stress Disorder (PTSD) after release from prison.
- All prisoners struggle to keep their marriages and family relationships intact and undamaged by the separation.

"There has been a growing trend of criminalising accidents as part of a wider 'blame culture'. Accidental 'criminals' are treated exactly the same as deliberate criminals throughout all stages of the justice system. A prison sentence for accidentally breaking the law or unintentionally causing harm to others is as devastating to the prisoner and their families as it is to the victims of crime." PM

G = Greedy - Ambitious

A substantial percentage of the prison population can trace the point at which they broke the law to unbridled ambition or fear of loss.

Ambition and reaching ahead to goals are good things and should be encouraged. The UK has always been entrepreneurial. Where it becomes a problem is when the following phrases are used:

- I deserve it
- Never give up
- It's a grey area
- I have no choice

- Whatever it takes
- Beg, borrow or steal
- Rules are made for breaking

Taking short cuts, (such as repositioning the stickers on a Rubik's cube instead of solving it through effort), can become a long-term habit which gets bigger and bolder over time.

Greedy people often have little empathy; they enjoy the thrill of getting something for nothing or may have a deep routed sense of entitlement.

Some become jealous of other people and tell themselves things like "why should they have it when I have got nothing" or "they can afford to lose it, they've got loads."

Many people feel that they are making too slow progress, or that they don't have enough legal opportunities, but the truth is that if people do not work within legal boundaries they will end up in prison.

We live in an opportunity rich country. We can identify an opportunity and begin trading with very little reporting or compliance requirements in many sectors and earn legitimate money without recourse to crime.

If people do not consider the impact that their business or financial dealings will have on other people, then they could easily end up in prison.

I believe that our legal and regulatory framework has grown so much in recent years that an Introduction to UK Law should be taught in schools because ignorance of the law is widespread (yet it is well known that this is no defence). Everyone has an obligation to learn the laws and rules that affect their industry.

E = Evil - Cruel and/or Predatory

Evil is a very strong word but it is a word that many victims of crime and their families would use to describe the perpetrators of the most heinous of crimes.

The truth is that most of the worst crimes are hard to understand. This is right, we cannot hope to understand them because we do not think like the perpetrators of these worst crimes, what they did is inexplicable and irreconcilable to our way of thinking, so we will never be able to understand them.

It has been proven that people can change. We are all growing and changing as we progress through our lives.

There have been hundreds of examples where people have changed through combinations of education, opportunities, therapy, life experiences, faith, mentorship, maturing and personal development.

No one should be written off.

This is one of the reasons why we no longer execute people.

Whilst locked away, **ALL** people should be given opportunities to personally develop and to maintain a purpose to their life.

If we, as a society, rob someone of all purpose and all hope, then they may as well have been executed anyway. 'Death by prison sentence' is a phrase amongst the long-term prison population many of whom view death as preferable to their meaningless undead existence.

It would be wrong of me to hide from the fact that there are evil people in our prisons and in our society **but these are reassuringly in the minority by a long way**. It is irrefutably a good thing that these people are kept securely away from society for the protection of all.

It is important however that we don't 'throw the baby out with the bath water' and that we stop assuming all prisoners are the same. We mustn't categorise them all together.

"Many members of our society determinately hang on the outdated assumption that all prisoners are evil, wicked and cruel, a sub-species of humanity that is beyond any hope of reformation. They believe that the people in prison deserve neither compassion nor support and at best should be shunned or met with disinterest. Before grouping all prisoners together however we should consider that the majority of

people in our prisons are not there for crimes against a person (including violence, sexual harm and robbery)** Source: House of Commons, Prison Population July 2019. **When we look deeper into the circumstances and the minority of those perpetrators who have committed crimes against a person, most would still not merit the label 'evil'."** PM

D = Disillusioned (with society and/ or with life)

Too many people in our society end up disillusioned.

Disillusionment is more common than it should be within our communities, it robs people of hope and many give up trying and no longer care.

We often hear about gaps in our society such as between the rich and the poor, but there are other severe gaps and preventable circumstances which lead to perceived or real unfairness, bitterness and disillusionment.

There are at least 10 aspects of our society that create disillusionment and, in some cases, **Predictable Pathways to Prison**.

I explain these using the coincidental acronym - **Then Police**:

T.H.E.N.P.O.L.I.C.E.
Trauma, Homelessness, Education, Nothing (to lose), Parenting, Opportunity, Law, Inequality, Care, Enlisted

I elaborate on each of these areas of concern as follows:

T = Trauma

Many people in prison have suffered trauma at various stages of their lives for example, victims of childhood sexual abuse often come to prison as adults.

Traumatic incidents in our lives can do significant damage internally and externally. Emotional and mental damage can last for many years and long after any physical damage has healed. This deeper damage sometimes only becomes apparent when certain trigger points happen.

Many circumstances can act as triggers such as fear of loss, fear of rejection, fear of being hurt, being shouted at, feeling out of control, seeing a certain person again after many years, visiting an area associated with past trauma.

How this links in with criminality and disillusionment, is that unresolved trauma causes emotional distress which prevents people thinking rationally. Traumatised people act without forethought as if they are in panic mode and with less consideration for consequences of their actions.

"60% of gang members have anxiety disorders including PTSD and a third will have attempted suicide" (Source: London Southbank University, 'from postcodes to profit')

Counselling and therapies are invaluable at helping people to come to terms with trauma. The opportunities for such help should be made more widely available and publicised further. Stigma should be reversed because dealing with challenges head on rather than ignoring deep damage and hoping it goes away, is a sign of strength and should be encouraged.

"One evening I went to meet up with my former girlfriend but behind my back she had seen someone else and when I knocked at her house, he opened the door and stabbed me in my arm. This event left me scared and traumatised. I was only 19 and it seemed like this life was a new normal for me. From that moment, I carried a knife to 'protect myself' and I promised that I wouldn't let myself be vulnerable like that again." DM

H = Homelessness

It is widely acknowledged that we have a housing crisis in this country and it has been allowed to continue for far too long.

This crisis has been unresolved in favour of a small number of entrenched vested interests instead of being allowed to benefit the general population and bring immeasurable benefits to society.

More than 170,000 people are currently experiencing extreme homelessness, with the highest ever recorded number of rough sleepers at 12,300 known people (Source: BBC News 23/12/2018)

Everybody should be able to have a basic home, not necessarily in the area they want and not necessarily the type of property they want but no one in a civilised country should be homeless or vulnerably housed.

"After I was made redundant, I lost my job and then lost my flat too. I was told that I was not a priority to the council and I became homeless. I lived in my car for two months, which was freezing and I stole to get some money to eat and to tie me over until my benefit claim was sorted out. I regret what I did and I am very sorry." LA

I defy anyone to come up with a realistic, legal plan if they are homeless, freezing cold, starving hungry, maybe craving for drugs and completely alone.

"I believe that housing should be treated as an essential utility - I would ask why people in our country are protected from having their water supply disconnected (they cannot legally be left without running water) yet they can have their housing disconnected and be left without a roof over their heads? Perhaps this is an oversimplification but why the difference in policies? What help is running water with no home? Surely a modest home and protection from the elements is a basic human right - as essential a utility, as water?" PM

Personally, I spent 10 years working in the property industry and developed an interest in sustainable housing. We will always have the gaps between the rich and the poor due to different ambitions, work ethic, skill sets, connections, opportunities etc. but everyone deserves a home of their own - protected and supported by real safety nets.

The number of people being released homeless from prison is particularly an urgent problem. Some people are released after being held on remand and have never even been convicted of any crime.

Many released prisoners are keen to have a fresh start and turn their lives around but without a stable home the chances of this are slim indeed.

"I am 63 years old. I am now homeless and slept six nights on the street. I came to prison because of an accident 3 years ago and handed the keys back to my council flat which I had kept immaculate. Going to prison meant that I have been classed as 'intentionally homeless'. I am 'not a priority' because I am not female, a parent, disabled, a drug addict, nor mentally ill (despite the horrendous anxiety caused). I was released from a so-called resettlement prison and had ROTL to visit the council but they did nothing for me. I told them I would live in any room anywhere in the country. My probation officer ignored me right up to the point of release and now makes me feel guilty because I have nowhere to live. I am vulnerable and scared right now." QD April 2019

Mr D's story above is scandalously common:

Between 2017-2018, HMP Highdown released 50% of people homeless (Source: inspection report May 2018)

Between 2017- 2018 HMP Norwich released 72% of people to unsettled or unknown whereabouts (Source: Ed Davey Liberal Democrats home affairs spokesman, FOI request)

According to the Ministry of Justice, between 1st May and 8th June 2020, in just 5 weeks, during the coronavirus pandemic and lockdown, 947 released prisoners were identified as homeless on their first night out of custody, 98 of whom were young offenders (aged between 18 and 24).

"Some prisoners are being supplied with tents in a survival pack in place of accommodation upon release, something which is totally unacceptable for the 21st century."
Independent Monitoring Board (IMB) 2018

Councils do not have an obligation to help with housing if they decide that a person is intentionally homeless.

The policy of labelling released prisoners as having made themselves intentionally homeless makes a mockery of the government's stated aim of reducing reoffending.

> **Two examples of circumstances in which councils may label a person as being intentionally homeless are 1) Being convicted of a serious offence and 2) Not paying rent whilst in prison** (Source: Shelter 2019)

We can see that almost all prison leavers are caught by one these two circumstances; the first applies to anyone who has received a long sentence and the second applies to the majority of those people who receive a short sentence.

The other option for most people is privately renting but this is also closed to most prison leavers. Due to the national shortage of property, landlords can afford to be choosy about who they rent to. Like most other people they use Google as part of their tenant pre-checks. it is simply easier for them to decline to rent to an ex-offender than to take any kind of unnecessary risk.

According to the Ministry of Justice, 66% of people sent to prison are first time offenders, yet 48% of people released from prison are re-offending.

Put simply, this means that prison, the devastating effects of prison and the lack of any real support for life after release are creating repeat offenders (at least 14% more re-offenders than expected).

Homelessness is a Predictable Pathway to (or back to) Prison.

E = Education

Schools discourage and ostracise many learners when they almost purely promote academia. Many schools do not support other types of intelligence and often stifle individuality and creativity.

When a school can celebrate a practical person, who has great kinaesthetic ability as much as an academic student who can recite the periodic table, then we will have progressed to an education system that celebrates each person and stops destroying the self-esteem of most young adults.

> **"We need to get better at identifying which is the right education for children. Performance targets and academic results come at a deep expense of the broader educational experience."** Amanda Spielman, Chief Inspector OFSTED

Schools often get exclusion wrong; my own daughter Joy was almost excluded at the age of 15 for her disruptive behaviour caused by me coming to prison. Joy and I worked through it; she agreed that she could work through challenges at school if I could get through challenges in prison and we supported each other. Just before her 17th birthday Joy got her GCSE results. She achieved 10 A grades (including 1 Distinction, 4A** and 2A*).

My experience was that the school completely failed to support Joy and inappropriately responded with detentions and 'isolation' instead of offering her counselling and support, engaging her high intelligence and accommodating her Asperger's.

Schools expel a lot of pupils between the ages of 13-15 and many of these are not offered any other provision.

"I was excluded from school because I was labelled as disruptive. Actually, I have ADHD which means that I get bored easily, that I learn faster when shown one to one and that I have quite a bit of restless energy. I know how to manage this but at the time before my diagnosis, the school really were looking for an easy way out. Exclusion in my early teens was bad for me because it led me to hang around with other excluded boys and young men; we found acceptance in each other and became what other people would call a gang. I hid the truth of my associations from my parents; as their behaviour got worse, I couldn't seem to get out of it; who else would welcome me in with open arms? This 'road' life seems glamorous, they had money and I joined them in smoking cannabis." CA

The link between exclusion and imprisonment is irrefutable and although other behaviours and factors are apparent, it would be hard to argue that exclusion is not a contributory factor to imprisonment.

42% of adult prisoners report having been permanently excluded from school. (Source: House of Commons, Work and Pensions Committee 2016-17)

"I am a high functioning autistic person; this means that I take a lot of things literally and sometimes I do not adapt quickly enough to change. I also experience anxiety when faced with difficult or unfamiliar situations. When I was at school, they were not interested in providing any Additional Learning Support (ALS); I was left behind and I gained no qualifications whatsoever. When I came to prison, I really wanted to stop accepting excuses from myself and so I began to study, I wanted to make up for all the missed opportunities. With the right help, I completed several personal development and academic courses and gained qualifications." LP

"I disengaged from school, messed around and was eventually expelled. It is only recently that I have been diagnosed with Dyslexia which means that it takes me longer to learn than others because letters and words jumble up. I wish that I had known this earlier. After I was excluded, I fell in with a group of similarly disconnected young men who made their own rules and normalised criminal activities. I had a youthful arrogance and felt like I would never get in trouble. Fortunately, my crimes didn't result in anyone coming to any serious harm. When I came to prison, I was determined to change and not waste time. I had left school with no qualifications but after getting my dyslexia diagnosis, with the right support and hard work, I passed 8 GCSE's and 2 A Levels." KM

There is a causal link between poverty/ social deprivation and exclusion.

Children from deprived areas and troubled communities are disproportionately excluded, with a 43% increase in exclusions in just 4 years between 2013 - 2017 (Source: BBC News 13/11/18)

Expulsion leads to a mind-set of *not fitting into society* and to teenagers with unstructured and unsupervised time on their hands.

> **"The wasted talent in prisons could be helped a lot earlier in the education system, if schools changed their approach to excluding pupils."** Sir Richard Branson MBE

Excluding children without initiatives in place for further education, effectively abandoning them, is a Predictable Pathway to Prison.

N = Nothing (to lose)

When people lose everything, they become willing to do anything or risk anything, because they feel that they have nothing left to lose.

Normal objective thinking disappears and in the absence of support from family, friends or helpful agencies, many people come to prison after a major catastrophe. Consider these examples:

- "My wife was killed." CL
- "After a business failed." IV
- "I was made redundant." YN
- "I ran away from home." WA
- "I was homeless and freezing." FH
- "My marriage of 19 years failed." NT
- "My partner kicked me out of our home." KD
- "My daughter was snatched by a paedophile." NR
- "I couldn't bear the pain I was in and self-medicated." HP
- "My long-term partner stopped me seeing my children." EL
- "Delays with Universal Credit meant I couldn't pay rent." FA
- "My children were going without the things they needed." PA
- "My dad became disabled and I found myself in between work. We lost our flat to repossession; this was a terrible thing to experience; I found myself sleeping in my car." RM

Is our society doing more or less to help people in such crises?

People who are released from prison are amongst the most vulnerable people in society. They are being released, more often than not with no home, no job, damaged family ties and poor continuity of medical care. By taking everything away from a person and not helping them to rebuild a meaningful life, the prison system is short-sightedly perpetuating a cycle of nothing to lose in most released prisoners.

P = Parenting

Parenting must be mentioned because neglectful parenting plays a large part in children failing at school and failing in society.

Parenting classes should be taught in school. Rather than just teaching "sex education", we should impart useful life information and values to the next generation; teaching children about future families and positive parenting.

It does seem as if values are no longer proactively taught and that virtually all moral frameworks are considered outdated. Positive and proactive parenting should be taught to our next generations alongside society values.

In many communities, we have normalised the idea that men can have multiple "baby mums" and deliberately father as many children as possible whilst being an absent or occasional parent.

"I have a wife and 3 different baby mothers, 12 children altogether, I do like to spread it around a little bit." RB

"I have 5 children with 4 different baby mums. The mothers know if they have a baby with me, they can't be having a baby with anyone else after that; no way. I drop money around and I make the effort to see all my children at least once or twice every month." LH

If people do not want to be there for their children and do not want to proactively parent, then they should make the responsible decision to not make babies.

"A multiple 'baby mums' model or a 'scatter-bomb' approach to parenting, is not in the best interests of any of the children being created. It is neither appropriate, nor biologically necessary for any civilised society. It should be discouraged by education and by raising awareness of the importance of positive parenting and a focus on the unique value of every individual child. The most important thing that children need from their parents *is their presence; not their presents*." PM

With many parents unsure of their rights and responsibilities and living a distracted life which does not focus on family, it is left up to the dramatic and extreme media, fashionable trends, peer-pressure or trial and error, to educate children on right and wrong.

If our society continues to drift in this manner without leading and guiding our future generations, we will create many more children suffering from neglectful parenting, low self-esteem and poor self-control who get excluded from school, link up with other associates who are also disconnected from society and then end up in prison.

O = Opportunity

When a person from a deprived area or disadvantaged background has the same opportunities to access education or employment then they are less likely to miss out and end up resenting those who are successful.

"As a child, my Mum worked multiple jobs and we still didn't have enough. As a teenager, there just wasn't enough money and no opportunities to get it. Growing up it wasn't a question of we can do this, this or this. The problem with our environment and the way we viewed things, our thinking, was the only thing you can do is crime." DR

The UK has the highest income inequality of any country except the US (Source BBC News 14/5/2019)

When people feel that society is unfair to them, they become angry, they attack society, they join up with others who feel the same way and they hit out in the form of crime in our communities.

"We don't see opportunity. People are depressed, angry and fearful in my community. The dream of peace, a good job and decent home is gone." MT

L = Law

Bad experiences with the law or perceived injustice can result in disillusionment and / or rebellion against rules.

"I was arrested by the police and remanded when I was 17 years old. I never committed a crime but was falsely identified as being part of a gang that had robbed people. Some family and friends didn't believe me and my parents suffered abuse. When I was released innocent, I felt angry and upset and went off the rails believing that if the police can behave unfairly, I might as well commit crime. I know it was stupid and the wrong reaction but at that age prison affected me a lot. I know that if I hadn't been falsely accused, treated as a criminal, refused bail and sent to prison unfairly, then I would have stayed on the straight and narrow law-abiding path. Maybe if I had received counselling, I wouldn't have lost my way after that first brush with the police" LE

The police regularly refuse to investigate crime or abandon investigations early and this is disheartening for victims of crime.

> "The police are the public face of the justice system. If people lose belief in the police, they lose confidence in the justice system altogether." PM

Some victims become vigilantes and in so doing break the law themselves.

"My Sister's ex was harassing her and being physically abusive. The police dropped charges against him and refused to investigate further. My Sister rang me in distress and I took matters into my own hands, assaulted him and hurt him. I pleaded guilty. I have never been to prison before." SG

Some turn detective themselves but this usually does not help matters.

"I was a victim of robbery with violence. The police said there was not enough evidence to pursue the criminals. A few days later I searched online and found my property for sale but the police still said there was not enough evidence. I contacted the sellers and got the details of the people who had robbed me. I went with a couple of friends to get my stuff back and then I was the one who ended up in prison." AL

The police often find themselves under pressure to achieve convictions at any cost and their conduct during investigations fails to attract support from the falsely accused and their families, and in many cases the general public.

Corruption or malpractice allegations against police officers have leaped 33.5% in just 6 years to 2018. The number of police officers who were accused of a lack of fairness or impartiality also rose. In total, there were 61,000 internal police investigations in 2018. (Source: The Independent Office for Police Conduct, March 2019).

There is too much of a 'them and us' attitude in many communities who do not want to support the police and who do not believe that the police are there to help them.

Apart from when it relates to the most shocking of crimes, the police would benefit from more positive PR and bridge-building before the disenchantment with police becomes multi-generational.

I = Inequality (and inconsistency)

In recent years, we have made great steps to promote social inclusion and this is very important. People must feel that they are valued by society, both individually and in groups and communities. If we are all on the same side in this way, we do not foster "them and us" attitudes.

"Prison is bad, right 'course it's violent and unpredictable, but it's still safer than street life for a young black man in some postcodes. I wear the wrong tracksuit or walk down the wrong road outside, that's me, I'm dead. I don't see society or community, what they doing for me? nothing so I don't care 'bout them. Yeah disillusioned tsst, that's just the start of it, no one cares, and nothing changes, what's the point?" SA

When people feel that they are discriminated against (whether this is real or imagined) by people or processes, they will turn their back on the system that appears to discriminate.

"I am only 23 years old and since I finished studying, I have really wanted to work. Unfortunately, I attended numerous job interviews and became disenchanted with not getting any offers. It was like no one wanted to give me a chance. At the time, I believed that I was being pre-judged because of my age and my ethnicity. (I am a young, tall British born black man). I lost hope and fell in with a bad crowd of people who were into various ways of making money illegally. This was my fault and I am not 'passing the buck' but I do feel with hindsight that I gave into peer-pressure when I should have been more determined to work legally. If I had been given a chance to work and not been judged by aspects of my appearance which I cannot change, I do not think that I would have come to prison." JJ

When discussing inequality, we should also consider the importance of **procedural justice** because when a person feels that the process of justice is fair, they are more likely to accept the judgement and follow the rules in future.

> **"The process of justice is as important as the outcome."** PM

Procedurally there is very little consistency within our justice system and many people feel wrongly targeted, misunderstood or treated unfairly.

Black people are now NINE TIMES more likely to be stopped and searched for drugs in England and Wales than white people (Source: Release, Stopwatch, LSE, Political Science July 2019)

Black men are 26%, and mixed ethnicity men 22% more likely to be remanded in custody at the Crown court than white men. (Source: BAME disproportionality in the criminal justice system in England and Wales, Ministry of Justice 2016)

On the same day decisions are routinely made that treat people differently based on one person's, albeit highly experienced, opinion or decision.

Consider these three real cases, which are not mentioned to lessen or justify criminal activity, but to illustrate a lack of consistency:

1) Two first time offenders both aged in their 40s were sentenced for a business fraud.

One was a female professional accountant and the other was her male client. The woman had higher culpability, being the professional; the man had followed her advice. The woman had one adult child; the man had three young children.

The judge sentenced both of them to 20 months' imprisonment. The woman had her sentence suspended and did not go to prison. The man was immediately imprisoned.

2) A man was fined £1,000 and yet in the same week another received 5 months' imprisonment for the same offence with the same severity.

3) Two prisoners serving the later stages of their sentences in open conditions, with similar histories and similar custodial behaviour were caught with unauthorised mobile phones. Phone records showed that both had used the phones to keep in touch with families and not for any nefarious purposes. Both admitted their offences, accepted responsibility and pleaded guilty on the same day.

The first prisoner had been caught with a smart phone which had the additional capability to take photographs and access the internet. He was punished with 12 days added to his prison sentence. The second prisoner had a basic 'Zanco' phone which can only call and text. He expected logically to receive a lesser punishment but was instead punished with 18 days added to his prison sentence. He questioned the judge, explaining that he knew the sentence that the first person had received. The judge dismissed him by saying that sentencing was entirely at his discretion. The second person thinks that his harsher treatment (50% more) was because he was of Indian descent. Without other reason to the contrary, it is difficult to explain any other justification for the difference in sentencing.

"Coming from an ethnic minority background or having mental health problems makes you statistically more likely to have force used against you in prison." Peter Dawson, Director, Prison Reform Trust

Accused people feel angry and bitter if they do not believe that the process of justice is fair. When the process of justice is fair and transparent, people are more likely to accept the outcome, respect authority and accept personal responsibility for their mistakes.

There are further real-life examples of judicial and societal bias in my first book entitled *'If criminals can change then so should society and our prisons'*.

C = Care

The Care System, despite caring for a child's physical needs, has since its inception, absolutely and irrefutably failed to care for the mental and emotional needs of the most vulnerable in society.

I am convinced that we could do a far better job, than we do at present, of raising children in care to feel that they have an identity, that they can contribute to society and that they are valued.

Care Leavers make up approximately 27% of the prison population; they are approximately 40 times more likely to spend time in prison than people who have never been to care.
(Source: HM Prison and Probation Service 2018)

Without dramatic and significant changes, the Care System will continue to act *as a feeder school to prison.*

It is essential that we put steps in place to reduce the institutionalisation and abdication of responsibility that children experience so that as young adults they do not develop the subconscious yearning to return back to an institutional life i.e. prison.

"If you want to cultivate a negative belief system about yourself then being in care is the place to be." Gethin Jones, Founder - Unlocking Potential

There are 8 known areas of disadvantage which have been identified by HM Prisons and Probation Service as follows:

- Low self-esteem
- Lack of trust in others
- Lack of support network
- Becoming institutionalized
- Low educational achievement
- Absence of positive role models
- Sense of abandonment and loneliness
- Poor practical independent living skills

More than half of children taken into care have already suffered abuse or neglect. (Source: BBC News 27/11/2018)

These children have often been taken from traumatic environments and continue to have little stability, security or real care shown.

"My Dad killed my Mum when I was 9 years old. I was taken into care but was offered no counselling or help to cope with the trauma of what had happened. I was shown no kindness and breaking the law became my way of rebelling, screaming at society. Crime became a way of life for me. I was taken into Young Offenders Institution at 13 years old. I didn't really know any different. I didn't get a purpose and direction until my daughter was born. I have a burning desire to turn my life around and create a good life for myself and my daughter. As an adult in prison, on this sentence, I have worked constantly to improve myself and faced the challenges of therapy head on. I have come to terms with what happened in my past, learnt to manage my thoughts and emotions better and how to maintain healthier relationships. I am now a more balanced person." AE

People leaving the care system are effectively abandoned from age 18 and sometimes even earlier at 16.

"Having come through the care system, I had to move 8 times between the ages of 15 - 19 and even experienced homelessness during this time. I had no stability, no help and no role models. I felt unwanted and I knew that I was unwanted. I turned to crime after not eating for two days." EN

The Care system is unfortunately a **Predictable Pathway to Prison.**

E = Enlisted

People leaving the armed forces need a lot more support than is presently offered. These people have complex resettlement needs; many suffer from mental health challenges and struggle to adapt to civilian life.

Many people leaving the armed forces have non-mainstream qualifications and struggle to secure employment.

"Conflict changes you and gives you scars deep inside. You never forget terrible events and they can come back and hit you hard years later." MB

Most ex-service personnel are used to having a regimented structure to their lives and rules to follow. In the absence of such a structure, many dwell on their experiences and slip into despair; others display unhealthy behaviours including drugs and alcohol or crime.

10,000 UK armed forces veterans are in prison, parole or on probation.
(Source: Liz Saville Roberts, justice spokeswoman, Plaid Cymru)

In 2018 a 24-hour helpline was established for former service personnel who need help with health, housing and money problems. We have yet to see the impact that this helpline will have on people, but unless there is substantial help provided after each telephone call ends, then a helpline in isolation will be of limited benefit.

Veterans who are suffering from diagnosed or undiagnosed PTSD make up a surprisingly high percentage of the prison population.

"At the age of 19 when I was a serving soldier, I completed two tours of Afghanistan. I have seen people shot and blown up and I assumed that these things didn't affect me. I wasn't offered any counselling or resettlement support. On one occasion, my comrades and I had been drinking in the barracks and whilst under the influence of alcohol I started fighting with an officer. I lost self-control and I am sorry to say that I punched him in the face and broke his jaw. This was Grievous Bodily Harm and I got a 10-year prison sentence meaning I have to spend 5 years in prison and 5 years under supervision. I really regret what I did; at 27 years old, I am now a much more mature individual and more in control of my thoughts and emotions." CK

Years ago, many politicians promised armed forces personnel a career in the prison service after discharge. Unfortunately, those promises were not delivered; a large number of the dedicated people who were made that promise did come to prison, not as prison officers after all but instead as prisoners themselves.

In just one year - 2016, more than 2,500 former members of the armed forces entered the prison system. (Source: The Guardian 2017)

We urgently need an increase in the provision of support, counselling and structured career pathways for our armed forces leavers.

"I was trained in combat, how to kill and survive war. However, at no point are we advised or trained in adapting back from this. We remain 'activated' even after discharge. Personally, 14 years after discharge from the military - having served three visits to prison and a lengthy stay within a psychiatric hospital, psychologists explained how I was still activated. I relied heavily upon structure and I was completely in the wilderness without this. The only time I receive help or support from military organisations is after I was convicted and residing in prison!" DM

Resettlement support and help to cope should not be left solely to those voluntary organisations that do a fantastic job but the military and regiments themselves should take a proactive approach in following up on individual progress at resettling into civilian life.

"Our country should feel desperately ashamed at how we still spit people out who have given their all in military service, unwanted and virtually unsupported." PM

Serving in the armed forces is unfortunately a **Predictable Pathway to Prison.**

Summary:

After reading examples of the people who have ended up in prison and the pathways that led them there, we begin to understand that if we want to stop people going through life trampling over the rights of others (creating victims) and breaking society's rules, then we need to offer more help and support to the most vulnerable in society, particularly at crucial junctions in their life.

The pathways that lead someone away from crime are different from the pathways that lead someone into crime.

Many people leaving prison have complicated needs and fit into more than one of the categories above.

"I was taken into care at the age of 11 years old after my mum had been unable to cope. I missed my mum and my siblings (who had been placed with foster families and other homes) and I struggled to adapt to the trauma, distress and disruption. I was offered very little support and my school were unable to handle me. I lost interest in studies and the teachers labelled me as disruptive; they were too busy to give me the help I needed. When I was a teenager, I was sent to a Pupil Referral Unit which rather than helping me, exposed me to other troubled young people. I started smoking cannabis, fell into the drug culture and moved on to harder drugs. I had to fend for myself from a young age and with no qualifications and little support I turned to supplying drugs as a way to live. I accepted responsibility by pleading guilty. When I came to prison, I wanted to change for the better and I really did." KB

We can see that KB experienced four of the categories I have explained in this chapter - the care system, exclusion from school, desperation and addiction.

This young man will not only need what is deliberately and loosely termed 'support' (in reality monitoring and supervision) post-release, but he will also need real care and practical help, to actually meet the potential that he, so obviously, has.

KB has taken responsibility for gaining basic numeracy and literacy skills and he really wants to stay crime-free in future.

I sat down with him and got to know him as a person; he believes that he has turned his life around; but that is now, whilst he is in a structured environment.

I would be gutted if he is released into chaos with no structure and support. This would be like giving someone a job as an air-traffic controller without any training or hand-holding.

The outcome is as unthinkable as it is inevitable.

People in prison need practical help; both prior to release and continuing after release to avoid them returning, by default, to past patterns of behaviour which are destructive to them and destructive to society.

Quotes - If I hadn't come to prison...

"I needed to get my head straight, I was a mess. I had to get clean from drugs, gain self-respect, learn new skills and find a new positive purpose in my life. I couldn't do that on the streets. Prison probably saved my life, or rather a few key people who gave a shxx about me, even when I didn't care about myself, they saved my life." SA

Quotes - If I hadn't come to prison...

The following quotes were given by serving prisoners who had spent a wide range of time in prison from 1 - 18 years in numerous prisons and who were now in the final few months of their prison sentences.

They were asked to give complete the phrase "If I Hadn't Come to Prison..." whether good or bad.

"I might have started a family." RD

"I would probably be in a bad way." BH

"My wife wouldn't have died alone." VE

"I might never have learnt my lessons." JS

"I wouldn't have been attacked inside." PE

"I wouldn't have met a lifelong friend." AD

"I wouldn't have discovered the real me." SP

"I wouldn't have grown up and matured." EM

"I would never have started self-harming." HR

"I would have seen my daughter being born." LP

"I don't know where I would have ended up." GS

"I would still be lost and living a chaotic life." JM

"I would never have learnt to read and write." MG

"I would have owned my own plastering firm." SB

"I would be working hard to support my family." DG

"I would be working and getting on with my life." CB

"I wouldn't have grown my communication skills." GI

"I would have got married instead of breaking up." PS

"I wouldn't have gained all the qualifications I got." IR

"I would have married my girlfriend and started a family." AD

"I would have been home to see my new baby twins arrive." EP

"I wouldn't have been so resentful of the in-justice system." WB

"I wouldn't have lost all of my friends and support network." LR

"I would have been healed and recovered in the community." DH

"I wouldn't have found my inner strength and determination." MF

"I wouldn't have found my talent for mentoring and teaching." BR

"I wouldn't have rediscovered my faith and felt so purposeful." MK

"I wouldn't have got off drugs and got my personal health back." LJ

"I wouldn't have missed out on so much important family time." MC

"I would have been a successful businessman and had a family." KY

"There is a chance that I could have carried on and ended up dead." RM

"I would have been with my mum when she died young from cancer." PH

"I would still be very selfish and not consider other people's feelings." NE

"I would have still been lonely, but now I have a few lifelong friends." BN

"I would have built my career and I would have married my girlfriend." AJ

"I don't do 'ifs' and 'buts', I learnt a bit and changed a bit for the better." SJ

"I would have got in the habit of selling drugs and probably ended up dead." JB

"I would have worked on my marriage and we would have stayed together." TA

"I would be with my family and wouldn't have missed so much of their lives." AS

"I would have been unemployed and probably continued to commit crime." MD

"I wouldn't have learnt from my mistakes and valued what I have so much." DS

"I wouldn't have lost my job of 15 years and would be happy with my family." AH

"I wouldn't have got qualifications, realised my mistakes and improved myself." SS

"I wouldn't have felt so low that I gave up and tried to take my own life in prison." JR

"My career would be further forwards and I wouldn't face stigma and prejudice." CU

"I would have been a lot more stable emotionally, mentally and financially." SL

"I would have had a lot more time with my baby girl and helped to parent her." TS

"I wouldn't have been reunited with my parents and rebuilt our relationship." WC

"My tenants wouldn't have been evicted from the properties they rented from me." VP

"I would be so much further ahead in my life, with a business and a family of my own." CC

"I would have been there to see my children grow up and would have supported my family." PC

"I would not have enhanced my abilities and completed courses for potential employment." DT

"I might not have learnt the consequences of my actions and the impact of crime on victims." JE

"I would have a long-term career as an entertainer but now my reputation is permanently ruined." RS

"I wouldn't have realised how serious my experiences had affected me and had the strength to seek counselling." HA

"My shop and warehouse business would not have had to close and I would still have at least six people employed." PE

"I would be doing well in the fitness industry and made a name for myself as a top personal trainer and referral instructor." LD

"I wouldn't have developed a love of drama and would have missed the chance to perform in several plays and have a new direction in life." JG

"I wouldn't have had time to stop and think about my life and the lives of others like my family and the community and the impact I can have on their lives." TA

"For me prison led to qualifications and my qualifications led to a job, actually a career; so, it helped me, but I think my story is a bit unusual in this respect." FF

"The noise is unbelievable, on a whole different level and after 3 years my hearing has been permanently compromised. I am in my 30s and have the hearing ability of a person twice my age." MS

"I am suffering from PTSD because I shared a cell with a man who was very badly assaulted (beaten within an inch of his life) in front of me and I could do nothing because there were three big men and no officers on the wing." KE

"I was living in a very small dangerous circle. My world actually got bigger when I came to prison. If I hadn't come to prison and made a decision to change, I would have been dead. Even when I was three years into my sentence some people came and shot at my house. I would have been dead if I hadn't come away and changed my life." JV

"The impact of my crime and my own reckless behaviour affected so many people that it is difficult for me to contemplate. My partner and I have been together for 15 years and this separation has caused so many challenges for her and for my children. They lost the family home and had to move at short notice. This caused financial problems for them and the children struggled badly at school." CY

Chapter 2 - The Potential for Prison to be a Catalyst of Change

"I don't like the phrase "product of the environment." It is not just about the environment, it's about your attitude; you can affect and change your environment. If my mind-set hadn't changed, it wouldn't have mattered where I had gone, where I had lived or what I had done. But change takes time, it doesn't happen overnight and it must be supported."

Robyn Travis, author and ex-offender

The Potential for Prison to be a Catalyst for Change

Most people who come to prison know that they have to change in multiple ways.

In many cases, these interventions could have happened outside of prison, but the individual definitely would not have been as motivated to change without prison.

Prison can be a catalyst for change. It is a bit like in the old-fashioned movies where someone in hysterics receives a slap around the face to break their thought pattern and snap them out of an emotional whirlwind. I am not saying that this is a good thing but the idea of a short sharp shock can be enough to spur someone on to change.

Personally, I prefer positive motivation, for example where opportunities and incentives are provided in the community, people can and do progress.

"Coming to prison destroys a person's life. If we do not help, support and empower the prisoner to rebuild a new life on solid foundations, then they will inevitably be released into chaos, confusion and crime." PM

There is a somewhat contradictory stance in many areas of prison. Money is invested on course provision to improve family relationships but the prisoner cannot act on the information they have learnt because many establishments provide little support to keep the family together and in fact put many barriers in the way such as relocating regions, oppressive visits and poor telephone access.

Some of this can be logically traced back to **security** overriding **rehabilitation**. There is frequently a conflict between security and rehabilitation and in these instances, security must prevail.

To ensure security concerns are satisfied, sweeping generalisations are made; large swathes of prisoners are treated the same as each other, when in reality they couldn't be more different. 89% of prisoners are not in prison for crimes against a person. (Source: MOJ 2017).

This situation is made worse by the fact that the previously effective categorisation system is struggling to remain functional in some establishments due to overwhelmed Offender Management departments.

"The biggest obstacle that prisoners face in trying to turn their lives around and not reoffend is insufficient staffing levels, leading to shrinking of prison regimes and 23 hour bang-up. Rehabilitation is wholly impossible from behind the cell door." PM

Despite the shortfalls of the prison system, there are thousands of committed people working within it.

With the help of these staff and their own motivation, numerous prisoners do make significant personal progress every day, week, month and year.

I have identified the following 20 areas where people change and progress in prison:

1. Tolerance
2. Future Goals
3. Personal Fitness
4. Caring for Others
5. Appreciation of Family
6. Overcoming Addictions
7. Personal Responsibility
8. Emotional Intelligence
9. Counselling and Therapy
10. Contribution and Community
11. Functional Skills Education
12. Higher/ Further Education
13. Leadership and Mentoring
14. Charity Awareness and Fundraising
15. Work Ethic, Skills and Experience
16. Work (Vocational) Qualifications

17. Understanding wider impact of crime
18. Understanding Criminal Urges and Triggers
19. Sharing Lessons Learnt and Discouraging Crime
20. Personal Development

I am pleased to elaborate on these 20 areas, with real life examples as follows.

1. Tolerance

Many people enter prison having spent the greater part of their life in a close bubble surrounded by people who are similar to them.

Over time people develop stereotypical views and entrenched ideas about people from different backgrounds, cultures, ages and areas.

In prison however, people are all thrown in together and have to try to get on. Inmates can meet people from every county in the UK, of every faith, every ethnic background and countries as wide and varied as Albania, Canada, DRC, Hungary, Russia and Vietnam. This widens a person's circle and improves their understanding of others. Some people build lasting friendships and learn to be less judgemental or closed minded.

"I was born in London to Caribbean parents. I met a white Russian man who spoke little English but in time we became friends. He introduced me to different foods, told me about his culture and we played chess. I missed him when he was released but will keep in touch with him. It is surprising the different people you meet in prison; I am more worldly wise now." RZ

The first question people typically ask each other in prison is "Where you from?" in the hope that the other inmate may know similar people or be able to reminisce about the home area.

Some prisons do have a gang culture where groups stick together to stop problems, support each other or intimidate other groups, but this does not preclude the hundreds of different interactions that occur every day between people from completely different demographics. To counteract this and to encourage tolerance, acceptance and diversity, prisons try to build bridges between different cultures and promote equality. Serving prisoners are trained to act as "Equalities Orderlies" helping to raise awareness and resolve problems.

"With extra training I became an Equalities Orderly and developed procedures with Officers, Prisoners and Civilian Staff to ensure that all 9 protected characteristics of the Equalities Act were complied with." WJ

The best run prisons hold events promoting cultural diversity and bridging understanding, these are well attended by prisoners.

"I attended "Crystal's Vardo", a play about the history of travellers seen through a young girl's eyes. It moved me, I learnt a lot about their culture and I understand travellers better now." NV

"Black history month at HMP Coldingley was excellent; a variety of inspiring speakers, good music and unusual food. Everyone was welcoming even to us white guys, I never felt out of place. It was a good event." MA

2. **Future Goals**

Goal setting is an important part of people beginning a crime free future life.

Goals give people something to aspire to and aim for in the future, a direction, but they also provide motivation NOW when it is most needed.

"I have a goal to gain permanent employment and live a stable life where I can be there for my family the way that they have been there for me." LD

Goals also help people to know what actions they should take today to live the future life they want.

"I have goals to be a family man with a partner and children as well as build a career around the gym and fitness industry. With this in mind I have been studying and building on my Active IQ and REPS gym-based qualifications" SW

Many people in prison will not have been told the importance of goals or how to set them; most will also be lacking confidence and self-belief that they can achieve them or that they deserve to achieve them.

Offender Supervisors and college tutors help prisoners to set positive goals for the future and the most effective ones provide on-going encouragement and motivation.

3. **Personal Fitness**

Gym equipment in prisons and accessibility are generally good and, in many cases, excellent. It is treated as a priority because of the popularity and the benefits to the entire prison community.

There are plenty of opportunities for people to use physical exercise as a way to release pent up tension and frustrations, to de-stress in the short term and also to become fitter and healthier in the long term.

"I came to prison as a "morbidly obese" man suffering from diabetes and I decided to treat it as a chance to change. I attended gym twice per week, I was given an extra remedial gym session. I also started doing yoga which I still struggle with now but I know it helps. 11 months later I am no longer diabetic and my weight is almost within normal range. I feel 10 years younger. Prison was a bad thing but I have probably gained more years of my life back that I have lost so it worked out okay for me." JW

Other people use their passion for weight-lifting and gym workouts as a way to help other people and make friends.

"I have voluntarily helped and supported many people in the gym and with personal coaching to help them to live healthier lives." MB

Some gain gym qualifications and develop a career in sports and personal fitness training.

"I used my skills and qualifications to help other people in remedial gym sessions. These were special classes and coaching sessions for people who have been physically injured in car accidents, recovering from operations or addiction or who were struggling to retain their independence during old age. I showed a great deal of patience, understanding and compassion and have received references and positive comments for my contributions to helping others. I became a GP Referral Fitness Instructor which is a prestigious accolade in recognition of the consistent results which I helped my 'clients' to achieve." PJ

4. Caring for Others

In the absence of sufficient social care provision and with overstretched healthcare departments, many necessary caring roles are delegated to other prisoners.

Roles such as Health and Wellbeing Champions (HAWCS) and Buddy Action Teams formalise this care by creating an employed prison job which may include extra training and the opportunity to gain qualifications.

"I served as a HAWC and helped to save the life of a man who hanged himself. I also gained additional qualifications and provided emergency health care assistance and personal support to vulnerable people." ME

"I joined a 'Buddy Action Team' and helped other prisoners in partnership with the healthcare department. I assisted people who, through ill-health or infirmity, required assistance with day to day activities, such as washing, dressing, laundry, library or basic mobility." ID

Caring roles do provide prisoners/ carers themselves with a range of benefits including:

- Friendships, respect and appreciation of peers.
- Greater freedom within prison regimes, less bang-up.
- Vocational skills, qualifications, experience and references.
- Personal development, improved communications skills and patience.
- Proof of trustworthiness - aiding progression through prison categories.
- Discovery of an increased range of personal emotions including empathy.
- A sense of responsibility and pride, the feeling that they are using time, for purposeful activity, that would otherwise be wasted.

"I am a HAWC and recently helped a man to stop self-harming. I continued to mentor this person until he was released. I attended NHS and governor meetings and designed self-harming prevention initiatives." EL

Caring and showing compassion reduces risk factors and may in some cases support eventual release in parole-sentenced prisoners.

"I helped to look after a man who had stabbed himself really badly. As HAWC, I was the person that residents to go to when they had healthcare complaints or concerns. I made referrals to healthcare, mental health teams and drug rehabilitation agencies." JA

In many establishments, there would be a shortfall in care provision, virtually equivalent to neglect, if other serving prisoners did not take responsibility for other peoples' day to day social care requirements.

"I speak sign language and I personally helped deaf people to communicate regarding urgent personal matters." KC

"I qualified in Health and Social Care awareness which enabled me to support elderly prisoners. I have found it very rewarding helping other people in need. For the first time in my life I feel like I am appreciated and valued and that I am not to be despised" WG

"I decided that instead of seeing prison as a dark and scary place (which it is very easy to do), I would instead approach it as an opportunity to help people who were in a worse position than me. I started a project to help prisoners to read and write letters, to rebuild their relationships that were damaged by their imprisonment and to improve their self-esteem. I particularly invested a lot of time with a man who lost his sight through diabetes during the time I knew him. This was really the definition of a person in crisis. To not only lose one's sight but to lose it in one of the most unfamiliar and potentially dangerous place imaginable. So, I became his support and helped him with personal care and decency. We wrote letters together to agencies to gain practical help and to plan for the future." DB

There is generally a large amount of caring and help provided between prisoners and sometimes between prisoners and staff.

"I saved a Prison Officer's life by performing CPR for several minutes until the paramedics arrived. I was highly commended for this." PN

These are of course not portrayed in the media who like to show all prisoners as violent thugs - a widely perpetuated myth which is wholly inaccurate.

"I saved a female Prison Officer's life when she was having a dangerous seizure whilst sitting. I laid her down, placed a pillow under her head and stayed with her until healthcare arrived." JL

5. Appreciation of Family

Prisoners can gain a new found appreciation for family members and people who support them.

"Every one of our long-term friends abandoned us, yet family I hadn't seen for decades rallied around, much unexpected. Positives and negatives!" LD

It is true that we don't always appreciate what we had until it's gone and we notice its absence. This is profoundly true with family who we see every day, naturally taking their presence for granted until we are in a position where we have to feel the physical, mental and emotional aches of missing them.

"I am really glad that I have help and encouragement from my mum." SB

When those prison doors bang shut each night, it is not unusual to hear muffled sobbing for the loneliness and sense of loss. Most prisoners I have met have admitted to crying at some point in their sentence, primarily due to being away from their family.

"I am fortunate to have a stable home life and a supportive family. I am looking forward to being back with my partner and our three children." KJ

The impact on families of prisoners is significant. It is widely document that in almost all cases, the children of prisoners suffer more than the victims of the actual crimes committed.

"Being in prison has been very traumatic for my family; they have lost the family home and had to move away from relatives. My teenage daughter has fallen into the grip of anorexia as a result of me being away. I will never commit crime and cause so much distress to my family again." DN

These impacts and the pain of being kept apart from families is a major deterrent to further crime being committed.

"Being sent to prison messed everything up for my family but I have changed for the better and I am rebuilding my relationships." RM

"Coming to prison was a big wake up call. It was very difficult for my children and my partner, who has been a tower of strength to me, she has found it in her heart to forgive me and our relationship is strong. I will never abandon my family intentionally or unintentionally in future." TN

"When I came to prison, I was very disappointed with myself at making such a huge mistake and one that warranted me being separated from my partner and our two sons. I was devastated and I knew that I had to take on board the essential life lessons from this dark chapter in my life." RH

Maintaining family links and rebuilding relationships damaged by the crime and punishment, must be an important focus of any rehabilitative prison system.

"In the 6 years I have been away from my family I have missed many milestones in my children's lives. I made my own family into victims. Not a day has gone past that I do not feel remorse for what I did. I will never commit crime again." RB

6. **Overcoming Addictions**

Many prisoners need to detox from substance misuse or other addictions and learn how to prevent themselves from relapsing by being aware of factors that increase their risk of relapse such as certain areas, people, events and circumstances.

"I sought help for my addiction and have now recovered. I no longer gamble. I have joined Gamblers Anonymous who provided me with a lot of help to overcome my very real addiction." YL

Overcoming addiction plays an important part in restoring self-respect and setting positive goals for the future.

"I have completely turned my life around. I have committed to physically and mental self-improvement, I consistently pass all drug tests; I have no interest in drugs and no longer even smoke." IW

There are a wide range of addictions, some are little more than a habit that should never have started but then becomes difficult to break. It is said that habits begin as cobwebs but end up as chains.

"My addiction was unusual but it has got a name it is called Kleptomania. I was a kleptomaniac; I stole and shoplifted for 12 years because I got addicted to the endorphin releasing thrill of getting away with something. It started by accident when I had missed paying for something in my shopping trolley and then I found myself trying to get one or two things each week. Then one day stupidly I walked out with a shopping trolley of shopping. Not getting caught was the worst thing because it just escalated from there. I had to get help. I know how bad crime is and how it makes everyone pay more for things and disrupts society. I have taught myself to get the same thrill from paying for things. That is much better for everybody, especially for me and my family. I am grateful for the help I received during my most difficult times and I would like to apologise for my completely unacceptable behaviour." GM

Breaking habits and overcoming addiction are achievements that should be celebrated because they are demonstrable signs that a person has moved on from where they were. It may not always be a big thing to other people but we all start from different places and all achievements are worthy of celebration.

7. Personal Responsibility

When prisoners have:

- ✓ Appropriate ideas for initiatives
- ✓ Skills, qualifications or experience
- ✓ A track record of being worthy of trust and responsibility

Then the most progressive Governors welcome such initiatives and provide support for prisoners to run their own projects.

"I have mentored many other people to gain the carpentry skills that have been so central to my life since my childhood. I have helped dozens of younger men to achieve NVQs in site carpentry which will help them to gain employment upon their release. I have been supported by the prison service in my efforts to do this and I have been highly praised for the good work that I have done and for the positive spirit I have shown in helping these people who have struggled to find employment before." DS

Many of the best ideas in prisons have come from prisoners themselves.

"I created and facilitated courses which educated people of the risks of New Psychoactive Substances (NPS) and general drug use. I personally taught around 500 people in my classes and wrote worksheets that will stay behind helping people long after I have been released." JE

"I qualified as a Yoga teacher (Level 4). Whilst in prison, I established my own classes which were very well attended by both residents and staff. I have written a 10-week Yoga and mindfulness course. My classes help people to improve their physical wellbeing and to find balance and peace. I intend to use my skills, qualifications and experience to build a future career earning a legitimate income whilst following my passion." NM

I personally experienced the idea of a Listening Governor when I wanted to formalise my resettlement help and support to prisoners after National Careers Service (NCS) closed. It all started with a letter explaining my plan to the Governor which he supported. Later with the help of a Deputy Governor I was up and running within about 5 weeks. I intend for this concept and all of the templates to eventually be emulated in all resettlement prisons.

> "Listening to prisoners and considering their ideas is not the same as giving them a 'cushy ride'. No-one is better qualified to know the best way to stop committing crime than the criminal themselves. If we listen to the most sensible ideas and trial them, we can then copy successes to other prisons for the benefit of all." PM

There is a journey of personal responsibility too; often from being in denial and blaming other people to accepting responsibility and being honest with oneself.

"I was dishonest, selfish and untruthful; in all honesty, I did it because I didn't expect to get caught. I thought it was behind closed doors and no one would ever find out. I could live with myself as long as no one else discovered the real me. I am ashamed of my behaviour and how I defrauded others. I am sorry." RN

8. **Emotional Intelligence**

   Some people in prison struggle to experience a full emotional range or are habitually concentrated on certain emotions, for example disgust or anger.

   Over the last few decades, we have seen an evolution of excellent courses in prisons which are designed to help people to understand their emotions better and to express them more appropriately.

   "I took part in an alternative to Violence Project and gained a Certificate in Understanding and Handling Conflict. I related so much to the course that I mentored and helped other people to complete it too, it was life changing." TJ

   People also learn how their thinking and their unique perspective can influence their emotions; they discover emotional management techniques.

   These people develop empathy for others, with a knock-on effect of healing family relationships and helping them to plan for a crime-free future.

   "I would say that the Resolve (formerly Controlling Anger and Learning to Manage - CALM) course changed my life for the better. I couldn't express myself properly before. I viewed everything through negative glasses. I thought everyone was attacking me. Now I understand that we each think and interpret things differently depending on our own experiences." PP

9. **Counselling and Therapy**

   Some people need help to overcome emotional distress, to cope and come to terms with their past, as well as skilled guidance to stop it affecting them so much in future.

   "The first time I was offered counselling was when I came to prison. I accepted this help and I have now come to terms with my past." NT

   "I completed 5 years of therapy which helped me to understand my traumatic past, to deal with my thoughts and emotions and to communicate and manage relationships better." GK

"I spent 7 out of my 24 years in therapy, a secure therapeutic community called HMP Grendon. This was life changing for me. I learnt to express myself and explain things better and began to understand what drove me. Until I came to prison, I never had the ability or the courage to talk through my experiences. I spent most of my life not being able to trust other people, I would ruin relationships myself, not believing that I could be worthy of authentic love and affection. Unless you move past your past and understand your own emotions, you cannot live fully." DI

10. Contribution and Community

Some people in prison give significant amounts of time on a voluntary basis to helping other people.

"With formal training from the Samaritans, I trained as a prison listener and helped other people whilst they were at their lowest points, self-harming or contemplating suicide. I just really wanted to help people. As I was helping others, this also made the time go quicker for me. I volunteered to become a Wing Wellbeing Representative; this was a new idea that I came up with. I gave up my own time to help distressed people. There was one young lad I met who was a serial self-harmer, I had many conversations and spent a lot of time with him. He had no family support and was facing a long sentence; he felt that he had no future. I tried to give him support and encouragement. I helped him plan goals for a positive life after release. He did take strength from our friendship. When I last saw him, he hadn't self-harmed for 9 months which was a big milestone for him. I got a letter from him a few days ago and he has now hit 12 months without any self-harm. This is a big difference for someone who was self-harming most days. I take comfort and feel a little pride that I have been able to make a difference to others. I do feel like I am putting good back where there had been harm from my reckless behaviour before." CM

Prisoners gain a lot personally when they take the focus off of themselves and begin to concentrate instead on helping and supporting other people.

"I have served other people in prison and learnt humility. I taught other people to read, following the system created by a brilliant charity called the Shannon Trust. I went through training with them to be able to help other people in this manner and it is rewarding teaching adults to read. They never knew what they were missing out on or what an essential life skill it was, until they discover what all these letters and words mean!" WK

In these support roles, prisoners develop greater empathy and practical skills

"I was a representative for over 50s. I identified the problems faced by the growing elderly population in prison and liaised with management to improve conditions, communications and quality of life for everyone." JA

They often have an opportunity to study for vocational qualifications that can be transferred into future employment.

"I worked as a Charity Advisor, liaising between prisoners and a number of resettlement and employment charities which helped prepare them for housing and work after release. I gained qualifications and skills and hope to have a job in the third sector when I am released." DB

Many take on extra responsibility themselves and realise the difference that a little help can make; this also helps them reflect on their past behaviours.

"I developed a better understanding of the impact that drug supply has on individual users and society. I have seen drug addicts first hand in prison and it woke me up to the thought that by making drug supply easier, I contributed to their suffering and degradation. I helped some of these struggling people first hand to overcome their challenges and tried to support them as much as possible." JW

They learn to accept responsibility and prove worthy of trust.

"In prison I became a Charity Co-ordinator. I built relationships with charities that support adults in difficulty. I liaised with many voluntary sector organisations including St Giles Trust, MIND, RAPT (Drugs and Alcohol), BASS Housing Trust, Family Matters, Citizens Advice and the Job Centre, amongst others. I made referrals and sign-posted prisoners to the most appropriate agencies for help. I aided resettlement by assisting with jobs, housing, bank accounts, restorative justice and relationships problems; all with a view to reduce re-offending and build a stable life. I gained organisational skills, learnt about record keeping, trust, confidentiality and complying with the Data Protection Regulations. When I left prison, I got a full-time job with one of the charities. By helping change lives for the better, my life also changed for the better." CA

These roles make a significant difference to the wellbeing of other prisoners and contribute to a sense of community on prison wings.

> *"In well run prisons, correctly categorised and with settled and stable populations, prison wings can become inspiring places where people know each other and look out for each other in a more neighbourly way than they do in some modern communities."* PM

"I served as a Foreign National Representative. It is surprising how many non-UK residents get in trouble with the law when they are here. I helped people to prepare for seeing Home Office Representatives by explaining procedures, completing paperwork and arranged translation services. I basically supported people, guided them and gave them personal attention when they were really struggling or preparing for deportation." LW

11. Functional Skills Education

There is strong reluctance from some people in prison to learn functional skills (Maths and English). There can be significant 'mental monsters' to overcome.

Past bad educational experiences can create a very strong aversion to classroom-based education; people feel that they are unable to learn or that they are stupid, and others may see themselves as manual people not academic people. Overcoming this aversion takes strength of will on the side of the student and patience by the teacher.

47% of prisoners are estimated to have no school qualifications, including GCSEs. (Source: House of Commons, WAP Committee)

The third-party college teachers across the prison estate are excellent; they are generally highly experienced professionals who are dedicated to helping others and have seemingly unlimited patience.

"I achieved Level 2 qualifications in Maths, English and IT. These are equal to GCSEs and put me on a level with other job applicants. I am not going to say it was easy, level 2 is challenging, but it was better than leaving prison with what I came in with - nothing!" JM

Frequently, prisoner students begin to enjoy classes after a couple of weeks, some gain functional skills qualifications for the first time, still others develop a love of learning that they build on and then encourage other prisoners to learn as well.

"I became an Education Orderly, signposting people on to courses that would help them to progress. I also informally helped less articulate people to word letters to family and professional contacts." PH

More than 750,000 people in the UK speak English so poorly that they will find it difficult to get work
(Source: The Times 2017 quoting the Office of National Statistics)

Functional skills are essential to access most jobs and so gaining these are made a requirement of progression in the sentence plans of many prisoners.

The biggest challenge is getting prisoners to classes in closed conditions when regimes are limited due to insufficient staffing or security concerns leaving prisoners banged-up.

"I used my prison sentence to improve myself, a striking example of this is that I hadn't gained any GCSE's at school because I worked instead; in prison however, I persisted until I gained Levels 1 and 2 certificates in both Maths and English, these are the equivalent to high GCSE grades." YS

12. Higher/ Further Education

The level of support for further education in prison varies a great deal between establishments. Some education managers are excellent, they really go out of their way to arrange telephone tutorials, computer time and help with stationary provision, others do very little to provide the support that distance learning requires.

"I have worked consistently throughout my prison sentence and also studied to improve myself. I have gained GCSEs and am 2/3rd of the way through a degree course having completed 240 Credits towards BA (Hons) in Social Sciences and Criminology through the Open University." LE

Frequent and unexpected prison transfers cause severe disruption and work is often lost. Nevertheless, it is admirable that so many prisoners do achieve life changing qualifications, supported by exceptional organisations like Prisoners Education Trust (PET), the Open University (OU) and Stonebridge College.

"You couldn't have much more adverse conditions in which to try to study and achieve a degree. Within the chaos of the current prison system, to get your brain to function well enough to secure a university degree is no mean achievement; I think it is a crowning achievement for any prisoner to improve themselves to that extent in such dire circumstances." Jon Snow, broadcaster and Ch4 news presenter.

Higher education massively improves individual self-esteem, enhances employment prospects and dramatically reduces reoffending.

"I have gained educational qualifications and yes I am now even doing a degree! Something that was unthinkable a few years ago." CI

"I achieved well in my GCSEs and A Levels and should never have got involved in any criminal activities. When I came to prison, I was devastated, in part because I had to leave my degree course. I was supported to enrol with the Open University, determined to continue my studies and I did eventually gain my degree." NR

13. Leadership and Mentoring

The concept of peer mentoring is a formalising of the core principles of encouraging and empowering others, whilst also teaching them and providing practical support. It is an educational and support provision which is facilitated by someone who has typically been through the same experiences and learning curves as the mentee(s).

"I have been a mentor to young men coming into prisons helping them to steer away from gangs and violence." OE

This is a natural progression for many successful prisoners who go on to share what they have learnt and help others.

"With help from College staff and after gaining Art and Mentoring qualifications I ran my own art classes which helped people to improve their mental health and to express themselves emotionally." LC

The mentor will generally have a great deal of natural empathy for the mentees because their backgrounds are similar and they have more in common that many other student teacher relationships. Mentees are often more receptive to learning from one of their peers.

"I have guided and supported many people to progress personally; I now speak to small groups and larger audiences about the power of positive change and the value of education." GA

Typically, high levels of support, signposting, handholding, and encouragement lead to better than average results. Peer mentors are an excellent resource that can and should be used consistently to improve efficiency and outcomes for prisoners. The best prisons have systems in place and specific roles that allow experienced or skilled prisoners to mentor, train and coach other prisoners.

"After overcoming addiction, myself, I became a drugs and alcohol Peer Supporter/ Peer Mentor who provided guidance, direction and personal attention to people who were often in distress, or coping with mental health challenges. As a sign of my commitment to change, I worked hard to gain a qualification in this role too." BY

Peer mentoring can be very effective because mentees feel camaraderie with the mentor. This means that they are more willing to listen to them and more likely to take direction or heed guidance.

"I became a Prince's Trust Mentor and, in this role, I was able to guide young people away from crime and gangs and instead help them to educate themselves and become employed." JC

Generally, peer mentors can dedicate time and attention to mentees which is far in excess of that which they would usually receive. Personal attention doesn't let anybody slip through the net; one gets left behind. The relationship between mentor and mentee also has demonstrable benefits to mentors; peer mentors grow their communication skills as well as their subject knowledge and understanding. Having such a worthwhile purpose, contributing to the success of others and being part of an effective team really helps peer mentors to grow in confidence and self-esteem.

"I developed barbering skills, gained qualifications and taught barbering to other residents. As a peer mentor I provided demonstrations and feedback to students as they cut residents' hair. I supported my mentees to progress from absolute beginners to formally qualified skilled barbers." SL

Mentoring fosters personal pride and responsibility in the mentor and it provides comfort and more compliant behaviour on the part of the mentee.

14. Charity Awareness and Fundraising

The more that people in prison feel they have a value and that they are included in society, despite their incarceration, the more likely they are to be productive members of society and not reoffend.

When televisions were first provided to prisoners, there was a public outcry, but in fact these are very important indeed. Prisoners locked away from society for years in a fast-moving technological era, are able to keep up to date and keep informed of societal trends prior to release.

When prisoners decide to raise money for charity, it helps them to develop self-esteem and empathy.

Despite most prisoners only earning around £12 each week, they can be surprisingly generous.

"I have organised several gym-based charity events. In recent years, I have raised thousands of pounds for charity for children with special needs. I held events including a 12-man team undertaking a "million-mile row" and a fun day for residents of a secure establishment which included an obstacle course and an "extreme" bench press event." HC

"I started a charity fundraising event called "Weights for Breaks". Along with 20 other men, we help a sponsored weight-lifting event that raised £3,200 to send disabled children on holiday to Disneyworld. The event really took off and is now held annually. I felt so happy that I was able to co-ordinate and promote such a worthwhile event and I am pleased that it has become an on-going project raising money for children's charities." GY

Even if they are not raising money, many people in prison feel strongly the pull of helping a good cause.

Some prisons have workshops operated by charities which inspire people to work hard and to their highest standards.

"I worked in a dedicated factory unit on behalf of a children's charity carrying out bicycle repair and maintenance. I disassembled, refurbished and rebuilt high volumes of bicycles which were donated by police recovery and by generous members of the public. Each bike would be repaired and given a full service. High value bikes were sent to auction for fundraising and low value ones were donated by the charity to families in difficulty. The staff and management cared deeply about what they were doing and I was a valued member of the team." LE

Community links like these between society and prisons are bridges to understanding. They encourage acceptance of prisoners back into society and help people in prison to feel like they still have a value, despite their past crimes.

Other charities offer support roles which are popular with people in prison.

"I gave my time as a charity support worker for Turning Point charity. I facilitated group therapy sessions, made appointments for people to see case-workers, gave out clean user kits and encouraged users to come off of drugs. I provided additional information, advice and guidance with a view to reducing re-offending and helping clients to build a stable life. I displayed trust, confidentiality and empathy. I know that people don't stop using until and unless they are ready so I made sure that I was there for them when they were ready. I have success stories of people who turned their lives around. I have many personal letters and a very complimentary reference from my time in this role." AH

15. Work Ethic, Skills and Experience

Working prisoners have the opportunity to gain a wide range of skills depending on the job role.

"I have used my skills to improve the surroundings for others, undertaking cleaning, cooking and maintenance tasks, completing all of these to a high standard. I received an award for fully refurbishing a prison wing." TM

The best run prisons have employment approaching 100% of eligible residents the poorest run have employment rates of around 20% - 30%.

There is a direct correlation between high unemployment and high drug use (and violence) in individual prisons. Unemployment is statistically a causal connection for problematic drug use both inside prison and outside of prison in our communities; this correlation is mirrored after release.

"I maintained a consistent work record despite my imprisonment, by working hard every day in prison jobs." SS

Although wages are in the region of 40p-60p per hour, prison jobs help prisoners to gain valuable work skills and they can look very effective on CVs.

"I came to prison at a young age and have spent a long time inside. I hadn't completed a CV before. Work wise, I felt that I hadn't really achieved anything worthwhile in my life. HOWEVER, it was explained to me that a lot of the prison jobs I have done have taught me real skills which I can use. I now see my potential in a completely different way and know that I have a value to an employer." PA

"The trusted positions that I have held during my years in prison involve good communication skills and time management and have opened the door to a job offer before my release from prison." LE

The work choices which are available to individual prisoners depend on their individual trustworthiness and the availability of jobs at each establishment.

Examples of the jobs available to serving prisoners include:

Activities Coordinator. Allocates prisoners into workplaces, giving guidance on most suitable roles and promoting availability of jobs.

Appliance Repairer. DHL. Restores and repairs domestic appliances.

Art Teacher. Organises and facilitates art classes.

Baker (Bad Boys Bakery). Works as kitchen porter and bread and cake maker.

Barber Shop Mentor. Gains barbering qualifications, helps in barber's shop and teaches others barbering skills.

BICS Biohazard Responder. British Institute of Cleaning Sciences. Cleans blood and bodily fluids and makes safe all surrounding areas.

B.I.C.S. Industrial Cleaning Operative. Cleans various settings using cleaning equipment, chemicals and machinery.

B.I.C.S. Industrial Cleaning Supervisor. Organises and supervises a team of qualified cleaners.

B.I.C.S. Trainer and Assessor. Facilitates workshops for people new to BICS, trains and assesses them.

Bicycle Repair and Maintenance. Repairs, refurbishes and rebuilds police recovered bicycles on behalf of charity.

Braille Studio. Programmes machinery and creates indentations in paper, card and packaging for blind people to be able to read.

Call Centre Operative. Calls customers to solicit their opinions on products and services for market research purposes.

Call Centre Trainer. Teaches new employees the systems, processes and scripts for calling customers for research and telesales purposes.

Careers Adviser. Helps people to produce CVs and disclosure letters, advises on job applications, interviews and careers.

Carpenter. Manufactures pre-built furniture units, installs, maintains and repairs wooden fixtures and fittings.

Carpentry Instructor. Facilitates workshops and supports carpentry students leading to recognised qualifications.

Car Wash Manager. Operates a hand car wash including moving vehicles, hand and jet washing, polishing, vacuuming and valeting.

Chapel and Mosque Orderly. Manages multi-faith chaplaincy provision, maintains chapel diary, cleans chapel and halls and serves refreshments.

Charity Advisor. Provides Information, Advice and Guidance on the availability of charity help and grant funding.

Charity Co-ordinator. Liaises with a range of voluntary sector organisations, informs them of need and distributes their literature.

Charity Project Leader. 'Keep Out' - crime diversion scheme. Hosts prison visits from groups of young people at risk of engaging in crime to educate and discourage them from crime.

Charity Shop Worker. Release on Temporary Licence. Charity shop voluntary work performing customer service and shop support roles in the community.

Charity Support Worker. 'Turning Point'. Facilitates group therapy sessions, makes appointments for people to see case-workers, issues clean user kits and encourages users to come off of drugs.

Classroom Assistant/ Peer Mentor. Business Enterprise Class. Teaches business skills and compliance and helps individuals to complete their portfolios and business plans to a high standard.

Classroom Assistant/ Peer Mentor. Catering Course. Teaches and assists on accredited catering courses. Aspects include food safety and allergy awareness, cookery and customer service.

Classroom Assistant/ Peer Mentor. Functional skills (Maths and English) classes. Encourages reluctant or struggling learners and gives personal attention, teaching and support.

Classroom Assistant/ Peer Mentor. Graphic Design Class. Teaches Graphic Design software (Adobe suite) and general PC skills to small classes of adults.

Classroom Assistant/ Peer Mentor. IT Academy. Teaches MS Office, Cisco networking and general PC skills in groups and one to one.

Classroom Assistant/ Peer Mentor. "Resolve" Violence Reduction programme. Facilitates informative training sessions within an anger management programme lasting several months.

Clothing Manufacturer. Manufactures jeans, shirts, sports clothes, blankets, quilts, sheets, bags and underwear in a factory setting.

Community Shop Assistant. Release on Temporary Licence. Charity warehouse work loading and unloading furniture, interacting with customers and donors, testing and demonstrating white goods.

Concrete Manufacturer. Making precast concrete blocks and bollards for road and street use.

Drug and Alcohol Support Worker (Peer Supporter). Supporting problematic drug users to rehabilitate from drug use, detox from drug addiction, identify personal triggers and resist relapse.

Employment Orderly/ Recruitment Consultant. Interviews residents to assess their skills and identifies opportunities to fill roles with the most suitable people.

Engineering Workshop - Welder and Fabricator. Fabricates high security locks, doors, windows, large gates, secure metal shutters and grills

Engineering Workshop - Paint-line operative (Powder-coating). Powder-coats doors, windows, large gates, secure metal shutters and grills and then conveys them into a high temperature oven to set.

Engineering Department Worker. Fabricates high security locks, doors, windows, large gates, secure metal shutters and grills

Equalities Orderly. Mediate in disputes and helps to develop initiatives and events that raise awareness of equalities issues.

Fabric and Material Recycling. Converts former healthcare clothing, bedding and fabrics into multi-use cloths and rags typically for equine use.

Floor Laying. Installs hard wearing linoleum in residential units including measuring, cutting, fitting, gluing and snagging.

Foreign National Representative. Liaises between international residents and prison staff or other officials to resolve a wide range of issues.

Gym - Cardio-Vascular (CV) Training Orderly. Explains safe use of gym equipment, maintains register and maintains the training area and equipment.

Gym Course Mentor. Organises and assists on structured gym courses.

Gym Instructor (Remedial). Provides remedial gym classes and coaching sessions for people with limited mobility or recovering from health problems.

Gym Orderly. Responsible for ensuring the smooth running of the gym.

Healthcare Orderly. Practically supports elderly or people with social care needs and liaises between healthcare staff and service recipients.

Health Trainer. Educates and coaches gym members on nutrition, fitness and healthy lifestyles.

Health and Wellbeing Champion (HAWCS). Registers healthcare complaints or concerns, makes referrals to mental health teams and drug rehabilitation agencies and provides social care support on prison wings.

Hearing Aid Refurbishment. Cleans, repairs and packs hearing aids and glasses to be sent to third world countries on behalf of Sight and Sound Charity.

Induction Orderly. Welcomes, reassures, registers and interviews people as they arrive into prison and explains what to expect in a new establishment.

Job Centre Orderly. Helps serving prisoners to prepare for release into the community by signposting them to their local job centre. Organises resettlement fairs, helps people to complete forms and paperwork, provides information, advice and guidance related to employment and benefit claims.

Kitchen Porter. Food preparation and bulk cooking to provide two meals each day including general cleaning, loading and unloading deliveries, monitoring storage temperatures, labelling and stock rotation and safe handling of food.

Kitchen Servery Worker. Serves food directly to residents, ensures compliance (through separation of serving trays and utensils) with religious requirements and special dietary needs, cleans and maintains servery,

Kitchen Supervisor. Oversees and co-ordinates a team of kitchen porters. Monitors food safety and hygiene, resolves short notice challenges, attends management meetings and organises catering for special events such as group visit days and religious festivals.

Landscape Gardener. Routine grounds maintenance including planting, mowing, trimming, weeding, edging and pruning as well as ad-hoc grounds development such as pond excavation and creation.

Laser machinery operator (Lasers Workshop). Manufactures finished shapes out of wood for jewellery, toys and early years' puzzles

Laundry Operative. Washes, dries and presses prison laundry and in some establishments, laundry for outside contracts (such as hotels). Works in an industrial laundry department using large driers, washing machines and presses.

Laundry Orderly. Performs service-washes for residents. Washes, dries and folds clothing and bedding, maintains a waiting list and manages urgent loads.

Lawnmower repair and maintenance. Repairs and reconditions lawnmowers and garden machinery.

Library Orderly. Supports the management and operation of a lending and reference library.

Life Skills Orderly. Develops and recommends courses to help prisoners resettle successfully in their communities upon release.

Mental Health Supporter and Peer Mentor. Signposts and make referrals to agencies and provides distraction packs, talking therapy and personal support.

Minibus Driver. Release on Temporary Licence. Drives residents and staff to outside appointments such as hospital or community work placements.

Motorbike and Scooter Repairer. Disassemble, refurbish, repair and rebuild police recovered items to be later sold on behalf of charity.

Music Orderly. Responsible for the smooth running of a music department, sound studio and music events.

Offender Management Unit (OMU) Orderly. Liaises between prison staff and prisoners to ensure that messages are delivered, appointments are attended and paperwork is completed accurately and on time.

Office Administrator/ Education Champion. Enrols learners onto a wide range of courses and offers encouragement and support to study.

Officer's Mess. Makes and serves hot drinks and food to staff and prison visitors.

Open University Orderly. Guided students on the most relevant courses for their future life plans, helped applicants to complete student loan forms and enrolled them onto access modules and degree courses.

Painter and Decorator. Refurbishes cells and carries out general internal and external maintenance.

Pallet Manufacture. Manufactures and despatches pallets for heavy use industrial and logistics purposes.

PC Refurbishment. Disassembles, wipes, repairs and refurbishes computers for charity to be sent to schools and villages in Africa.

Peace and Community Engagement (PACE) Representative. Facilitates discussion, mediation and conflict resolution between parties.

Plastic Manufacturing. Manufactures high impact multi-use and recyclable knives, forks, spoons, cups, bowls, plates, jugs and trays.

Print-shop Operative. Operates printing, cutting and folding machines to produce literature and signs for prisons and government departments.

Prisoner Information Desk (PID) worker. Helps fellow prisoners with signposting, letter writing, applications, information, advice and guidance.

Programme Coach / Course Facilitator. Encourages and practically helps fellow prisoners to complete all modules of an anger management and violence reduction programme called "Resolve".

Programme Coach / Course Facilitator. Facilitates informative training sessions and gives demonstrations on a food-safety and catering course.

Radio Production. Conducts interviews and radio shows for National Prison Radio (NPR). Trains in interview techniques, audience engagement and how to use adobe audition software as well as studio equipment (hardware).

Reception Orderly. Welcomes and interviews people as they arrive into prison. Cleans the prison reception area and assists staff to ensure smooth admissions.

Recycling and Waste Management Operative. Collects, sorts, crushes and bales waste ready for recycling.

Recycling Operative (Plastics). Shreds and grinds CDs, DVDs and other small plastic items to create plastic chips for reuse.

Rehabilitative Culture Representative. Helps management team to develop initiatives which support rehabilitation and aid resettlement after prison.

Resettlement Representative. Provides practical help and signposting to serving prisoners to prepare for release into the community.

Restorative Justice Facilitator. Hosts meetings between prisoners and staff when they are at loggerheads or angry and upset with each other.

Segregation Orderly. Responsible for cleaning, general maintenance and food serving of a Care and Separation Unit (CSU - aka Segregation/ The Block).

Segregation Support Worker - Project Unite. Provides additional pastoral and practical support to people held in the Care and Separation Unit (CSU - aka Segregation). Operates mobile library, mediates in disputes, monitors well-being, documents safety concerns and listens to grievances.

Shannon Trust Mentor. Teaches adults to read and write and provides English as a Second Language (ESOL) support.

Sign Manufacturer. Manufactures heavy-use signs for motorways and prisons.

Social-care orderly (Prison Carer). Provides personal care support to elderly people with dementia or restricted mobility, people with disabilities, learning difficulties and those coping with mental health challenges.

Stores Manager. Operates stores department, distributes furniture, personal care products, electrical items and clothing and maintains logs. Conducts regular stock takes and places stock orders with management.

Tool Repairman. Repairs, cleans and maintains power tools and plant hire equipment including heaters, de-humidifiers, portable lighting rigs, paint strippers, power saws, angle grinders, magnetic drills, hammer drills and all hand tools within a workshop operated on behalf of Speedy-hire.

Translator. Supports prisoners with reading, writing and spoken translation. Accompanies them people to important meetings with Healthcare and offender managers and helps them with general administration.

Transport Co-ordinator. Manages a small fleet of vehicles, co-ordinating drivers and journeys, and diarising MOT testing and maintenance.

Hand Upholsterer. I received and staples and stitched material and padding onto pre-built wooden frames to create heavy use chairs and sofas.

Vacuum Cleaner Refurbishment. Repairs and reconditions Dyson vacuum cleaners for resale by charities.

Violence Reduction Co-ordinator. Develops violence reduction initiatives, acts as a mediator between officers and prisoners and liaises between prisoner groups to de-escalate tensions.

Visitor Centre Orderly (Customer Service Assistant). Cleans and prepares visits hall, tables and chairs, serves customers hot drinks, food and snacks.

Waiter (Clink restaurant). Greets customers, waits on tables, serves hot and cold drinks, meals and snacks and cleans tables, chairs, floors and food services.

Warehouse Operative. DHL. Picks, seals and packs prisoners' canteen orders (primarily groceries and toiletries).

Warehouse Supervisor. DHL. Oversees a team of pickers and packers processing prison canteen orders.

Wheelchair Maintenance. Repairs and refurbishes wheelchairs within a workshop operated on behalf of a charity.

Woodworker. Manufactures a wide range of wooden items by hand and machine (including circular saws, band saws, routers, hand held and belt sanders).

Works Operative. Provides a reactive maintenance service dealing with urgent repairs as well as routine maintenance.

Workshop Manager. Coordinates and supervises a workshop team. Trains workers in all assembly line roles and ensures that targets are met.

Workshop Operative. Camouflage Netting. Manufactures camouflage netting on behalf of the Ministry of Defence.

Workshop Operative. Doors and Windows. Assembles UPVC windows and doors from component parts.

Workshop Operative. Electronics Workshop. Assembles complex wiring looms for use in the automotive industry.

Workshop Operative. Fixings Workshop. Manufactures and packs Rawlplugs, nuts, bolts, nails, screws and other fixings for sale in DIY stores.

Workshop Operative. Fragrance workshop. Manufactures room air fresheners on behalf of national retailers.

Workshop Operative. Headphones. Refurbishes and repackages headphones and small consumer items on behalf of Virgin Airlines.

Workshop Operative. Lighting Assembly. Assembles complex parts into finished light tubes, tests and packs them for retail sale.

Workshop Operative. Plumbing Workshop. Assembles component parts into finished plumbing assemblages and guttering for retail sale in Wickes DIY stores.

Workshop Operative. Radiator Valve Workshop. Assembles radiator valves, packages the finished products and bulk packs for despatch.

Workshop Operative. Tea Pack Workshop. Packages tea, coffee, milk, sugar, cereals and sundries into hotel sized portion packs for issue to prisoners.

Yoga teacher. Facilitates yoga and mindfulness classes for prisoners and staff.

Availability of job opportunities varies significantly between prisons and attendance at workplaces is often negatively affected by prison regimes.

"I used my time in prison in job roles where I could work hard, gain new skills and also help many other people. I have served in many highly trusted support roles which taught me a wide range of interpersonal skills and helped me to develop an admirable work ethic." VM

For full CV descriptions of these jobs please refer to the book *"How to get a GREAT JOB when you have a CRIMINAL RECORD"* by the same author.

16. Work (Vocational) Qualifications

The best run prisons focus on helping prisoners to gain vocations qualifications as well as skills.

Many prisoners develop a strong sense of pride and self-worth through work and most have the intention to carry this through after release.

There are numerous vocational qualifications available across the prison estate ranging from entry level qualifications to full NVQ's and licences.

"I am so delighted to have gained a NVQ Level 3 Diploma in Engineering and Technology including Railway Infrastructure, Personal Track Safety and use of all small plant equipment. I have a Sentinel card and I am ready to work. This was a lot of money but I got a student loan. I am guaranteed permanent work at above average wage as soon as I leave prison. I am so grateful to the prison service for everything they did to allow delivery of this course. My future is stable and secure now." SP

"I am now 23 years old and when I came to prison age 21, I was determined to gain skills and qualifications. I wanted to change for the better. I achieved vocational skills including Level 1 and Level 2 bricklaying, a Forklift truck licence (counterbalance) and a Construction Skills Certification Scheme (CSCS) card including all Health and Safety modules." HH

There are even career pathways within the prison and many partnerships with forward thinking employers such as DHL and Halfords.

The British Institute of Cleaning Sciences (BICS) skills and career pathway is a good example where a prisoner can:

> Gain Level 1 qualifications whilst working as a BICS Industrial Cleaning Operative.
> Progress to BICS Biohazard Responder and BICS Industrial Cleaning Supervisor gaining a suite of Level 2 and Level 3 qualifications.
> Ultimately, whilst in prison, gain BICS Trainer and Assessor qualifications and be qualified to teach and certify trainers and assessors.

Cleaning qualifications may not impress some people, but we should bear in mind that:

> 1) Many people in prison have no formal qualifications. This may be the first time they have been recognised for achievements. Helping prisoners gain qualifications improves their self-esteem, encourages further study and reduces reoffending.
>
> 2) These types of qualifications are a pathway into permanent employment or self-employment. Bio-Hazard workers can typically earn £28k-£35k pa and almost never find themselves unemployed.

Vocational qualifications include, but are not limited to:

Art and design, Barbering, Barista, Block paving, Bookkeeping, Brick laying, Business enterprise, Carpentry (site and bench), Car Valeting, Catering, Ceramics, Cleaning (industrial and biohazard), Computer networking (CISCO IT Essentials), Confectionery, Cookery, Creative writing, Customer service, Domestic appliance repair, Drug and alcohol mentoring and counselling, Electrical installation, Exercise Referral, Fire warden, First aid, Fitness instructing, Gas cutting, Graphic Design, Health and safety, Heating installation, Horticulture Skills, Hospitality, ICT Systems Support, IAG (Information, Advice and Guidance), Kitchen fitting, Laundering, Learning Support, Machine setting, Mediation, Microsoft Office, Motor vehicle maintenance, Music Technology, Painting and decorating, Peer Mentoring, Photography, Personal Track Safety (PTS), Personal training, Plastering, Plumbing, Portable appliance testing (PAT), Retail, Sales and Marketing, Risk assessing, Roofing systems, Sewing and stitching, Solar panel installation, Sports coaching, Steel Fixing, Street-works, Textile manufacture, Upholstery skills, Warehousing (Storage and Logistics), Waste and recycling, Welding, Workshop management, Window installation,

Availability of courses and qualifications varies tremendously between prisons.

"I secured a place on a carpentry course which gave me a purpose for six months and led to me gaining formal qualifications. This new focus means that I can now gain legitimate employment and stay away from criminals and criminal activities." KR

17. Understanding wider impact of crime

Being in prison can open people's eyes to the impact of crime and criminality on individuals.

"I met some drug addicts in prison who had wasted their entire lives because people like me brought drugs into society. This makes me ashamed and also makes me feel responsible. I have also met people who have self-harmed or even committed suicide because they were unable to get the drugs that their bodies craved. I have taken a long hard look at myself and grown up. I know that I need to stop living such a selfish and irresponsible life; I have to think about the wider implications of my life choices." RP

There are a number of Victim Awareness courses available in prison ranging from general in-cell, self-study packs with limited value to a powerful intervention course called 'Sycamore Tree'. This is a non-faith promoting course run by Prison fellowship volunteers, typically accommodating 20 attendees and run over six three-hour sessions over six weeks. Attendance can be voluntary or made compulsory as part of sentence plans.

"I have had time to reflect on and understand the harm that I had caused to individual people as well as society. I am truly very sorry for what I did and I am determined to stay crime-free for good." TJ

This course encourages personal responsibility, reflecting on root causes of crime and it helps people to change their thinking. Attendees meet courageous victims of serious crimes (usually parents of murder victims) and they learn a lot about the impact of crime on other people and on society.

"I voluntarily completed an accredited Victim Awareness course called Sycamore Tree and other personal development programmes. I met victims of crime and this gave me profound insights into the harm of crime." GW

Many people start the course believing that they haven't created victims, but they discover the ripple effect of crime and how it affects the criminal, their family, victims, their families, communities and society as a whole.

"I now realise how serious the consequences of my actions were. Previously I had always been there for my wife and children but now my wife has to manage everything by herself and my children are suffering without me being there. Crimes such as mine can have far reaching ripples into society too. I needed to mature and change." SC

Having completed Sycamore Tree and mentored on five courses, I can vouch for the dramatic changes that attendees go through. Unfortunately, like many essential interventions, it is under-resourced and over-subscribed; some people have to wait 2-3 years to get a place.

18. Understanding Criminal Urges and Triggers

People in prison are encouraged to reflect on their personal motivators for crime. Understanding these personal triggers is important so that people know what to avoid.

Simple changes like disassociation from criminal associates, changing area and walking away or counting to ten before losing their temper, can help people to avoid crime.

Once they understand why they committed their crimes, many people make a decision to break-away from past problematic lifestyles.

"I have cut off all contact with past criminal associates and formed a support network of family and friends who all live decent, positive and law-abiding lives." JD

"Now I have put prison behind me, I work full time and even more hours than my contract requires me to. Boredom was my biggest trigger for crime so now I make sure I am never bored." TG

Helping people to understand the root causes of their mistakes and their crimes and then helping them to replace their thinking and behaviour with alternative thinking and behaviour can make a dramatic difference.

"I had to grow up fast and scared. I was convinced that I was worthless. I was angry and I wanted to hurt people and hurt the world. I don't want that for my children. So, I had to change. I focussed on gaining proper qualifications so I could work and be a role model for my children. How can I tell them to study if I didn't do it? I don't want them following my path so I need to show them how I have changed." FY

19. Sharing Lessons Learnt and Discouraging Crime

The majority of prisoners, (certainly more than half of the people I have met) are motivated to teach other people the lessons they have learnt, the consequences of their crime (s) and the impact of imprisonment.

"I have made arrangements to speak at driving awareness courses and tell my story to warn other people of the dangers of mobile phones and other distractions whilst driving." DR

People who have been punished for their crimes are a vast resource that is underutilised in terms of teaching their cautionary tales and the great benefit this could bring.

"I set up a drug mentoring programme which helped addicts to detox and to understand risks of relapse. I met with dignitaries from the Ministry of Justice who were particularly interested in the good work I was doing." FM

There is no one better to teach the pitfalls and lessons than someone who has actually lived through the subject being taught.

"I held business start-up classes in which I shared my experiences of the right and wrong ways to run a business to avoid falling foul of the law. I taught people who have their own small business ideas, such as being self-employed tradespeople, or starting online ventures, upon release." VL

Many people become very vocal, enthusiastic and passionate about telling their story and encouraging others not to make the same mistakes. They are particularly keen to share their lessons with young people and try to guide them not to make the same mistakes.

"One project that has been important to me is called 'Inside-out'. In partnership with Hampshire Constabulary, young offenders or teenagers identified as being at risk of becoming involved in crime are brought into prison for a day or for a few sessions. We sit down with these children, listen to each other's stories and show them what prison is really like; doing all we can to discourage them from crime and steer them towards a positive life, as valued people in their communities." GT

"I was very influenced by music, I took it to heart and tried to live that lifestyle, but that's no good. Now I share my story with the youth and tell them to enjoy music, like they enjoy films, but don't try to live that life - it's no good." SP

"I served as a lead facilitator for a charity project called 'Keep-Out'. In this role, I worked with deprived young people who were identified as being at high risk of engaging in crime and I discouraged them from crime by explaining the awful consequences, how to avoid negative peer pressure and how to set goals for a positive and crime-free life." KD

"I invested time working with troubled young people in a crime diversion scheme called 'Last Chance'. I explained to them that they must do anything possible to avoid prison and stay crime free. I removed all of the ridiculous glamour and allure of crime and prison and told them the truth, however hard-hitting. From the looks on their faces I know that I have helped to steer some of these troubled kids back onto the right path." MF

Some people are handed long prison sentences supposedly to deter other people from committing similar crimes. A far more useful deterrent would be to share the backgrounds to crime, the thought processes, the triggers and the lessons that individuals and society can take away from each crime.

"The project I am proudest of being a part of is called MVP-The Mentors in Violence Project. I was able to host visits from young people most at risk of committing crime or who were interested in helping their peers to avoid crime. I gave a series of talks, sharing my story and my personal journey of rehabilitation. These young people really listened and I know that I had a big impact on them and that if anyone could, then I could certainly discourage them from crime. I would tell them "Look, coming to prison is about as low as you can end up in your life, there is nothing big about it. This is not a big-man place, this is a place for losers and loners and you don't want to end up here. Do anything you can to live a clean and good life and never commit crime. Crime destroys your family and it destroys society." Some of the young people were influenced by their friends, by music and by media; they needed to be told the reality, the harsh reality to understand it. So, I am determined to carry on my good works and never commit crime. I have changed for the better and learnt many lessons." DC

20. Personal Development

Overall, there are 8 primary drivers for personal development in prison which I explain using the coincidental acronym - **I'm Past It**.

I.M.P.A.S.T.I.T.
Intervention, Mentors, Pain, Age, Self-Image, Time, Incentives, Training

These are powerful drivers for change and self-development which work in combination to accelerate change.

I elaborate on each of these drivers for personal development as follows:

I = Intervention

Prison itself is an intervention and it is essential that such interventions occur so that they can serve as a catalyst for change.

Other inventions include transfers, therapy, counselling, mandatory courses and the provision of opportunities for change and personal growth.

"I was reluctant about completing the Getting It Right course at first because it was forced on me, but I actually got a lot out of it and I went and got a book on Cognitive Behaviour Therapy so that I could understand how to make permanent changes." RE

Depending on the crimes that people have committed, some interventions are compulsory as part of their sentence plan.

"I felt angry when I was made to do a self-change intervention called 'Kaizen'. I stropped and said very little for the first 2 sessions. By the third one however when I realised that this could actually help me, I unfolded my arms and got into it. This course really turned my life around. I learnt so much from this; the person who graduated was not the same person who enrolled on it. I feel so good and positive now; I discovered self-talk and positive thinking, considering consequences, managing emotions, choosing personal associations carefully and other life skills." DB

"I completed a course called 'Positive lifestyles' which helped me to improve my relationships and the way I see other people. I no longer feel the need to control so much but try to understand them better." AF

The timing of interventions is also important, much like when teaching children, interventions must happen swiftly when people are most receptive to change.

"I completed a comprehensive programme called Addressing Alcohol Related Offending (AARO). This helped me to understand why I drank and why drinking changed my behaviour. I drank socially at first, then I started drinking for the sake of it; it became an addiction. I developed a problem with alcohol, it magnifies my emotions and increases my likelihood of criminal behaviour, that's why I no longer drink at all." KP

People need to be treated as individuals and require an investment of time and attention to help facilitate change.

"I graduated from TSP-Thinking Skills Programme. This is a widely recognised and praised programme it really is a game changer. It woke me up to the idea that I could live a crime free life, that I can be better than I have been, that I can make better decisions and that I deserve a chance of happiness and normality too. I worked hard on this programme and I was praised for my commitment to engage wholeheartedly and complete the course." SL

M = Mentors

Mentors, role models and positive family members help individuals to develop an image of who they want to be, but more than that, they hand-hold and guide the person.

"I was embarrassed to learn until I was approached by another prisoner. He offered to help me and I felt equal to him so I listened to him and started to accept his help. He became my mentor and now I have achieved Maths and English qualifications. Because I found school tough, I was un-teachable at first, I couldn't be taught by a teacher but learning from a mentor worked for me. Now I feel able to learn and have joined a business class and will be doing bookkeeping after. Having a mentor made a big difference to me and got me started on learning." Al

Mentors are listened to more intently as real-life examples of what is possible, who care and are usually part of the peer group, having *natural authority* rather than *imposed authority*.

P = Pain

The pain caused by the punishment of prison and the consequences of their crime (s) is a major catalyst for change and desistance.

"I do not think the same way anymore; I am not the same person. I am so acutely aware of consequences and I think before I act" JC

"My wife is so stressed she got shingles really bad and all my children and my mum are distraught, I never want them to go through it again." PI

"In shock and despair, I tried and failed to take my own life, nothing this bad had ever happened in my life before and it was very hard to come to terms with. I feel such terrible remorse and guilt for causing the sad death of another person." WN

"Looking back, I am angry with myself and ashamed that I got involved in criminal activity. The pain I have caused my family and the victims is difficult to think about but I have to think about it so that I never sink so low again. I have been away from my wife and children for a long time. This is my first and last time in prison." GL

A = Age

Maturing, gaining life experience and changing biologically (a reduction in the level of testosterone in men) leads to more considered behaviour.

"I was wild in my youth. I was physical, aggressive and ready to boil over at the slightest thing, but I have calmed down a lot. It is like I am a different person now." GL

"I have grown up so much since I committed my crime. I do believe that people do change. I know that I have a long way to go, but I have something to aim for, positive life goals and things to work towards." CT

S = Self-Image

People need to believe that that change is possible and that they deserve a better life.

We need to guide and help people to develop the idea of a different future life, a desired self which is very different from before.

"I have broken ties with undesirable past associates. I don't have anything in common with them anymore and don't want to be around them." KL

It is important that people develop a vision of the kind of person they aspire to being.

"I don't see myself as a criminal anymore. That is not the life I want. I want to be a positive role model, working and providing for my family." BE

"Coming to prison was a depressing shock but contrary to this, it was also a highly motivating wake-up call. I have taken a long hard look at myself and reminded myself constantly that I was here because of my own decisions. I have been very inspired to change for the better." JJ

T = Time

Time for self-reflection and soul-searching eases understanding and helps people to reach powerful conclusions.

"I have had a time for self-reflection and personal development; I am a more positive person, in a better place mentally and physically than when I committed my offence. I am determined to start a new chapter in my life, free of crime and I want to make a contribution to society." SU

Silence, stillness and solitude have philosophically, been thought for thousands of years, to be the pathway to self-actualisation.

> "Away from the busy-ness of society,
> many people find themselves." PM

Too much alone time, can however lead to isolation, loneliness and despair; in many people it increases the risk of self-harm and destructive behaviours.

I = Incentives

The opposite of pain, this is the carrot rather than the stick. Incentives are proven to work in a prison setting and help to facilitate habitual good behaviour.

"One prison gave students a small bonus of £5 or £6 on their canteen each time they graduated from a course or gained an educational level. When people earn £12 a week wages, extra money is really appreciated for phone calls, toiletries or treats. The maths and English classes were always full because of this. I have not seen that anywhere else. In most prisons, people are dragged kicking and screaming into classes, some would rather stay banged-up because they don't see any benefit to them." HP

Enhanced behaviour incentive programmes reward good behaviour with additional visits, increased canteen spend (money for telephone calls, toiletries etc.) and special visits called "family days".

"When I first came to prison, my partner and I were arguing constantly. She would visit with the children and we would sit across the table from each other, struggling to adapt to the situation and hardly saying a word. The first family day I was given however was totally different, we had private time to talk and cuddle and play with farm animals with the children. After that day we were fine again. That family day gave us hope that our relationship could last and it has. Family days are priceless." VT

Of particular consideration is the impact of family on helping prisoners to change. Prisoners are generally acutely aware of the pain caused to their families by their behaviour.

The more they see their family as a positive force in their life and the more contact they have with their families, the more motivated they generally are to develop personally.

"After I completed 'Resolve', my family were invited to attend the awards day. I am so pleased that they were allowed to attend and see how much I have progressed. They have agreed to give me a second chance in my life. I will not let my parents, siblings or my young son down ever again." JS

T = Training

It is overwhelmingly worthwhile to provide prisoners with vocational courses, educational opportunities and support for personal development.

"Since coming to prison I have learnt what is expected in any workplace and I have gained the habit of work. With a lot of determination and some late nights, I am now a fully qualified Railway Engineer with a solid career ahead of me." MF

Education is a proven way that many people change their lives around.

"I have completely turned my life around. I have passed accredited self- development courses and I am a more rounded and positive person." WN

"I was fortunate that I met a Prison Training Officer (Simon) who ran a horticulture course and he became a mentor to me. I was able to talk to Simon and he cared enough to listen, he inspired me on the path of self-improvement. With his help I went on to mentor other people and I gained a qualification in Learning Support and Peer Mentoring. Simon coached me and I worked hard to gain a range of vocational qualifications (including garden machinery, forklift truck and CSCS card). I believe that this man helped me to change my life for the better." AJ

The potential that someone has is not, in isolation, enough for them to change.

A person has to want to change and be ready to change before they gain the necessary motivation and become receptive to new ideas and influences.

It is important none the less to recognise the potential that every individual has to develop and change for the better, to behave differently in different environments and with different people, and to strive to bring the best out of themselves.

Recognising and respecting this inherent potential is the first step to supporting and encouraging positive change.

"The moment you begin to make excuses for yourself, for your behaviour, that is when you start on the pathway to prison."
Stan Williams, founder of the notorious Crips gang, Nobel peace prize nominee, Nobel prize winner for Literature.

Quotes - The things that would help me to never come back to prison

"The things that will stop me from coming back to prison are not really things. They are the people that I care about and who care about me, as well as my own attitude and actions.

I know that I am responsible but I also know that I need a hand sometimes. If you just land back out there and you have no family or support, then yes you will need things, basic things, like food, shelter, maybe clothing.

If people don't have their basis needs met (see Maslow's hierarchy of needs) then they have no choice but to commit crime just to survive.
That's not an excuse, that's reality, no one should be expected to starve or freeze when they have already paid the price for their crimes." AL

Quotes - The things that would help me to Never Come Back to Prison

The following quotes were given by serving prisoners who had spent a wide range of time in prison from 1 - 21 years, in all different prison categories, and who were near the end of their sentences.

The following quotes were given by serving prisoners who had spent a wide range of time in prison from 1 - 21 years in prison (in all different categories).

They were approaching the final stages of their sentence and were asked to name the things that could stop them from coming back to prison.

"**Family support.**" HA

"**Being drug free.**" TD

"**Sticking to rules.**" YG

"**Personal motivation.**" SP

"**Family relationships.**" JB

"**Earning legal money.**" GS

"**A roof over my head.**" HA

"**Remaining drug free.**" WY

"**Controlling my temper.**" LM

"**Being able to earn a living.**" KB

"**Having a family of my own.**" RM

"**Making a stable family home.**" BE

"**Having full time employment.**" RR

"**Stability in work and finances.**" KI

"**The people who care about me.**" RJ

"**A permanent job at a living wage.**" CB

"**The thought of freedom and fresh air.**" LV

"**Nothing is bringing me back to prison.**" SB

"Not drinking, staying away from alcohol." BR

"Having goals and working towards them." KW

"A stable, long term partner by your side." GD

"Moving to a new area and getting a fresh start." JR

"Avoiding the people, I used to hang around with." SH

"Staying away from drug dealers and drug users." FO

"Building bridges with estranged family members." LY

"My own determination and the support of my wife." AC

"Spending time with my children and grandchildren." HP

"My determination to set an example for my children." TB

"The fear of being locked up again for 23 hours a day." KS

"Helping me to cope with my mental health challenges." SC

"Having my own home, where I can shut my own door." MR

"Not being lonely, joining things and making new friends." LF

"Changing myself through personal development and study." JG

"Employment, stable home, family life and positive mind-set." SP

"If I stay away from drugs, I stay away from trouble and crime." RV

"The church community have accepted me, despite my crimes." HE

"Myself, as I know not to be stupid and repeat similar mistakes." KB

"Not reacting emotionally but taking time to think things through." PA

"Being given a chance; not excluded by employers and landlords." BR

"Staying away from the people who hurt my brother + their family." ME

"The lack of freedom and the overwhelming despair of being in prison." NS

"Being reunited with my children and being able to be involved in their life." MI

"Employment and help to survive (housing and food) until first pay check." KA

"It is a waste of life, that's the loss, that's the deterrent, those years wasted." NY

"Following regulations that affect my businesses and paying for legal advice." MS

"If I am financially self-sufficient and can make money to support my family." JW

"I won't re-offend, no matter what, I have seen enough from one time in prison." DS

"Getting a job that I enjoy and that I can bury myself in to keep busy all the time." BA

"Support from my family and me thinking of them and considering them more." MF

"Focussing on family instead of so-called friends who are just out for themselves." TP

"I will not be coming back I just want a fresh start and to make everyone proud." MW

"An employer giving me a chance, I would take it and not let them down, I would give it 110%." KB

"The ability to work as much as I want to without being bored and be trusted with some responsibility." MK

"Society accepting me and being given a job. I am willing to work and I will work hard but I need a chance." BR

"Getting a desk type job without being rejected due to my age, because I can't do labouring work anymore." SW

"My own determination will stop me coming back, not slipping into old habits and making the same hasty and stupid decisions." ID

"Understanding the impact of my crime on my victim personally and also the effects of all crime of people and society in general." KS

"Getting my foot in the door and gaining a good training job or apprenticeship so that I can build a future with permanent work." LE

"I will be a very careful driver. In the future I will allow extra travel time for each journey and have a working dash camera and sat nav at all times." AL

"It's the little things that matter so much, taking my children to school, eating meals with my wife, you can't put a value on seeing your seeing your family." BH

"My children, my family and the thought of the time I have missed and will never get back. The thought of being away from my family again is the ultimate deterrent" LH

"With a job, I am less likely to re-offend in the future. I know that Rome wasn't built in a day and I am a work in progress, but a job will be a big step forward for me." RC

"If I have structure and stability then I will not have chaos and I won't be involved in crime. A job and a place to live within an hour of my family are most important." KS

"People tell me that I can forget prison, but I don't want to. I want to remember the awful experience as long as I live so that I remind myself never to come back. Those memories will stop me coming back." DP

"Having meetings with probation recorded so that there are two sided versions of events, rather than decisions made by individual people. Police interviews are recorded, why aren't probation ones, they are just as important if they can lead to prison." NF

"Provision of secure housing, not even just temporary hostel places but permanent little homes where people can settle into regular life after so years of stress, upheaval and uncertainty, would definitely be a big factor in stopping me and many others from coming back to prison." LH

"You have to believe that it is possible to bring people round. I think most people who go to prison are capable of making the journey to a better way of living." Jon Snow, broadcaster and Channel 4 news presenter.

Chapter 3 - The Vital Role of Pastoral Care and Faith Provision in Prison

"Whilst in prison, I discovered my faith and in this I found fulfilment and hope." CT

"The Chaplaincy team pulled me out of an unimaginably dark place that I never could have got out of on my own." WG

The Vital Role of Pastoral Care and Faith Provision in Prison

Faith provision in prison is generally excellent and in most prisons is made a priority.

Chaplaincy teams provide a huge amount of unconditional help and support to people in prison. I needn't mention any specific religion because all religions are represented and supported and pastoral care is provided by multi-faith chaplaincies.

Life-changing pastoral care is proactively and wholeheartedly given and there are very few barriers put in the way (other than restricted regimes in closed prisons) making chaplaincy a truly unique feature of the prison service.

Most people in prison have to come to terms with:

- What they have done, their crime.
- The complete destruction of their previous life, through the imprisonment.
- Life stresses that continue despite their imprisonment, including but not limited to, bereavement, divorce and parental disputes.
- What happened to them in the past; most people in prison have suffered abuse or neglect as a child or been victims of terrible crimes themselves.

The modern prison experience itself is demonstrably damaging to an individual's wellbeing and mental health.

Particular problems come from 23-hour bang up, overcrowding and violence, as well as regular transfers away from individual support networks.

There are many occasions where it is simply impossible for a human being to cope without help.

Prison chaplains really do go the extra mile and offer a great deal of comfort and practical support to people in prison and their families. This is particularly appreciated and necessary in times of sadness, grief or crisis, such as bereavement or newly arriving in prison.

"My son tragically died whilst I was serving my prison sentence. The chaplain came to see me with the awful news. I do not remember how I responded but I do remember being picked up off the floor by the chaplain who sat with me throughout the small hours of the morning. He then took me to a private room where I could phone home. Later he organised all the paperwork and liaised with the governors so that I could go to the funeral. I have never even been to church in prison, yet I was treated as if I was the most committed and valuable member of the church community. I wasn't judged I was genuinely cared about and I am very grateful." GE

Chaplains also communicate with family members when the prisoner himself is in crisis.

"Early in my prison sentence I self-harmed and tried to take my own life. I became addicted to a powerful drug - NPS/ Spice, which sent my mental health in a tortuous downward spiral. At one point the prison officers thought I might die. The chaplains didn't only support me, they rung my next of kin and arranged two visits. Eventually they even helped me to get transferred so that I could have a fresh start in a different prison away from the drugs, the debt and also near to my family. I would not have got through my prison sentence without the chaplains, I would be dead. I do owe them my life." NH

Faith can be unifying but it can also be divisive if not managed correctly. I consider faith to be very personal indeed. I neither encourage nor discourage anyone from learning about and following any faith or religion.

The excellent team work shown by the faith leaders in prison sets a great example to prison residents of tolerance, acceptance and help.

"When I first arrived in prison, I was crying for 3 hours. I was bewildered and couldn't cope; I didn't know where I was physically or mentally. Historically I was Christian but the Muslim imam came and sat with me. He listened to me, comforted me, helped me to phone home and also upon my request, prayed with me. He noted my faith and the next day the priest came to see me and each day a representative of chaplaincy came to see me to make sure I was okay. Their compassion helped me beyond words, I am not sure that I wouldn't have taken my own life without their attentiveness and care." PJ

When people have available time, such as when they are serving a prison sentence, faith can give them a focus and it certainly becomes a solid foundation on which to build a more complete life in future.

"I became committed to my religion in prison and discovered the power of prayer. This gives me strength and I have now have friends inside and outside of prison. I feel accepted, connected and able to turn my life around. I am very grateful to the faith leaders I met who helped me." PB

When people in prison do make a decision to explore their spirituality and religion further a whole new world opens up to them.

"I never knew that I could sing until I joined the small singing group in prison, now I have my own favourite hymns and I practise in my cell. I feel so much more stable and happier. I have a bit of my old optimism and light heartedness back. Something I haven't felt since I was a child." TK

As well as religious services and festivals, there are many social activities such as singing groups, prayer groups, courses and religious study sessions that people can choose to be a part of.

"Going to regular prayers has helped me to change for the better; I believe that there is a power greater than myself, that I am accountable and answerable to. I have developed a clear moral framework and I have many people who are like brothers in my faith community. This can only be a good thing; I know that out of everything that happened to me and the bad that I did myself, the one good thing that has come out of this is that I now have renewed faith and belief. I am a worthwhile person; I am a good human being, who can do good for others." JC

These regular activities fill people with hope, help them to pass time in self-reflection and study and also give them something to forward to.

"Getting unlocked for church on Sunday was the highlight of my week in prison. I shaved, showered and dressed as smart as I could. We had live singing from guest church groups as well as audience singing. I loved the singing and the positivity. After service we had coffee and biscuits and met and chatted with volunteers from the community. I felt like I wasn't worthless, people cared. For those couple of hours, it was like I wasn't in prison. Did it help me tangibly? yes and no you see for a few days after church I was calmer and more positive and for a few days before church I was looking forward to it. So, it helped me yes to get through each week, but tangibly means did I change, well I didn't see myself as a criminal before, I came to prison as a one-off thing, so I haven't really changed. But if I hadn't had that lifeline of church and the love from those genuine people, I may well have got more and more depressed. I was certainly feeling it." MS

It is apparent that chaplaincy provision in prison provides numerous benefits to people, these make the coincidental acronym:

F.A.I.T.H.C.A.R.E.

Fellowship, Acceptance, Inspiration, Teaching, Help, Community, Accountability, Rehabilitation, Empathy

I elaborate on each of the benefits as follows:

F = Fellowship

Building friendships and relationships is very important in prison because people can soon find themselves depressed, isolated or even ganged up on.

The hardest part of the prison sentence for most people is the separation from family. Friendships amongst faith members can be a great comfort and go some way to filling the huge void left in a person's life.

A = Acceptance

In restricted circumstances, where it is hard to change anything, acceptance becomes an essential factor for mental health and well-being.

Faith groups promote acceptance of:

Situations - Helping people to come to terms with reality of situations and concepts that are difficult to grasp, to see that they will be able to handle it and that there may be a greater purpose that hasn't been revealed yet.

Other people - They learn forgiveness and how to appreciate other people and treat them with decency and respect. All people are precious manifestations of the creator, even if they are flawed or imperfect, they should all be valued and accepted.

Themselves - They learn that they are valuable, that their past does not have to define who they are and it does not need to affect the future or be repeated in it. Self-esteem, as well as thinking and behaviour, improve when people begin to accept themselves.

<u>Themselves by other people</u> - They learn that they are as good as anyone else, unique and valuable as they are and deserving of being treated with respect, decency and even kindness. Acceptance is the opposite of the rejection which many people in prison have experienced throughout their lives.

Reaching a point of acceptance of the reality of where a person finds themselves helps them to get through each day.

A big part of acceptance is forgiveness and learning to let go of anger, hate and negativity. Faithcare helps people to discover and embrace this concept.

I = Inspiration

Faithcare providers give people hope and inspire them to develop a vision for the future.

They begin to get direction in their lives and this direction keeps them going even when things are tough.

The inspiration from stories of other people who have overcome personal challenges (both historically and more recently) is a powerful driving force for positive change.

"Chaplaincy have been the main source of comfort to me in a very difficult time. They have helped me to build a relationship with God and to see good in everything and everyone." RR

T = Teaching

Many people in prison are missing the moral framework that others take for granted. Faithcare teaches this moral framework and people begin to develop ethical values based on religious principles.

These standards, values and life lessons often become the new foundation upon which people can build more successful and law-abiding lives.

H = Help and support

Practical help and support are essential for people in crisis.

Faithcare providers give a huge amount of real help at key points in people's lives such as when they first arrive in prison, when they suffer bereavements and relationship breakdowns and they also arrange positive events like weddings and baptisms.

C = Community

The long-term benefits of being part of a faith community are well documented.

Feelings of disillusionment, a perceived inability to fit in (misfit) or being unwanted are often precursors to criminal activity.

When people feel more connected to their community and wider society, they are substantially less likely to commit crime against that society.

Faithcare providers foster healthy links between prisons and communities. Prison chapels and faith celebrations are often the only exposure that people in prison have to guests from outside of the prison and vice versa. The warmth and acceptance shown by visitors from outside the prison is humbling and enlightening to prisoners.

Faithcare providers also signpost outside groups prior to a prisoner's release so that they can continue to worship and study with like-minded people upon release.

A = Accountability

When people in prison begin to engage with Faithcare providers the relationship often becomes that of a mentor and mentee.

This leads to greater accountability on the part of the mentee and a desire to please the person who has shown belief and trust and who has invested their time.

Faith itself and the belief in a higher power create accountability, leading to people holding themselves to higher standards of conduct and behaviour.

R = Rehabilitation

Faithcare providers play an important role in the rehabilitation of offenders.

Rehabilitation means positive change, change for the better. It means guiding people and practically helping them to break bad habits and not return to past problematic or unlawful behaviours.

Sycamore Tree victim awareness programme is probably the best example of Faithcare making a demonstrable difference and a measurable contribution to rehabilitation.

This is a 6-session course facilitated by external 'Prison Fellowship' volunteers. Attendees learn about the wider ripple effects of crime on individuals and on society, they meet victims of crime and they learn to accept personal responsibility.

People who complete this course express remorse and gain a greater understanding of their personal triggers; their reasons, circumstances and thought processes that led to crime and imprisonment.

> "I joined a course that other inmates had told me about. It was run by outside volunteers who cared about helping people to change and gave up their own time. This course was called Sycamore Tree and it is widely recognised for helping people to change their attitudes, thinking and behaviour. Courageous victims of crime came in to speak with the 20 attendees of the course. The programme lasted 6 weeks and I didn't want it to end. I completed the course and all of the workbooks, I graduated with a Level 2 certificate in restorative justice which I was proud of. More than that however, the course helped me to draw a line under the past and begin planning a more positive law-abiding future." JD

Sycamore Tree is widely recommended and leads to a recognised Level 2 qualification in Understanding Restorative Justice.

Faithcare has an important role to play in the growing emergence of Rehabilitative Cultures across the prison system and in helping people to change for good.

> "At the end of Sycamore Tree, I publicly spoke to audiences about my crimes and the regret that I feel. Now I also mentor other people." MA

> "I liked being part of Sycamore Tree which is an accredited Victim Awareness programme. I qualified as a mentor and became a classroom assistant supporting learners on 7 further six-week courses. By repeating the course so many times myself, I really learnt my lessons and began to accept full personal responsibility for creating more positive ripples into society." ES

E = Empathy

As more care is shown to an individual and as their self-esteem improves, they develop greater empathy and understanding of other people.

Empathy is an essential building block of a pro-social life. A life that asserts the rights of the individual but also respects the rights of other people.

Many people in prison have missed this important milestone of their emotional development or have an underdeveloped sense of empathy.

Faithcare is built on empathy; through the deliberate teaching and also through the examples of support and compassion shown, the recipients of Faithcare develop demonstrably greater empathy of their own.

"The chaplaincy team were superb they really helped me a lot with a wide range of issues; not just faith but my family relationships and mental health too." EY

Faithcare is a powerful force for improving self-worth and reducing re-offending.

Faithcare provision is as important, or perhaps as essential, as traditional healthcare provision. It can often be more effective than healthcare in ameliorating mental illnesses, such as depression and anxiety. When considering the proven links between mental health and physical wellbeing, it is apparent that **Faithcare** can and does dramatically improve physical health too.

I would like to express my personal admiration and appreciation for all the good work that is done by prison chaplains and volunteers and I would urge all interested parties to support them wholeheartedly in all possible ways.

"By merging the life-changing pastoral care, support for families, religious teachings and worship into a formalised range of services called 'Faithcare', it will be possible to reach more vulnerable and isolated people within prisons and also attract greater support from a wider range of people and organisations, both inside and outside of prison." PM

"Prison helped me to reform, it stopped me being an impulsive person, but it also tore my family apart." HW

Quotes - I could have coped better with My Prison Sentence if...

"If I had been better informed of what to expect in advance, it would have helped me to prepare or even if the judge had given me a week or two to get some things together. Being thrown in at the deepest of deep ends made coming to prison more traumatic than it needed to be." CT

Quotes - I could have coped better with My Prison Sentence if...

The following quotes were given by serving prisoners who had spent a wide range of time in prison from 1 - 27 years in a multitude of prisons and who were now in the final few months of their prison sentences. They were asked to share those things that would help them cope with their prison sentence.

These are not necessarily the views of the author; a wide range of replies have been included for perspective and to help understand a wide range of thought processes.

"More family times." PA

"Being treated fairly." SS

"If I had a single cell." SB

"More positive people." EO

"More time out of cell." HC

"Positive encouragement." SL

"Therapy and Counselling." RC

"If I had more family visits." EB

"If the staff were more positive." JR

"I had been helped and supported." LH

"If sentence plans were better organised." PD

"More support for families and more opportunities." MC

"Better food instead of potatoes and rice every day." TN

"If I had spent my whole sentence in open conditions." KA

"Officers to understand that prisoners are not all the same." DV

"If I had come to terms with it and accepted where I was sooner." NS

"If I was in prison nearer home, I could have visits from my family." EA

"Better affordability of phone calls home and more access to phones." SA

"Coming to prison with clothes, a radio and books would have helped." PP

"Having parent's rights to see my children even as a serving prisoner." LB

"More available ROTL to access full-time work and send money home." GT

"If I could have prepared my family in advance it would be less shock." MY

"I had been easier-going with my partner and family and not taking out my stresses on them." KS

"Visiting the gym more would have made me healthier and made me feel better about myself." AN

"If I had stopped rebelling against education and courses quicker and embraced personal change sooner." DL

"Making Release on Temporary Licence for rebuilding family ties more accessible, regular and predictable." ER

"Use the prisoners more, get them out to work, it is better for everyone if they feel valued and are kept busy." CB

"If more help was provided for rehabilitation and resettlement so I could have begun planning and imagining a life after release." JE

"If there was more equality in prisons, I found it unfair as a traveller, I was treated very differently and with distain by most officers." RN

"I was given courses to do earlier in my sentence and employment throughout, it would have helped me to use my time better." MS

"If I had spent time with more positive people, instead of trying to people please and impress the idiots (there are plenty of these in prison)." PK

"Being treated like a human being instead of a prison number - a number that means we are scum and lowest of the low; there to be bullied, intimidated and despised." CH

"If I had understood more about the reasons for getting the sentence I did I would have coped with it better. I still think that the length of sentence is made up on the spot." GS

"If there was more help on the outside for families of prisoners then they wouldn't be suffering so much, people in prison would be less distressed and relationships less strained." OA

"Having windows that open instead of useless vents, on hot bang-up days it felt like I was being cooked in my cell. I couldn't even get undressed because of rules saying that we have to stay dressed in case female officers are doing checks." BT

"I see first hand how hard it is for people to cope with prison and how destructive the entire system is.

So called 'induction' wings and courses do little to prepare people or their families for the difficulties ahead.

We need a more joined up approach to supporting individuals to get through prison unscathed and achieve rehabilitation so that they can return back to society.

There is so much more we could do, if only we had the time and backing to do it."

Prison Officer, 8 establishments, 15 years.

Chapter 4 - Mind-set Milestones; The 5 R's of Change

"I pleaded not guilty because initially I did not believe that I was guilty of the charges as suggested. I was however guilty of the irresponsible and dangerous behaviour that led me to this point. I had to accept responsibility otherwise I knew that I could never change and live a normal life. I had to take a long look at myself and get to the point where I said "It's my fault" only then could take control of my future." LD

Mind-set Milestones - The 5 R's of Change

This chapter first appeared in "If criminals can change then so should society and our prisons" ISBN 9781696356565. It is included here for relevance and because it introduces chapter

There are a number of **Mind-set Milestones** that a prisoner or ex-offender must go through to effect a real change and to live a law-abiding life.

I call these milestones **the 5 R's** and explain them as follows:

- **R1 Remorse**

   I am sorry for what I did, for the impact of what happened and I do regret my crime(s).

- **R2 Reasons**

   I now understand the reasons/ triggers why I committed my crime and the circumstances around it.

   I have a clear insight into the circumstances, my thought processes and my emotions at the time.

   I know exactly where I went wrong.

- **R3 Responsibility**

   I admit that it is my fault and I am not passing the blame.

- **R4 Rehabilitation**

   I won't do it again; I have learnt lessons and changed.

- **R5 Reconciliation**

   I want to make up for what I did wrong and contribute.

   I am committed to living a rule following and law-abiding life.

   I have goals for the future and I consider the impact of my goals on other people and society.

There are people in society that will accept me. I know that there is a place for me in my community and that I can have a job and a home and a chance of a fresh start.

"If all the 5 R's of change - Remorse, Reasons, Responsibility, Rehabilitation and Reconciliation, are adopted by an individual, then change can be as permanent as if it was set in concrete." PM

I have learnt the following 2 important considerations:

1. The **5 R's of change** are each of equal importance, to secure lasting change.
2. People can be helped and encouraged, but not forced, to discover each of the **5 R's of change**. They have to be ready.

Achieving **all 5** of these Mind-set Milestones guarantees ex-offenders a more positive future in which they are not weighed down by guilt or shame from the past, not recalled back to prison and not convicted of new offences.

The previous chapter will clearly end and a completely new one will begin.

"John's" story, which follows, includes and demonstrates the 5 R's.

As you read it, tick each one that you can spot:

Mind-set Milestone		Tick
R1	Remorse	
R2	Reasons	
R3	Responsibility	
R4	Rehabilitation	
R5	Reconciliation	

I was sentenced to 12 years' imprisonment for being involved in a conspiracy to supply drugs. This meant spending 6 years in prison and 6 years under supervision in the community.

I would like to share some background, not to justify what happened, but to explain a little.

I have always been a hard-working professional person. At the time of committing my offence I was working as a Construction Site Manager.

My partner and I married and had 2 beautiful children. We bought a modern car and our first home all within a very short space of time. As my expenses grew, it was clear that I had taken on too many financial commitments in this short space of time before my wife could return to work.

I got myself into a lot of debt and I tried to deal with it all by myself instead of discussing things with my family or seeking proper advice (which I now realise I should have done).

I was working as many hours as possible in my job but couldn't seem to get in front. I became fearful that we could lose our family home. I confided in someone I thought was a friend who introduced me to a couple of people with a "business opportunity". They were in fact drug dealers.

At first, I was shocked by this, but it is only years later that I can now admit to myself that I felt excitedly "naughty" and like a big man meeting these criminals.

Really my attitude was immature and irresponsible; looking back I am ashamed. With hindsight, it is clear that I should have said no straightaway, but in my desperation, I thought I saw a way to get out of the problems I had put my family in and I got involved in the conspiracy.

Predictably, I was caught after just a couple of months. I put my hands up, accepted responsibility and pleaded guilty.

My crime was totally out of character for me. This was my first offence.

I apologised to my family and to the judge and I decided to face my prison sentence courageously and as a positive opportunity to change my outlook.

Whilst in prison, I have committed to self-improvement, continued my work ethic (my CV still has an unbroken work history despite coming to prison) and tried my best to help other people in difficulty or distress.

I voluntarily completed an accredited Victim Awareness course called Sycamore Tree, as well as other personal development programmes. I met victims of crime and this gave me profound insights into the destructive effects of crime.

I became a drugs and alcohol peer mentor where I saw first-hand the nightmarish struggles that drug addicts go through. I supported users through detox and helped them to understand their risks of relapse. I also made referrals and signposted them to healthcare and to mental health teams.

With formal training from the Samaritans, I trained as a prison "listener" and helped other people, whilst they were at their lowest points, (self-harming or contemplating suicide). I am now a more understanding and humble person.

My intention is to build a productive life and put the past behind me. I really regret my previous criminal activity and I have learnt many lessons; I am a different person now. I have just finished the custodial part of my prison sentence and I have been reunited with my family. We currently live in

Stevenage; Hertfordshire and I am willing to commute or even relocate for the most suitable employment opportunity. I know that I can contribute to the community as a decent and law-abiding citizen again and I have every intention of doing so.

Hopefully you are able to see that the Mind-set Milestones - the 5 R's, form part of "John's" journey and they are embedded throughout this person's experience. John will be highly unlikely to ever re-offend again because he has instinctively and now consciously hit all of the 5 Mind-set Milestones.

John also has 2 of the 3 most important elements for successful resettlement namely **Support from Family** and **Long-Term Accommodation**.

The other important element being **Stable Employment** was being worked towards at the time of writing the letter.

By way of an update, **"John"** *is now working full-time again* **(March 2019)**.

> "Forgiveness and reconciliation are possible
> in an enlightened society." PM

The 5 R's of Change

R1	Remorse	I am sorry for what I did and I do regret my crime(s).
R2	Reasons	I understand the background circumstances and my personal buttons/ triggers well enough that I can explain to others if necessary.
R3	Responsibility	I admit that it is my fault and I am not passing the blame.
R4	Rehabilitation	I won't do it again; I have learnt lessons and changed.

R5	Reconciliation	I want to make up for what I did wrong and contribute.

"Most people in prison want to change but they need help and support to do it. Those who are chained by habit cannot usually break those chains by themselves. People need practical help and emotional support to change." PM

Chapter 5 - WHY I went to PRISON

(By 150 people who are determined never to return)

Hindsight reflections into how and why people ended up in prison

"I am so sorry for the harm that I caused." KE

"The life I had chosen was not a healthy one." RP

"Once the adrenaline kicked in, I went completely ott; I saw red and was consumed with rage." TA

"It was like quicksand that I got more and more sucked into, I will never get involved in that world in future." KS

"This was an accident that I will regret for the rest of my life." JL

"Since I committed my crime, I have changed a lot for the better." CR

WHY I went to PRISON (By 150 people who are determined never to return)

Background narratives can serve as a bridge to understanding that people in prison are not dissimilar to the people in our communities.

They also show that the convicted person has a better understanding now, of what happened and that they are unlikely to make the same mistakes again. A few of the explanations that follow were mentioned to judges in mitigation, most however were only revealed years later with the benefit of hindsight and a listening ear.

None of the background reasons included in this book are given to make less of their crimes or to shift blame in any way. Reasons are very different from excuses and rehabilitation cannot happen until and unless a person takes responsibility. If you think that you are reading an excuse, then at the very least it will give you an insight into the mind-set of a convicted criminal, perhaps one of the many who do struggle to accept responsibility or admit that they caused unjustifiable harm to others.

In truth however, there are often multiple narratives that fit the facts and if we are interested in crime prevention then it is useful to hear the convicted person's perspective.

From my viewpoint as interviewer, I believe that the writers of these personal statements are genuinely remorseful about what happened.

Even in cases where people maintain their innocence (which they are entitled to do), they have been encouraged to accept responsibility for their involvement, for decisions they made and also to explain how they have been improved or affected by imprisonment.

If you find these stories interesting and insightful, then I would also recommend my book entitled 'If CRIMINALS CAN CHANGE then SO SHOULD SOCIETY' which contains 100 further narratives.

WARNING

The following pages contain stories, explanations and events, which may be distressing to some readers.

NB: Most prison sentences are known as **determinate**. This means they have an end date. Prisoners serve **HALF** of their time in prison and half under supervision in the community (subject to compliance with licence conditions).

Indeterminate prison sentences have a tariff (minimum sentence) rather than an end date. Prisoners serve their **ENTIRE** tariff in prison and only then become eligible for consideration for release (parole). It is common for prisoners to serve substantially more than their original tariff. After eventual release, they spend the remainder of their life under supervision in the community (subject to compliance with licence conditions).

◆

GBH wounding with intent (S18) - 4 years' minimum imprisonment for public protection (IPP), **indeterminate**, served 9 years and 6 months

My Dad died suddenly and traumatically, when I was 14 years old and as a developing teenager, this had a catastrophic effect on me. I ran away from home, got involved with the wrong group of people and I turned to drugs and alcohol to numb the pain of loss. Whilst in a fog of drugs I hurt my victim and now I am so very sorry. I accepted responsibility by pleading guilty. The first time I was offered bereavement counselling was when I came to prison. I accepted this help and I have now come to terms with what happened in my past. I sought help for my addiction; I am now clean of drugs. I have completely turned my life around and want to put the past behind me.

◆

Robbery - 8 years

In my early twenties I was associating with a group of undesirable people in a deprived and challenging housing estate. Unemployment was rife at the time and boredom was a big issue for many people. I became a drug user and both drugs and alcohol have plagued my life ever since. The craving for drugs has stopped me from being my real self and has driven me to behave in ways that I am truly ashamed of and which I am sorry for now. I accepted responsibility for what I did and pleaded guilty. I knew that I had to change the people I was associating with and that if I didn't break free of drugs now, then they would always control my life. I underwent detox, completed a number of courses and now I engage with all of the professionals; accepting help and support to overcome all of my personal triggers and urges. I consistently pass all drug tests and have been drug free for two and a half years. I know that this is a cliché but I do believe that I have turned over a new leaf.

♦

Conspiracy to supply class A drugs - 9 years and 6 months

I had built a waste-management business which was doing well. I had two trucks out and four staff working. I unexpectedly lost a contract due to a competitor under-pricing the work. I am convinced that they would only have been able to manage such a low rate for a short while and then would have had to renegotiate because they would have been losing money. In the refuse business drugs are quite prevalent and although I never allowed it in my workforce, I was aware of people who had been involved in drug supply. In desperation to keep my business afloat, not make redundancies and keep providing for my family I became involved in drug supply.

In prison I saw the terrible effects of drug supply on the most vulnerable people in society; I feel ashamed that I even considered being a part of this. This was my first ever criminal offence and it is certainly something that I will not be repeating. The impact of imprisonment on my family was catastrophic, my children have really struggled and needed counselling and I will never put them through this ever again.

♦

ABH and two counts of GBH with intent (S18) - 6.5 years' indeterminate sentence (IPP) 9.5 years served so far

A local man kept making threats towards me and despite avoiding him I bumped into him when I was visiting a former girlfriend. We fought hard and I seriously hurt him with a glass bottle. I was remanded into prison straight away. I knew that I had to see prison as a turning point. I came to prison angry, violent, misunderstood and lost.

I was struggling to come to terms with my sexuality and I knew there was something missing. In prison I joined a "Buddy Action Team" which is a voluntary project to help others in partnership with the healthcare department. I assisted and cared for people who, through ill-health or infirmity, required assistance with day to day activities, such as washing, dressing, laundry, library or basic mobility.

Now I want to take my care skills and help more people in the community.

◆

S18 GBH, Violence - 4 years' minimum imprisonment for public protection (IPP), indeterminate, 9 years served so far

My Mum sadly died from leukaemia when I was a teenager. I was offered no support or counselling and really had to cope on my own. My Dad was a very angry man and he expressed his feelings as violence against me and others. I tried to spend as much time away from home as possible and joined up with a group of older boys and men. I had no direction in life other than wanting to impress these people who I put on a pedestal, for no real reason other than the fact that they accepted me.

I became a drug user and my associates encouraged me to live a criminal lifestyle. When I came to prison, I was given counselling which helped me to come to terms with my traumatic past and to deal with my emotions better. I also learnt to reflect on and understand the harm that I had caused to individual people as well as society. I am determined to stay crime free for good and I am very selective about the people who I associate with.

◆

Possession with Intent to Supply Class A drugs - 3 years

A close family member had got into serious financial debt and trouble and I tried to help them out of their distressing and frightening situation. Unfortunately, it wasn't the kind of debt that could just be paid, these people were adding interest onto interest and they said I couldn't pay money but would have to carry a parcel for them instead. I recklessly did this hoping that it would be the end of the matter. I was caught in the act and arrested. I was convicted in court because I was unwilling to give the names of the people involved in supplying the drugs. I didn't feel that I could do this because that would have put my family's life in danger. Despite my criminal act and my involvement with these people, I was able to present good character references to the court including one from a serving police officer. All of whom said that my offence was out of character - I had never been in trouble or in court before.

When I came to prison, I decided to make the best out of a bad situation. I formalised my barbering qualifications, gained B.I.C.Sc cleaning qualifications, passed a bricklaying course and achieved a Construction Skills Certification Scheme (CSCS) card. I decided not to accept excuses from myself but achieved these whilst also working in prison jobs. All of these extra qualifications are to ensure that I never come back to prison again.

♦

Conspiracy to supply Class A drugs - 13 years

I was made redundant when construction work dried up. I became desperate to provide for my family particularly because my wife was pregnant. I let myself down by breaking the law over an 8-week period. At the time I did not think about the possible consequences to society or my family.

My crime was out of character for me; prior to this I had worked consistently for 15 years. I will never abandon my family like this again.

♦

GBH Section 18, wounding with intent - 5 years and 9 months

A group of friends and colleagues were out on a VIP night at a night club when a man punched someone in the face. My girlfriend/ partner said "why did you do that?" and shouted "stop it!". The man grabbed her around the neck, picked her up by her throat and threw her. I felt that I had no choice but to intervene. I punched him and when he fell to the floor I stamped on his side. His two friends then hit me several times also using a belt which split my head.

I was taken straight to hospital and the following day as I was recovering from my injuries, I was charged with GBH by the police. The instigator and his friends were not charged with anything. Despite us asking for them to be charged, the police said there was no point pursuing charges against the attacker/ victim and they couldn't identify the two accomplices who had committed the GBH against me.

My girlfriend/ partner who had been almost strangled was however charged as an accomplice under a rule called joint-enterprise, albeit the slightly lesser charge of GBH S20, meaning that it was without intent. I had no choice but to appoint solicitors under the legal aid scheme; this doesn't pay much for the solicitor's or barrister's time and they were not really interested in defending the charges against me. They convinced me to plead guilty. This entire sequence of events was crazy and surreal. It is true that we could have called the police earlier and I shouldn't have stamped on the attacker's side once he was on the floor but my girlfriend and I were the actual victims of crime here.

◆

GBH S20 (wounding without deliberate intent) and causing death by dangerous driving - 11 years

I was experiencing a period of great turmoil in my life and had suffered bereavement. I went to a party with some friends and had not intended to drive so I had been drinking. At some point in the small hours of the morning a friend came to me panicking because he had missed his last train home and he asked me to drive him. I wasn't thinking straight and I made the irresponsible decision to drive him home. It was on this journey that the terrible tragedy happened. I hit someone with my car and they sadly died.

I was arrested and bailed for this crime. I hadn't realised how such an accident could also affect the driver; I was experiencing flashbacks, lack of sleep and trauma. A few weeks after the accident I was in a McDonalds when a man I didn't know started assaulting a friend of mine, I stepped in to stop the fight and calm the situation down but I got hit too, so I hit him back. The girl I was with took me outside the restaurant because she knew that I was already upset and distressed in general. Later on, everyone was arrested and charged because the attacker had been hit with a wet floor sign and it cut his eye.

I have never been in trouble with the police before; I pleaded guilty in court and accepted full responsibility. I deeply regret this whole period in my life. I have engaged with a number of support services which have helped me to come to terms with what has happened, to release pent up emotions and to express my feelings better. Being able to talk about what has happened has helped me to be able to compartmentalise that dark chapter of my life. My heart goes out to the family of my victim, I am so very sorry. If I could turn back the clock, I would but devastatingly I know that this is impossible. All I can do is try to live a better life and not waste this chance I have been given to turn my life around.

◆

GBH wounding with intent - 6 years

I went out with a group of friends to celebrate during the Christmas season. We left the pub in the small hours of the morning when a large man started attacking one of my friends. We were all intoxicated and my friend was particularly vulnerable. I stepped in to protect my friend. I went too far and hurt the man with a wooden fence post. I am so very sorry.

♦

Conspiracy to rob and conspiracy to burgle - 15 years

I have always worked but work in my field became sporadic and I had a period where I wasn't earning enough money. I began to get into financial difficulties and I shared my challenges with some friends. They suggested that I do some "work" with them and it was only as I began to find out more that I realised what they meant. I know I should have backed away but I felt that I was desperate for money.

I am a family man with young children and I so desperately wanted not to let them down, but that is exactly what I ended up doing by committing crime. I am truly sorry for what I did; I have learnt my lessons and changed a lot.

♦

Conspiracy to supply Class A and B drugs - 10 years

I sublet commercial premises to a third party who used the office to store cannabis. By the time I became aware of it, I knew that there was just one week left of the arrangement. I was shocked but felt that I couldn't do anything because I may have brought a whole world of troubles and problems down on my head if I had intervened. The judge agreed in court that I was only involved in the conspiracy for 2 days, but I was still sentenced to 10 years and became subject to confiscation proceedings, despite having not profited from the arrangement other than by my receipt of usual commercial rent.

I have never been in trouble with the police before and have certainly never been to prison before. Coming to prison really opened my eyes to how easily people can get swept along into committing crime and I met a diverse range of people.

When I came to prison, I decided to try to find ways to improve myself and help other people. I completed a crime reduction and victim awareness course and I am currently studying to achieve a BA (Hons) Degree in Politics, Philosophy and Economics with the Open University.

I have grown in humility and empathy due to my experiences and I used the time to help more than a hundred people in anxiety and distress in my Orderly, Advisory and Mentoring roles.

♦

Being concerned in the supply of class A drugs and GBH Section 18 wounding with intent - 6 years and 4 months

My parents became very busy with their own life and lost interest in me when I became a teenager. I fell in with a bad crowd and got distracted from my studies at school. The 'roadman' life only leads one way. Associating with the people that I was I developed a drug and alcohol habit, justifying this existence as a 'partying lifestyle'. With my current maturity I can see how misguided I was and how dangerous and unhealthy such a lifestyle was. One evening after I had been drinking, I got into an argument and I did hurt my victim and this resulted in my GBH charge; fortunately for me and my victim, the long-term effects were not extreme. I did plead guilty straight away to both of my charges and I am truly sorry for what I did. I also completely detoxed from drugs and alcohol and understood the root causes of my escapist behaviour. It has been time for me to accept full responsibility for my life and my effect in the world. I can honestly say that I have completely turned my life around since that dark chapter in my life. I have gained work related qualifications and a very strong work ethic. I know that I will be a good candidate for a proper job on release.

♦

Conspiracy to supply drugs - 12 years

I had a couple of tough years where I was in and out of agency work. Despite always being available to work, I had gaps in my employment and low paid roles, which left me struggling under a mountain of debt. Debt collectors were harassing me and bailiffs had given me a deadline to make payments or they would begin to take goods. I hid the true extent of the problems from my wife and family. A friend invited me to get involved in this drug supply chain (called a conspiracy) and explained that it would be easy money and that I could get in front quickly. I knew that I was doing wrong but I couldn't see any other way out, so I did get involved and of course I got caught very soon after. In the 6 years I have been away from my family I have missed so much. Many milestones in my children's lives have been and gone. I know that drug supply creates victims and I also made my own family into victims.

Not a day has gone past that I do not feel remorse. I will never commit crime again.

♦

Importation of Class A Drugs - 5 years and 8 months

We relocated from France to the UK when I was 7 years old. I come from a good family but we had moved to a challenging and deprived area (Haringey). I stayed out of trouble and away from negative influences and I achieved 7 GCSE's at school. Unfortunately, as a young man I was bullied into hiding a parcel of drugs in my house. The local criminals said that they would pay me to store the drugs or they would hurt me if I didn't. I was working and I had my own flat which I shared with my Aunty. Unfortunately, my Aunt found this package and didn't know what it was or suspected it was something untoward and flushed it all down the toilet. Now I was in even more trouble because this was treated like a life-threatening debt. I could be killed for this. I panicked. I should have gone to the police or got help much earlier but I was now told that I had to 'do a run' to Europe to bring in a consignment. I was at my wits end. I was stopped at the border; the drugs were discovered and I was arrested.

I pleaded guilty straight away. I was distressed, literally gutted at coming to prison and at the realisation that this was ALL my own fault. My family have been angry with me and my wife has unfortunately divorced me. I am so very aware of the consequences of crime as well as anyone else can be. I had so many dreams when I was younger, I enjoy drama, I wanted to own my own small business and after coming to prison for a long time I felt that I could never be worthy of achieving anything ever again.

I have however had a lot of time for self-reflection, I completed a course called Thinking Skills and I have set positive goals for the future. I have learnt about crime and victims and in future I intend to discourage other people from breaking the law.

♦

Breaches of CPR's - 18 months

I was prosecuted by Trading Standards for breaches of the recently implemented regulations known as the "Consumer Protection from Unfair Trading Regulations". I was a joint partner in a construction business and we overcommitted to work based on positive cash flow projections, which failed to materialise. I let some customers down when the business failed and I am truly sorry. I did not mean for anyone to lose money; my offence was not deliberate; but I just took on too much. I accepted full responsibility and pleaded guilty.

♦

Conspiracy to supply class A drugs - 9 years and 6 months

I was working in my own business as an electrical installer. I had worked on projects at a number of prestigious sites including Excel and O2 arena. The people that I was working with were involved in using cocaine to power through long jobs; I had stayed away from drugs until my long-term relationship at the time began to deteriorate. I broke up from my partner and I started using cocaine to boost my mood. Eventually the habit had grown to where I was using the drug to get through each day and I needed more and more to get the same effects.

I made multiple phone calls to the people involved in this conspiracy and got too deeply involved with them and that is how we were all convicted together. This was my first ever offence and I deeply regret my involvement in this conspiracy.

I decided to use my time to contribute to helping other people; I served in the highly trusted orderly roles both within offender management and at the induction (first arrival) stage of peoples' prison journeys. In these roles I provided information, advice and guidance and a high level of support to people who were often in distress or suffering from mental health disorders such as anxiety and depression.

I am pleased to have been able to help alleviate many problems and reduce serious consequences such as self-harming or stopping eating.

♦

Conspiracy to supply Class A and Class B drugs - 4 years and 6 months

I was a taxi driver but had some quiet months in summer and got into debt because my car was on finance. I was persuaded to deliver drugs and attracted to the money. I was called a courier and drove from London to Lincolnshire a number of times over a 6-week period. I do accept responsibility for what I did. I was trying to maintain a front. I have a wife and two young children. I didn't discuss my problems with my wife and I didn't think about the possible consequences of my actions.

I have learnt a lot since then and I will be open and honest with my wife and will not break the law again.

♦

Conspiracy to rob - 6 years

I came to the UK at 20 years old as an Asylum seeker because my life and the life of my whole family were threatened.

I worked hard in the construction industry on building sites and gained a number of skills including plastering, tiling and carpentry. I, alongside some colleagues were facing redundancy from a building site that had kept us employed for several months. These were undesirable people and I should never have listened to them. They told me about a way to make money and I allowed myself to get drawn into their scheme. I agreed to be a get-away driver as a way to get quick money.

I am sorry for what I did and for allowing myself to be led by other people instead of being strong enough to say no. I let myself and my family down as well as my community.

I accept full responsibility for my crime and I know that I would handle things so much differently in future - I am determined to never commit crime again.

♦

Grievous Bodily Harm (GBH S18) with intent - 8 years

I am very close to my Sister's family and I care deeply about my niece and nephew who I treat as if they were my children.

A former friend of the family who had previously helped a lot with babysitting and odd jobs became obsessed with my family and began stalking them. The family had to take out an injunction against him to prevent further harassment. After this we had no further contact with him until we discovered that my niece had been self-harming.

Sadly, we discovered that my niece had been molested by this man for a 3-year period between the ages of 11-14. I was furious beyond words. I went round to his house. His dog came to the door and he had given the dog the same name as my niece. He told the dog to sit and the dog obeyed, He then looked me in the eye and said "it is a shame that she didn't do as she was told like that", meaning my niece. Enraged by this comment and devastated by the harm he had caused to my niece. I reacted in a fit of rage and seriously hurt this person.

◆

Conspiracy to supply Class B drugs - 5 years

The agency that I was working for had no work placements available for me for several months and it left my family in a difficult financial position. I am not trying to excuse my behaviour but I did become desperate and I wasn't thinking straight. I have a partner and a young daughter and I couldn't bear the thought of leaving them so vulnerable. I got involved with a chain of drug supply in the hope of making enough money to carry us through the difficult time, but I was caught and arrested instead. As soon as I was caught, it was like a big weight had lifted off my shoulders, I hadn't wanted to be a criminal and I pleaded guilty to my crime.

I had never been to prison before and I knew that this would be a big test for me and possibly the biggest test for my family. I really regret having, through my own reckless stupidity, effectively abandoned my family. I have missed irreplaceable years of my daughter's life and this is a massive incentive for me to get my life on track. I worked in prison jobs throughout my sentence and kept my CV up to date. Even though these aren't prestigious or highly skilled jobs, they do show that I have not abandoned my work ethic, despite me finding myself in the darkest of situations.

◆

Burglary - 5 years and 6 months

It all started when my Mum became an alcoholic and didn't look after us children. We had no routine or stability. Mum struggled with alcoholism with many years, as long as I can remember. From the age of about 11-12, I got involved with a bad group of people, they were on glue and gas and then I turned to drugs. I committed a burglary out of desperation, to fund my worsening drug addiction. I accepted responsibility and pleaded guilty. I have worked hard to completely detox from drugs, I am no longer an addict and I am fully rehabilitated from substance abuse. I am ashamed of my past and I intend to build a productive life in future.

I am so disgusted with myself for what I did, I would say that I really was a scumbag. I am so sorry, I did it because I was a drug addict and didn't have anything good at all in my life at the time. I am so motivated to change, I have got small business ideas, which sound like they have got potential and I completed a business course so that I can get ready for self-employment. I hope I can start a new life, no scrub that, I plan to start a new life and do better in all areas.

♦

Conspiracy to burgle - 7 years and 6 months

I was introduced to a money-making scheme when I was in between jobs (I was working for construction agencies at the time). I became desperate for money and became greedy. I just saw pound signs and didn't think about the consequences, or worse I didn't allow myself to think or care about the victims of my associates' crimes. I didn't commit the robberies but my role was still criminal because I was involved in selling on as an agent. I took personal responsibility for how low I had sunk, I pleaded guilty in court and also publicly and sincerely apologised.

I have used my time in prison productively to gain additional work-related qualifications to ensure that I always have legitimate employment in future. I also took part in personal development programmes which improved my mind-set and life skills.

♦

S18 GBH - 4 years' minimum imprisonment for public protection (IPP), indeterminate, actually served 9 years

My father died suddenly and traumatically when I was 14 years old and as a developing teenager, this had a catastrophic effect on me. I ran away from home, got involved with the wrong group of people and I turned to drugs and alcohol to numb the pain of loss. Whilst in a fog of drugs, I hurt my victim and now I am so very sorry. I accepted responsibility by pleading guilty.

The first time I was offered bereavement counselling was when I came to prison. I have now come to terms with what happened in my past, I got help for my addiction and I am now clean of drugs.

♦

Importation and Conspiracy to supply Class A and Class B drugs - 18 years

I became too greedy financially. I was a taxi driver (London black cab), but became desperate to retire early because my wife was disabled and I was dedicated to her full-time care.

I recklessly got involved with criminals because I saw a way to make money and support us both for many years ahead. Instead we ended up separated by prison walls and I placed more stress and distress on her shoulders.

◆

Possession, with Intent to Supply, Class A Drugs - 3 years

I am a mature hardworking man; I have worked all of my life. After around 10 years of successful carpet fitting, I had to leave at short notice for alternative employment. I worked for several agencies labouring and delivery driving, but work was not always permanent and it became difficult to budget. I am a father with two children to provide for and I do take my responsibilities seriously. It was around this time that I was asked to do a favour for a friend. I say friend, but really, he was an associate; he asked me to deliver a package. I knew that that this wasn't entirely legitimate and I should have refused straight away, but in a moment of personal weakness, I agreed.

I thought that it was Cannabis (a class B drug) but when I was stopped by the police and the parcel was opened it contained class A drugs, much worse than I even realised. If I knew what was in the package, I definitely wouldn't have done it. Now, having gone through prison, I wouldn't do it again, even if I knew it contained cannabis, the lesser drug.

I wouldn't commit any crime again; it is definitely not worth it and there could never be any acceptable excuse whatsoever.

◆

GBH Section 18 wounding with intent - 5 years

My baby Nephew sadly died unexpectedly and I was distressed and grieving. I went out and got very drunk, I also stupidly took cocaine which is something that I rarely did, but I just wanted to bury these intense feelings. I was upset for my brother; I couldn't answer the question "why" and I felt powerless. Late in the evening a man started arguing with me and he pushed me, I do not remember this but apparently, I hit him with my pint glass. This resulted in a cut on the man's face so hence the charge of GBH.

I was arrested the next day, I did plead guilty straight away and I am truly sorry for what I did. This has been my first criminal offence and I have never experienced prison before.

I was scared and alarmed when I first came to prison. In prison I mixed with very different people from those which I would usually associate with. The diversity of the people in prison opened my eyes to different backgrounds. I became less judgemental and I now feel more empathy and understanding towards other people.

♦

Conspiracy to supply class A drugs and conspiracy to supply prohibited ammunition - 7 years, 6 months

I had an urgent need for money when I had a new baby after already having twin boys. Suddenly my financial outgoings escalated and I really wanted to provide well for my family. At the same time, I had found myself in between contracts (I am a carpenter), with an empty run in my work diary. It was at this time that I was introduced to a person who later became one of my co-conspirators.

What I did was stupid, dangerous and irresponsible, I accept this and I am very sorry. I accepted responsibility by pleading guilty and I completed a victim awareness course. I began to realise the effect of crime on society. I do not want my precious children growing up into this type of environment. I am now so very anti-crime. I just can't wait to be reunited with my family after being taken away from them through my own recklessness.

♦

Aggravated Burglary - 8 years

I was brought up in a good home and was doing well in school. My mum expected great things from me, but from about 14 years old I fell in with a bad crowd of young people. I had felt singled out and like the odd one out in school but these street kids accepted me and they felt like an extended family. I started carrying a knife for protection at first, but soon it became essential almost like a phone. I never used it but I did become involved in drug culture and unfortunately that life only leads one way - to prison.

I spent many years in prison on multiple sentences. Now aged 34 I have totally turned my life around. I know that the life I was living was not helping me, my family or society.

I completely stopped all drug use, I know that drugs actually poison the next generation, I despise them. I have worked hard to gain multiple skills and qualifications.

I have been practising my religion properly and studying my faith; this has helped me to hold myself to a high standard and kept me grounded. I have also been helping many other people with a wide range of issues (I even gained a Peer Mentoring qualification so I can be of more value to other people).

♦

Robbery and being concerned in the supply of drugs - 14 years and 6 months

I was brought up in a single parent family in a deprived area of Hackney, London. I was the man of the house from a young age. I gave up on school at the age of 15 and was picked up by a local group of older men. They groomed me into glorifying crime and drugs and told me this was the only way I could get a better life. We tried to rob a well-known drug dealer and got caught when the situation escalated out of control. I didn't know what other opportunities there were for me, but when I came to prison, I knew that I needed to change.

My Mum and family are devastated about me being away and I am truly sorry for my crimes. I have completed many courses and gained a folder full of worthwhile qualifications. I just want to work full time and stay away from crime for good.

♦

GBH and Attempted murder - Discretionary life sentence, indeterminate, minimum tariff 12 years

A friend introduced me to a group of people who were violent drug dealers but who wanted me to help them record rap music. I was unsure but felt a strange pull to the dark and murky world they were operating in. After a few months of associating with them, I was forced by threats on my family to collect an outstanding debt on their behalf. I was actually shot; I was in a coma in intensive care and then spent 2 months recovering in hospital. I do know that this was my own fault and that the life I had chosen was not a healthy one.

♦

GBH S18 - 5 years

When I had just turned 18 years old, I was out in town with a group of friends. I accidentally bumped into a man and spilt his drink; I did apologise straight away. Unfortunately, when I left the pub this man was waiting outside with his group and started angrily approaching me with a glass bottle. My cousin hit him and he fell over but I was still scared and enraged so I carried on kicking him.

In the heat of the moment, I know that I went too far.

This was not premeditated at all; I had not set out to hurt anyone and I am sorry.

♦

Conspiracy to supply class A drugs and perverting the course of justice - 16 years

I grew up in the Camberwell/ Brixton area of South London and saw people making what appeared to be a lot of money from selling drugs. I was attracted to this materialistic life and this warped way of thinking. I am certainly not going to try to excuse my behaviour. I grew up in a good family who are all devastated that I broke the law. I learnt a lot about the impact of drug supply on victims when I volunteered for a Victim Awareness course in prison; I knew that I wanted to change. I also committed 6 entire weeks, every day, to a life changing course called Thinking Skills Programme (TSP), I gave the course 100% and I was praised after completing this course. Whilst in prison, I have worked consistently and gained additional skills and qualifications. I served as a Chapel Orderly and in this role, I helped many people who were upset or at a crossroads in their lives, like I had been.

♦

Conspiracy to Supply Class A drugs - 11 years

From a young age I had an entrepreneurial mentality and worked in my family's small businesses. I was very keen to have my own income and was looking out for an opportunity that I could call my own. It was at this time that I started hanging around with the wrong type of young men. My family did say to be careful of those people but being young and immature, I thought I knew better. Before I knew it, I started selling drugs for them. Things very quickly spiralled to where I pretended that I had that proper business I had always dreamt of. Unfortunately, of course, my so called 'business' was built on sand not rock and was completely illegal and unsustainable. I was arrested when I was 25 years old and had to face up to my criminality.

Coming to prison helped me to mature and become wiser; I have learnt a lot.

♦

S18 GBH - 3 years 9 months' tariff, discretionary life sentence. Served 14 years

I was in a dysfunctional relationship and had been physically hurt. I acted instinctively but aggressively in a terrible moment of temper, in order to protect myself. I had never been violent before this time and I feel ashamed that I overreacted so much that I hurt my ex-partner badly. I administered first aid and called the emergency services. I was full of remorse afterwards; I accepted responsibility and pleaded guilty.

♦

Possession with intent to supply class A drugs - 5 years

I had a very turbulent childhood after my parents went through a difficult separation. I was taken in by my grandmother for a while but despite her efforts, I ended up in care and foster care. By my early teens I felt like I was an inconvenience and unwanted, I struggled for role models and had little direction. I fell in with a crowd of older men who seemed to accept me for who I was and I liked being part of this street 'family'.

Being moved around a lot mean that I left school with no qualifications and I was abandoned by the care system at the age of 16. I turned to my older associates who helped me get started in selling drugs. Inevitably I ended up in prison on more than one occasion.

Since those early years, I have grown and matured a lot. With children of my own and a long-term partner, I am more determined than ever to be a positive role model and to live a crime free life.

I know that people who leave prison without qualifications get drawn back into the streets, cuddled back; they need to fill their time with something and earn money. I don't want this; I have turned my back on that life and gained many qualifications and skills so that I can be legally employed upon release from prison and turn my life around.

♦

Conspiracy to supply class A drugs - 8 years

My Dad sadly died when I was a teenager and I was left with a big hole in my life. I started hanging around with some undesirable people and they made crime appear cool, glamorous and acceptable. I wish I had never got involved with this crowd because now my criminal record means that most people will prejudge, when I believe in my heart that I am a good person.

My Mum has been my rock and I really want to make her proud. I know that I have to turn my life around for my Mum, for my partner and our young son. I have broken all ties with past criminal associates and I know that I can achieve a worthwhile life without crime.

To this effect I have worked hard to gain new skills and qualifications and also completed several personal development courses. I believe that I am a better, more balanced person for having used my time in prison effectively.

◆

Common assault and attempting to inflict GBH (serious injury) - 3 years

I have always worked hard for my family and we bought our own house which I was gradually improving at the weekends when I was available from my job as an electrician. I was working in my front garden when a drunk man came past slurring his words. I ignored him and later on he came past again and started insulting me and calling me stupid for working on a Sunday. I asked him to leave me alone but he came back a third time and this time I felt nervous because my children were nearby too. I asked him to leave me alone and he said "Fxxx your wife and fxxx your children!" I believe that this was a racially motivated incident against me and my family - I am from Kosovo originally, but have been a British citizen for almost 20 years. He reached into his coat and came closer to me; I had no idea why. I stood up and pushed him away (that was the apparent assault). I then picked up my shovel and as he came quickly towards it, I swung it several times (allegedly this was attempting to inflict GBH), I deliberately did not hit him with it. That drunkard could have walked away at any time, but he kept coming to my own house. In his statement the man confirmed that he had been drinking for six hours and beyond all explanation the jury still found me guilty of both charges.

When I first came to prison, I felt very bad, not just for me but I have never left my wife and children before and I have been constantly worried about how they can cope. Day to day concerns like meeting the mortgage payment, helping with homework and driving to after school clubs. It has been very hard indeed for my family. I have never committed any crime before, have never been in trouble with the police or been to prison before and I certainly will never do so again. I regret this sequence of events and have used my time in prison to help other people as much as possible and I have also worked in roles that contribute to the prison community.

◆

Causing serious injury by dangerous driving - 20 months

I had just received a phone call to tell me that my Grandfather had sadly died. In my haste to get home to my family I drove above the speed limit and also went through a traffic light that had just changed to red. I caused a collision in which a lady got hurt. Fortunately, the lady has made a full recovery, but I am truly sorry for causing this accident. I am a considerate and respectable person; I have never been in any sort of trouble with the police before and I did plead guilty.

♦

Conspiracy to Supply class A drugs - 8 years

I got into serious money problems when I was hospitalised for 6 months and made redundant. I had endured almost constant vomiting, as well as stomach cramps and pains, in the weeks prior to being admitted to hospital. Eventually I was diagnosed with chronic Crone's disease. I had been unable to pay my bills and debt collectors were hounding me constantly. I was in fear of losing my home.

I am ashamed now of how I turned to crime to make fast money. At the time however, in desperation I turned to people that I knew were involved in drug supply and for a period of 6 months I made money illegally. With hindsight I wouldn't bury my head in the sand again. I know that I should have sought help and professional advice. I know that I would do this now, as a more mature person.

When I first came to prison, I was so shocked and scared that I couldn't imagine getting to the end of what seemed like such a long sentence. I didn't feel like I could plan for a future life, it was like my life was over because something so unimaginable had happened. Now however I do feel that I still have so much still to give. I also know that I have grown personally both in positivity and resilience. I do regret my crime and I have learnt many lessons.

♦

Money Laundering - 7 years

I am a successful businessman who regularly conducts high value financial transactions. I am in fact maintaining my innocence of this offence because I was actually receiving legitimate money from the proceeds of a sale of property overseas. My case was very poorly prepared because I had naturally assumed that I would not be found guilty. The jury did not reach a unanimous verdict, two people believed me to be innocent and the judge allowed that conviction to stand.

I am appealing my conviction, but this takes a long time. Meanwhile I must stay here away from my family, employees and customers.

Despite the injustice of what happened, I made a decision to see my sentence as a positive time. I committed to work, self- improvement and contributing to help other people. I am a more positive and determined person now and I fully intend never to return to prison.

♦

Conspiracy to supply class A drugs - 5 years.

With hindsight, I cannot believe what I did; having never been in trouble with the police before, it still surprises me how I came to prison. I look around and I am shocked at how I ended up in prison with a criminal conviction. I am actually a single parent to two lovely children a son and a daughter. Things have been tough for the three of us for many years after their mum had some serious personal problems, but we were a happy family unit. Me with my work and them with their school - and the evenings together, well that was our time.

I was labouring and working hard on construction sites. I was in-between jobs and I couldn't afford not to work because of my children. I took some temporary work for an old contact of mine. He asked me one day to collect a bag for him from someone. I knew this guy was dodgy and that something wasn't quite right. I should have refused but I just went along with it for an easy life. Thinking back, I should have refused straight away. Nothing happened for almost a year, by this time I was working steadily in a new job when the police came and arrested me as part of the conspiracy.

Fast forward to now and I have gained additional vocational skills in prison and I have become a fully qualified bricklayer. I have even trained other people in how to build fireplaces, garden walls, cavity walls, piers and window frames.

I am about to embark on a new and steady career in bricklaying with my own apprentice alongside me.

When I first came to prison, I was very worried about my children but fortunately my Mum and Dad came to the rescue and cared for them while I was away. I phoned my children every day and I promised them that I will never come back to prison, that I will never make this kind of mistake or commit crime ever again. I know that I have far too much to lose.

♦

Robbery and Malicious Wounding - 7 years

I let myself down badly when I started working with "road men" drug dealers. I was struggling as a drug addict and owed money to one of them. They tasered me and seriously hurt me and then forced me by further threats to commit the crimes of robbery and malicious wounding.

♦

Conspiracy to supply Class A drugs - 4 years

I was brought up in a poor and dangerous part of west London. I saw my friend tragically die from being stabbed. This really shook me up and it took me a long time to come to terms with. Partly for my own protection and peace of mind, I began associating with older men. I thought that they were my friends and they were accepting me but in fact they were using me and I hadn't realised that I was being exploited. My involvement in the conspiracy was limited to holding a phone for the conspirators; I did not sell drugs or hold drugs. This, my first time (and last time!) in prison has taught me not to get involved with anyone who is doing illegal things.

It has been hard being away from my family and they have been very worried about me. I know that I will never come back to prison. I have turned my back on crime and away from past criminal associates. I have three younger brothers and I am very close to them. I am petrified of them getting involved in crime or any trouble, so I really want to be a positive role model for them.

♦

Manslaughter by loss of control and **conspiracy to commit ABH** - 12 years

I achieved well in school and passed all my GCSEs but I started to fall in with the wrong crowd of people. I started smoking cannabis at a young age and my Mum would not allow this in the house. I naively thought I knew better, so after a number of arguments with my Mum I left home. I ended up in temporary, emergency accommodation; basically, I was homeless, but still full of teenage arrogance and ignorance, I was too proud to return home.

I turned to my 'peers' who made me feel respected and they got me involved in supplying drugs. This is a dark and dangerous slippery slope, I had no structure to my life; it was chaos really, looking back. I was 21 years old when this terrible chain of events happened.

A friend of someone I knew had been robbed and after some phone calls backwards and forwards, the person who did it agreed to meet and return the items he had stolen. I went with my friend not realising that this was a set up.

We should have suspected that something would go wrong because this was the type of life we were living then, but we genuinely thought we would collect the items and leave. When we got there, about 20 people were waiting for us with hammers and knives. They tried to hit my friend. One tried to stab him so I punched him but the whole group turned their attention on me. I fell to the floor, they tried to hit me with hammers and I knew that one hit could have killed me. The first man tried to stab me but dropped the knife. I picked it up in panic and tried to get away but they cornered me instead. Once cornered I thought it was all over for me so I began swinging the knife frantically but this didn't stop them coming for me. In my panic I thrust the knife and then managed to get away, not knowing the outcome. Later on, my victim sadly died and I am so deeply sorry.

I regret what happened with my whole heart and wish that I had never agreed to help my friend. I hadn't thought of the possible consequences, now I know that this type of life is not really living.

There are so many ways to live a decent and normal life. I have embraced the concept of self-improvement and completely changed my thinking and behaviour. I have gained a number of work-related qualifications.

I have nieces and nephews and one day I want to be a parent myself. I want to be there to watch them grow up and to be part of their growing up. I have broken ties with the people that I used to hang around with and I have encouraged others to reconsider their friendships and their lives.

◆

Arson with intent to endanger life - 4 years

I found out that my long-term girlfriend had slept with someone else behind my back and when I telephoned her to ask her about it, she laughed and taunted me by saying "what are you going to do about it?" In a moment of emotional distress, I set a small fire in her porch, because I was trying to gain her attention and couldn't cope with the wave of feelings that I was experiencing. I did plead guilty straight away and I am truly sorry for what I did.

I have completed a number of personal development courses which have helped me to understand my thoughts and emotions better. I also took part in a victim awareness and empathy programme and developed a greater understanding of the impact of crime on individuals and on society.

This was my first and last offence; I will never commit crime again.

◆

Money Laundering - 5 years and 3 months

For a number of years, I had been a successful businessman with a car rental business. To meet the growing needs of clients and compete with other providers I had to expand my business and took on a fleet of vehicles on finance. My business was based in Cyprus earning Turkish Lira but my finance payments were made in Euros. The exchange rate changed dramatically from 1.8 to 3.9, more than doubling in just one year and I couldn't meet the payments. Unfortunately, my income forecasts were not enough to meet these increased finance payments. In a time of personal distress and fearful about escalating threats of debt recovery, I made the reckless, selfish and criminal decision to launder money for a percentage fee so that I could pay off the finance and save my business. I am sorry for letting my financial problems get the better of me and for turning to criminality. I deeply regret what I have done and I accepted responsibility by pleading guilty in court. I have never been in trouble with the police before and coming to prison was a big shock for me. I am a very family orientated man with a wife, three children, one grandchild and another on the way. My family has been my life and it has been very distressing to not be with them as they go through the ups and downs of everyday life. I can state very definitely that I will never break the law again.

◆

Possession with intent to supply class A drugs - 8 years

I had an urgent need for money when I hurt my back and was unable to perform my normal work in construction. I have a wife and three children and we started to fall into arrears with all of our bills. I knew that ultimately, we would be evicted from our rented home, I didn't know where to turn, but I certainly took the wrong turn when I got involved in crime. I knew that what I did was wrong, I pleaded guilty. I know that drug supply contributes to so much degradation and crime in society and I am sorry.

Originally, I had tried to provide for my family, yet the consequences of my crime were that I have been taken away from them, removed from their lives for a long period of time and made things significantly worse for them. I had to see prison as an opportunity to change; I have completed many self-development courses and maintained a consistent work ethic, working to improve my employability.

◆

Manslaughter - discretionary life sentence, indeterminate, minimum tariff 13 years

When I was 23, I developed a problem with alcohol and got into a fight whilst I was drunk. I punched a man in the face; he fell and hit his head; he sadly died a week later.

I have regretted what happened every day, and will continue to regret it. I wrote to the family to express my sincere remorse and I cut alcohol out of my life.

◆

Conspiracy to supply class A drugs - 7years and 6 months

I was a very active father to two young children when my partner unexpectedly fell pregnant with our third child. We were very happy at the news, but inside I also began to worry about how I would provide. I had not long gained my formal plumbing qualifications and I was finding my feet working full time in my new job. When my new baby son was born, I was in awe of him and of my partner. Our relationship was good and our family was complete. I knew that my son needed so many things and I was as stretched as I could be in work. In a moment of weakness, I discussed my fears and worries with some associates I knew. They told me about how I could make money by 'working' with them. I should have said no and walked away but I gave in to the temptation to ignore the law and make money in this way.

When I was caught for my part in the supply of drugs, I accepted responsibility by pleading guilty. I had never been to prison before and coming to prison was a big wake up call. It was very difficult for my children and my partner, who has been a tower of strength to me, she has found it in her heart to forgive me and our relationship is strong.

I am determined not to let her down like this and will certainly never abandon my family intentionally or unintentionally in future. My family will always be forefront in my mind in future.

I have spent a large part of last year in prison doing charity work and was highly praised by the YMCA for using my qualifications as a personal trainer to help so many people. I am sorry for my past selfish actions; I have learnt my lesson and I have honestly changed a lot.

◆

GBH (S18) wounding with intent - 9 years

A friend of mine was in serious trouble with people who wanted to do him harm. He rang me in panic and distress and I rushed to help him. I stupidly took a knife with me, I didn't really think that I would use it, I just took it for protection and maybe to threaten if needed. When I got there to help my friend, things quickly escalated and I used the knife against one of the attackers. I regretted what I had done straight away, I knew that I should have rung the police and let them deal with it. Ever since that day I have felt awful about what I did but thankfully, my victim has made recovered. I learnt a lot of lessons and grew up. I did plead guilty straight away and I am truly sorry for what I did.

Since coming to prison I have made substantial progress in developing my mind-set, my emotions and I have totally changed my behaviour. I completed lengthy and detailed programmes such as "Resolve" and "Personal and Social Development" (PSD) which helped me in my own journey to personal change. I also took part in a structured programme in which I met victims of other crimes and this was a real eye opener to me, I will not treat life so cheaply or take the law into my own hands ever again.

◆

GBH wounding with intent (S18) - 2 years and 4 months' minimum imprisonment for public protection (IPP), indeterminate, actually served 13 years in prison

I visited a gathering at a friend's house whilst I was high on drugs and whilst there, I also drank alcohol. I was heavily addicted to drugs and have no recollection of events at all other than waking up in a police cell charged with this serious crime. I accepted responsibility by pleading guilty, I was full of remorse and I still am. I worked hard to completely detox from drugs, I am no longer an addict and I am fully rehabilitated from substance and alcohol abuse. I completed 5 years of therapy in a secure therapeutic community, this helped me to come to terms with my traumatic past, to deal with my thoughts and emotions and to communicate and manage relationships better. I also tried my best to help other people in difficulty and distress. I became a drugs and alcohol Peer Supporter/ Peer Mentor providing a high level of guidance, direction and personal attention to people who were struggling. As a sign of my commitment to change, I worked hard to gain a qualification in this role too.

♦

Conspiracy to supply Class A drugs - 16 years

I really regret my offence, which arose because I experienced tremendous financial pressure after moving house and faced unexpected bills for remedial works. I was working as many hours as possible in my job but couldn't seem to get in front; I became fearful that we could lose our family home. I got myself involved for a one-month period with the wrong group of people. I thought I saw a way to make money and straighten out our family finances. I accepted responsibility by pleading guilty at the first opportunity. My crime was very out of character for me. I am actually a mature and family orientated person and I feel ashamed now.

♦

Being concerned in the supply of drugs - 3 years and 9 months

After 5 years of stable employment, my employer became only able to afford me part-time and then eventually I found myself out of work altogether. I struggled to make ends meet on such a reduced budget and I became desperate to provide for my family (I have two young children). I got involved with bad people and I let myself down.

♦

Possession with intent to supply drugs - 3 years and 8 months' imprisonment

I had a serious motorbike accident which left me struggling both mentally and physically. Before my accident I had worked for a decade with the same employer, starting as a delivery driver and progressing to area manager level. I became unable to work due to my injuries and struggled financially. I had nerve damage in my left arm and reduced mobility. I was prescribed medication to ease the pain but this proved insufficient and the pain was unbearable. In desperation I began to self- medicate with illegal drugs and before I knew it, I was addicted. I struggled to make ends meet and became desperate to provide for my family (I have three young children). Torn between feeding the family and feeding my addiction, of course I didn't pay my drug supplier and got in debt to them. I got drawn into drug supply so that I could repay my debt. The whole drug experience was like quicksand that I got more and more sucked into; I will never get involved in that world in future.

♦

Manslaughter by Gross Neglect - 5 years and 3 months

I am a lorry and car mechanic with 30 years unblemished experience. I carried out a 6-week visual inspection of a lorry to ensure road safety. Three and a half weeks later, a young driver experienced challenges with the braking system whilst travelling downhill. The driver did not take any avoiding action but instead crashed at 15 mph and caused the tragic deaths of 4 people. The fault was identified as being due to "slack adjusters" which were not installed correctly. I was not the mechanic (who was convicted separately); I was just the visual inspector. VOSA did confirm during the trial that a visual inspection cannot tell whether slack adjusters were installed correctly but nevertheless the jury found me guilty of having a part in this tragedy.

Coming to prison is a damaging and very destructive experience but I am a positive and resilient person who tries to turn negative events into positives. I do believe in looking forwards. I have had to face up to the fact that I am in prison and make the most of it. I have used my time in prison to complete courses and gain a number of qualifications. I have proven worthy of trust and am allowed to live and work in open prison conditions where I will be gaining further trade related qualifications.

♦

Attempted murder - 8 years' minimum imprisonment for public protection (IPP), indeterminate, 12 years served so far

I grew up in children's homes and foster care with little stability in my life. The person I hurt had abused my brother and I over a long period of time when we were children. This had a very traumatic effect on me growing up and does still affect me. When I saw this person as an adult, I reacted with rage almost instinctively because I felt the same feelings of fear, anguish and upset that I had as a child. I do regret my crime. I also regret so much what this person did to me when they took away my innocence. The first time I was offered counselling was when I came to prison. I accepted this help and I have now come to terms with my past. I detoxed from drugs and alcohol and I no longer need to use these to cope with everyday life. I have been clean for 6 years.

Building on my commitment to positive change, I trained with the Samaritans as a prison "listener" and helped other people, whilst they were at their lowest points, self-harming or contemplating suicide. I progressed to become a listeners' trainer and I am pleased to have taught many other people how to carry out this worthwhile role.

♦

Conspiracy to supply drugs - 5 years and 3 months

I naively and recklessly went to support a friend who I knew was buying drugs. I had no idea that he would be buying so much and that by accompanying him I would find myself involved in something called a "conspiracy". I accepted responsibility and pleaded guilty at my first court appearance.

♦

Conspiracy to steal and rob - 9 years

I look after my wife who is chronically ill with anxiety and depression, anaemia, pancreatitis and severe back problems. Caring full-time for her and our four children took a massive toll on our family finances and my own mental health. I started to spend time with a group of undesirable criminals. In my distressed state I wasn't thinking straight and I joined them in their criminal activities. I deeply regret my offences and I accepted responsibility by pleading guilty. My crime was very out of character for me, I have never been to prison before. I am actually a mature and responsible and I am ashamed of my past actions. Since coming to prison I have completely changed my mind-set and sorted my head out. I have completed many courses and I have also had the courage to ask for help both personally and for my wife. Now my wife is now more supported and I know that things will be so much better this time when I am home again.

♦

Conspiracy to supply Class A and Class B drugs and money laundering - 8 years

I had always been an ambitious person and worked hard in my family business. As my young family started to grow, I wanted to provide well for them and I yearned for more independence and success. My ambition turned to greed and I recklessly got involved with a group of criminals who made crime appear clever, risk free and harmless. I look back and I know that drug supply is far from being harm free. I did plead guilty and I am truly sorry for what I did. Now I see that it is a stupid idea and that crime and prison takes you away from your children. I have missed so many milestones in the lives of my two daughters'. I would pay anything to have got the time back with them that I have lost.

It is said that you learn from your mistakes and I have certainly learnt from mine.

◆

Being concerned in the supply of class A drugs - 40 months

I had established my own small business as a car dealer. I would source part exchange cars and sell them to customers. This was going well but I let my love of cars get the better of me and I began to buy and sell high end sports cars. With hindsight this was reckless because I didn't have the financial resources to carry out mechanical repairs on such specialist vehicles and things went wrong when a car that I sold broke down. I had reinvested the sales proceeds into other cars so I couldn't refund the customer and I was sued for thousands of pounds. I was really sorry that this customer had problems with the car and I felt that I had let him down. In my desperation to avoid bailiffs and my reputation being ruined, I spoke to some local drug dealers that I knew. I had in the past been an occasional smoker of cannabis and I saw how much money they were making; I thought that I could get myself out the hole I was in by selling drugs.

With hindsight I realise what a ridiculous and dangerous decision I had made. I should never have got involved with such people. When I was caught after 3 months, I did accept responsibility and pleaded guilty. I realise that I have embarrassed myself and that I have brought shame to my family and I am very sorry.

When I came to prison, I wanted to study and improve myself. I completed courses including Personal and Social Development (PSD) and Positive Lifestyles. These helped me to really think about where I had been going wrong in my life and taught me more about the power of association. I had many realisations and insights on these courses. I have stayed away from cannabis for many years and I am determined to stay away from all drugs and drug supply; I have seen with my own eye the devastation that drug use and drug supply causes to people's lives and I want no part of this in future.

◆

Robbery - 7 years

I was addicted to gambling and lost all of my money in a local bookmaker's shop. I became desperate so I attempted to rob the bookmakers. I regretted my offence as soon as my head cleared and I did plead guilty straight away, I am truly sorry for my actions. Since coming to prison I have been determined to change, I have joined Gamblers Anonymous who have provided me with a lot of help to overcome my very real addiction.

◆

Possession with intent to supply class A drugs - 7 years and 4 months

I had been working for agencies when I found myself in between work. I have a family to provide for and I began to suffer severe stress due to financial pressure. In this time of personal weakness, I got involved in with some unscrupulous characters who agreed to lend me money in exchange for storing drugs and paraphernalia. I naively and stupidly allowed them to use my garage. As soon as someone came to collect their stuff they were arrested and so was I.

I deeply regret that I let my financial pressures get the better of me and I allowed myself to get sucked into criminality. I realised exactly where I had gone wrong and I accepted responsibility by pleading guilty. Coming to prison has caused severe hardship to my family and I have also seen the impact that drug supply has on users and on the wider community. I am highly motivated never to commit crime again, to improve myself in all areas and to focus on my future law-abiding life.

Whilst in prison, I have always worked or studied to improve myself. I served as an Offender Management Unit (OMU) Orderly and in this highly trusted role I helped many people in distress or coping with mental health challenges and emotional problems. I gained extra qualifications so that I could be more effective in supporting other people.

I have studied hard and completed many vocational courses in prison which will ensure that I always have stable employment after my release and will be able to enjoy my career and take pride in providing legally for my family.

◆

Violence (S18 GBH) - 10 years' imprisonment

I was grieving for my nephew who sadly drowned aged 13. I was very close to my nephew; this was a traumatic time for me and my family. I attended the wake and drank too much. I felt that someone was being flippant about the tragedy and I took serious offence. I got into an argument with them and totally lost my cool. I have never been violent before but I literally saw red, I lost my head totally and was totally over the top, aggressively attacking my victim in a terrible moment of temper. I was full of remorse afterwards; I accepted responsibility and pleaded guilty

◆

Possession with intent to supply class A drugs - 4 years

When I was 11 years old my parents separated and I went to live with my dad. I left school just before getting qualifications so that I could work and contribute to the rent. Over time my dad became disabled and I found myself in between work; the household income plummeted and we lost our flat to repossession. This was a terrible thing to experience, I found myself sleeping in my car and my dad moved up to Lancashire to stay with a friend.

Having suffered so much for not having money, having seen my dad lose his home and also losing the ability to spend so much time with my dad all hit me hard. I wasn't thinking clearly and I decided to do whatever it took to make money, hence my crime.

I feel deeply ashamed now for turning to crime and I am sorry. I pleaded guilty in court; it was a frightening thing being sent to prison for the first time but I knew I had to accept my punishment.

My dad's health worsened and whilst in prison I was given the devastating news that he had very little time left to live. I was given a choice to be escorted to see him in hospital or to attend his funeral. I chose to see him whilst he was alive so that I could say goodbye and hug him. Although this was very difficult to bear, I will always be grateful that I had the chance to see him before he passed away.

I believe that I have matured so much and that I have coped with my prison sentence well, I have developed resilience and positivity. I have certainly changed for the better and used all the opportunities available to better myself and become more valuable to employers.

One thing I decided to do was to improve myself, I achieved Literacy (English) and Numeracy (Maths) qualifications which I had missed out on at school, I studied nutrition, lost lots of weight and got fit, I gained the discipline of reading for the first time and have now read more than 50 books, I learnt to play chess and really developed my thinking skills.

◆

Conspiracy to supply class A drugs and being concerned in the supply - 7 years

After I left school, I became disenchanted with the poor availability of work and when I was in work, I wasn't earning very much money. I compared myself to some friends who had left school at the same time as I did and I saw that they were earning a lot more than me, they seemed able to 'flash the cash'. I immaturely thought that drug dealing would be a good way to provide for my children. Coming to prison I have realised that no money can replace the time I have missed with my children and that greed and criminality have far reaching impacts. My youngest son was just one-year-old when I came away and he will be almost five years old when I am released. My older son has epilepsy and has developed behavioural challenges, since I have been away causing him to lose his main role model. I am sorry for the affects that my crimes have had on my family and on society.

Since coming to prison, I have gained a number of work-related skills and qualifications which are in demand in the workplace. Stable and permanent employment means that I can live a successful life and provide legally for my family. I do regret my crimes; I have reached deep inside myself and matured.

◆

Importation of Class A drugs - 8 years

I try to travel home to Jamaica each year to see my elderly mother and my extended family. Unfortunately, some local criminals caught up with me and threatened me to carry some drugs back to the UK for them. They told me that they would hurt my mother and my sister if I didn't comply. My mother is in her 90's and I felt that I couldn't take a risk that they were serious and what was the harm, so I carried drugs for them. I realised almost straight away that this was a bad decision and that even if I was 'successful' the drugs are still damaging to society and to the individuals. I should have come up with an excuse why I couldn't carry the drugs or contacted the authorities for advice. I can't have been the only person to experience this type of thing and there must be procedures to deal with it. I was naïve and reckless and when I was caught, I received a long sentence. Coming to prison has been a big shock and disappointment to me and my family. I wish that I had never broken the law. I have tried to use my time in prison to improve myself and to be strong for everyone else.

◆

Conspiracy to supply drugs, importation and money laundering - 21 years

I initially started dealing in drugs because I wanted to build a business and couldn't see an opportunity that didn't require large sums of money which I didn't have. I was greedy to be honest, I was blinkered at the time, only thinking about the money and I didn't consider the knock-on effects of drugs on society. Nowadays I would do things so much differently and I would pursue a legitimate career and legal opportunities.

I felt ashamed for what I did and determined to accept personal responsibility, so I pleaded guilty in court. I also provided character references from people in my community who had known me as a decent person before I committed my crime. Since coming to prison I have personally witnessed the harm that drugs do and the chaos they cause to peoples' lives, wellbeing and mental health. Some people in prison take drugs to help them get through a sentence, to cope with problems and block things out. During my time in prison I have helped and supported several people to cope better with their pressures and find alternatives to drugs. I realised that drug use is similar outside of prison; it is the same type of vulnerable, traumatised and distressed people who turn to drugs and who get exploited by the drug dealers. I never want to be part of that life again. I very much regret my crime and I have learnt a lot from my time away from my family and society.

◆

Conspiracy to supply drugs - 5 years and 10 months

My Dad sadly passed away and I became the breadwinner for my family, responsible for my Mum and my little brother. I abandoned my law degree which I was studying at Birmingham University and I returned home. I am a very hardworking and motivated person; I grew my own successful loft insulation company from the ground up. The company had a significant contract with EON and were waiting for major funding via the government's flagship Green Deal project. Unfortunately, the government delayed implementation of the Green Deal by 2 years (and more recently scrapped it quietly) which had a hugely detrimental effect on my business. I was unable to keep staff employed and also maintain cost infrastructure. I panicked and in desperation turned to crime in the hope that I could keep my staff employed and my family fed. I accepted responsibility by pleading guilty. I have never been to prison before. I deeply regret what I did and with the benefit of hindsight, I know that I would do things so much differently.

♦

Robbery - 4 years

This relates to an incident which happened more than ten years ago and shortly after I had left the Army. I have matured and changed a lot since those days and have an unbroken work record as a decent member of society. Since coming to prison I have kept my work ethic by working hard in prison jobs. I have also helped many other people. I particularly dedicated my time to help a terminally ill man who was suffering with cancer. I helped him with personal care issues and to collect medication. I have many positive comments on my record for how much I helped other people in the very challenging environment that is prison.

♦

Initially ABH which later became manslaughter - discretionary life sentence, indeterminate, minimum tariff 3 years, 15 years served so far.

My local community were upset with a man because he had been filming children in our local area. This was not anything to do with me but as I was walking back home with a friend after a night out, this man thought I had been one of a group of youths that were troubling him. He came out of his flat and grabbed hold of me. I was drunk and I lashed out. Both my friend and I hit the man; the problem was I went too far. When we left the man, his neighbour was helping him up and he appeared okay. Unknown to me this man had health challenges and he had a heart attack after we had left and sadly died. I deeply regret my part in what happened. The sentence that the judge issued to my co-defendant and me reflected that we were guilty of Actual Bodily Harm (ABH) which sadly became manslaughter as a result of the victim's heart attack. We had not set out to kill this man or to badly hurt him.

♦

Fraud - 5 years

I deeply regret my dishonesty which I committed when I had overstretched financially. I was trying my best to support my wife whilst she gained a university degree after having our four children. I struggled to make ends meet and became desperate to provide for my family. I thought I saw a way out of my struggles, to gain some easy money and get ahead and I let myself down badly. I do accept responsibility for what I did. My crime was very out of character for me. I am actually a mature person with a strong work ethic and I am embarrassed by my crime.

◆

Fraud and Fraudulent Trading - 8 years

In 2010 my businesses failed and I went personally bankrupt. I was reckless, greedy, stubborn and far too optimistic. I addressed this mind-set and these behaviour issues before I came to prison, when I established a legal and compliant consultancy business. My family and I downsized our home and reduced our lifestyle and outgoings to a more realistic and sustainable level.

I am very sorry for my dishonesty and for causing people to lose money, I do regret my actions and I hope one day to be able to make amends.

◆

Conspiracy to supply drugs - 7 years

I struggled to fit in at school and was labelled as "naughty". I was suspended on my 15th birthday and I never went back to school. Without any qualifications I spent years as a labourer on building sites. The government introduced a compulsory test called Construction Skills Certification Scheme (CSCS) which all site workers have to complete and pass. Unfortunately, due to my academic challenges (and fear of tests) I failed to qualify for the CSCS card. This meant that I was never able to secure long term work and that I often found myself in-between jobs.

I have a son and daughter, when my son was born, I became desperate to provide for my family. There were so many things this little baby boy needed and I wanted to be a good father. I turned to crime, which I now know was the worst thing I could have done. Crime took me away from my family and has a terrible effect on society too. At the time I just saw my baby and wanted to give him the things he needed.

◆

Death by dangerous driving (2 counts) - 56 months

I allowed myself to be distracted and had a lapse of concentration, even though I am a very experienced and mature lorry driver. I unfortunately crashed into a queue of stationary traffic. My phone was checked by the police and I had not used it; to this day I do not know exactly what happened. I will live with the pain of what happened every day for the rest of my life but I know that my pain will be nothing compared to the suffering of those families involved. I am truly sorry.

♦

Armed Robbery - 10 years

I was a clever and enthusiastic child and at junior school age I achieved a scholarship to an excellent private school in Essex. Unfortunately, at 11 years old I had to go to a state school in Walthamstow where I lived. The contrast was very dramatic; within a few years I was exposed to swearing, violence, drugs and a completely different world. Growing up I felt like I had to sink or swim, but it became very challenging living and going to school in the same deprived area. I began to be very influenced by older people and I started down the path of selling drugs.

Over the years I tried to get out of that lifestyle by started my career path in music and script writing. I do have a talent in these areas and at one time I was under contract with a well-known music group. I poured all of my money into creating and promoting my work and when the money and debt ran out, I didn't know where to turn. I became stubborn and turned to my criminal associates for help. Looking back, I know that I should have stuck to legitimate means to earn money and I am very sorry but at the time I was selfishly just thinking of my own ego. I justified my actions by saying that I was doing it for my 3 children and my partner, but in honesty, if it was truly the case that I was thinking of my children, I would have got a job like any other decent person.

I decided to see prison as an opportunity to clear my head and sort my life out. I have definitely developed as a person and changed for the better.

♦

Conspiracy to burgle - 15 years and 6 months

I was working but I wasn't earning enough money and I got myself into financial difficulty. I thought that robbing cash machines was victimless and that I wouldn't hurt anyone if I made money this way. I couldn't have been more wrong. I have completed a victim awareness course that has helped me to understand the wider impacts of crime on society. I have used my time in prison to work and improve myself so that I will be a more stable employee upon release. I have also helped many other people in difficulty and distress. I worked with members of the travelling community and helped them to settle into prison and cope with the separation from their family. I also built bridges with other service providers to help them with reading and writing and overcoming personal challenges. I really regret my crimes and I have learnt many lessons; I am a different person now.

♦

Possession with intend to supply class A drugs - 8 years

I had been working really hard in my own takeaway business when my wife became badly ill with double pneumonia which meant that she was unable to work in her job as a care assistant for about 6 months and I had to take time away from the business to care for her. I had to trust employees to run my business but unfortunately, they stole from the takings and by the time this was discovered, the impact on the profitability of the business was seriously bad. Customer service levels had also fallen and the business started to struggle. It would have closed had I not found a buyer who was willing to invest capital into the business to bring it back up to a sustainable level. Selling the business left me with no income and only a small amount of capital and it is in this time of financial pressure, personal stress and weakness that I broke the law.

I have been out of trouble for more 30 years. I had a conviction all those years ago for handling stolen goods when I was a very young man of around 22years old. It was my wife who inspired me to stay on the straight and narrow for all these years. The strength of our marriage has been the foundation for my whole life and I was in an emotional whirlwind when she was so desperately ill, I couldn't bear the thought of not having her in my life. I am so glad that she recovered from her illness. Now this desperate period of our life is behind us, I have made a decision to focus on getting through this prison sentence and changing my life for the better. I am truly sorry for what I did; I accepted responsibility and pleaded guilty.

♦

Possession with intent to supply drugs - 3 years

After many years of stable employment, I was only able to secure part time work. I couldn't make ends meet on such a reduced budget. I became desperate to provide for my family (I have two young children). The situation came to a head when we were evicted from our home. In desperation, I recklessly got involved with an undesirable group of people who gave me the opportunity to sell drugs. I can't believe that I did it, having never broken the law before; I am ashamed of how I turned to crime. Whilst in prison, I have gained trade skills through work in plumbing and property maintenance as well as qualifications which I am still building on. I have turned my life around.

♦

Possession and supply of illegal firearms - 16 years.

When I was a teenager, I got introduced to a lifestyle that revolved around drugs. I developed a habit myself which led me down a dark path of supplying to fund my drug habit and protecting myself to avoid getting hurt or killed by rivals. I come from a good family and this life was hidden from my family. I was living two lives, doing good in my community on one side and the darkness of drug supply on the other. I discovered that you can't live both lives; one eventually catches up with you.

Surrounded by all that negativity, the odds were against me until I took responsibility. I shifted my focus from negativity to positivity and grew apart from those people, I used to know; I don't have the same goals or motives as those people anymore.

I started to learn things about myself and I have had time out to figure out who I wanted to be and what I wanted to do with my life. I was trying to find myself as a young man, but really, I needed to come to prison to change.

♦

Conspiracy to Import Class A drugs - 12 years

I was working as a freelance street works operative but unfortunately there was a gap in my employment and I became desperate for money. I began to panic as the last of my savings dwindled because my children were very young children at the time. I turned to some people who had offered me the chance to help them before. Previously I had stayed out of any trouble, dodgy deals or crime but in this time of personal weakness I gave in to the lure of easy money. Of course, in reality there was no easy money, I was predictably caught. I pleaded guilty was sent to prison for my crime.

I had never been to prison before. At first, I was shocked and distressed to be away from my children. When the door shut each night, I was lonely and literally pining for my family. I was a wreck of a man. One evening I looked in the small plastic prison mirror and reminded myself that this was my fault. I had broken the law and I had to pay the price. I decided to stop wallowing and feeling sorry for myself.

I knew that I could never change unless I accepted personal responsibility. What doesn't kill you makes you stronger and more resilient, so I used my time to learn and improve myself.

♦

Fraud by misrepresentation and perverting the course of justice - 6 years

I was involved in a property fraud because I became greedy for money. When I was offered the opportunity all I could think about was the difference that the money could make to my family's life and how I wouldn't have to be working so many hours any more. I was blinkered to the consequences of my crime and the impact that it could have on my victims.

I repaid all of the money back to the people who had lost out, so that in the end I didn't have any financial gain and they didn't lose out.

♦

Burglary - 6 years

I had some turbulence in my earlier years when I started hanging around with a bad crowd after my parents separated. This led to me doing some short sentences in prison for dangerous driving and handling stolen goods. I had grown up a lot and felt that I had sorted my life out when I experienced a bad episode after I split up from my former partner. We had twin sons together and despite me being on the birth certificate and having equal parental rights, she stopped me seeing my sons. Worse still she stopped my dad and step-mum from seeing them too. We had to go through the court process in which she constantly told lies and invented things, 11 allegations she made were proven in court to be false. She went as far as to change the children's surnames; which the courts have subsequently ruled she was not allowed to do. My dad is 70 years old and loved spending time with the twins so this caused a lot of anxiety for the whole family. Unfortunately, my dad had a heart attack and I almost lost him as a result of the emotional distress we were all going through.

Mentally, this period of time put a huge strain on me, I didn't seek help when I should have and instead, I started to self-medicate with cocaine. I had been working in a proper full-time job with a reputable company. Unfortunately, once my drug habit took hold, I didn't keep my job; I committed my crime when I felt I had nothing worthwhile left in my life. I have been determined to develop myself since coming to prison. With help, I stopped taking drugs altogether. I have engaged with several thinking and behaviour courses; I learnt to open up and talk my feelings through and to consider the consequences of my actions so much more. I am sorry for the trouble I have caused to people and I have changed a lot. I now have positive goals for a future crime free life and better coping strategies for when life's inevitable challenges come along.

♦

Possession with intent to supply class A and class B drugs - 33 months

I had studied and achieved good GCSE grades at school, but developed a cannabis habit in college. As a young man I didn't have the good a work ethic that I do now and my CV was incomplete. I did some agency work but for a long period of time I found myself out of work. This lack of employment became part of 'a perfect storm' of events which threatened to engulf my family. On top of this and hidden from my mum and me, my dad had developed a gambling addiction which got progressively worse. We suddenly discovered that the family home was about to be repossessed, I tried to step in to help. I rang a past associate who I used to get cannabis from and told him I need work urgently. This was the worst thing I could have done because it was illegal and also because this man was already under police surveillance; after a short period of time I was arrested.

I accepted full responsibility for my crime and pleaded guilty in court. This was my first ever offence and I am really ashamed with myself for turning to crime. I am determined to make amends to my family and to live a positive life free of crime. The family home was sadly repossessed and my parents now live in temporary accommodation. I completely stopped smoking cannabis and my dad has now sought help for his gambling. I have also broken ties with the criminal associates that I used to know and taken steps to gain more work-related skills and qualifications. I have definitely improved my employability and taken a lot of positive steps to become a better person.

♦

Conspiracy to rob and conspiracy to burgle - 11 years and 9 months

I spent most of the 1980s in the "care" system and endured psychological, physical and emotional abuse for most of that time. This had a serious impact on me. I felt alienated from society, socially isolated and it led to me spending many years in prison on multiple sentences. I was breaking up people's cars for parts and shipping the parts abroad. Brought up around crime, I didn't know any different as a child but as I have grown and matured, I realise now where I went wrong and how wrong my life has been.

I do regret my crimes and I am sorry for what I did. I hope that the victims of my crimes can forgive me. I have completed many personal development courses and vocational courses. Now I am about to start a Personal Track Safety course, all to ensure that I can gain legitimate employment upon release.

◆

Importation of class A drugs - 9 years and 9 months

I was succeeding as a self-employed air conditioning installer. I had worked on many diverse and prestigious projects and I really enjoyed my work. Unfortunately, I found myself working all the hours possible but I had hit a ceiling in my earning capacity. I became greedy. There is no excuse for it and I am not going to deny the truth, I was greedy and I broke the law. Things came to a head and I panicked when I received a large tax bill. This was subsequently proven to be a HMRC error but in the meantime in an impulse I had taken myself overseas and shipped drugs back thinking I would make a lump sum of money quickly which would get me out of trouble.

This was my first offence; I have never been in any kind of trouble with the police or the law before. When I came to prison, I was distressed but I had to "suck it up" and get on with it. I had got myself in this mess and it was up to me to make the best of it. I have worked or studied to improve myself throughout my sentence. I tried my best to help and serve other people. I became a classroom assistant in an IT academy where I taught people Graphic Design skills that would eventually help them into employment. I also served as an Equalities Orderly where I mediated in disputes and helped to develop initiatives and events that raise awareness of equalities issues.

◆

Grievous Bodily Harm (GBH S18) - 6 years

I was undergoing treatment for an inexplicable period of depression. My mental health took a turn for the worse causing me to have suicidal thoughts whilst on the prescribed medication. I did actually attempt to take my own life on more than one occasion. My medication was changed to avoid these distressing side effects, but it had not stabilised quickly enough and so I was sectioned under the Mental Health Act. I was released prematurely within a matter of hours of my section, a decision which has still not been explained. I committed my crime within 30 minutes of being released from the section unit.

There was no logical or explicable reason for me to attack my victim. I am full of remorse, I have apologised to my victim, I am truly sorry. But I really wasn't in a fit state of mind at all. I was remanded into prison straight away. After my mental health had improved due to my medication stabilising, I had the opportunity to attend court where I accepted responsibility and pleaded guilty.

♦

Possession of a firearm with ammunition - 5 years

I was brought up in a rough area of East London and was very distressed because many of my school friends became gang members. They became involved in criminality but I never wanted that life, I stayed away from it and focussed on working. I stayed with the same employer and progressed from a bricklayer and general labourer to become a site manager, overseeing property developments.

Tragically a school friend was shot around the corner from my house. This was a gang territory issue; they call it 'postcode wars. A few days later I received a phone call out of the blue from someone who knew the victim and knew me when I was younger; he said "I have left something for your protection in your garden."

When I looked in the bag, I saw a gun inside but didn't know what to do. I really didn't want to get sucked into this life of violence and crime. I have no previous criminal history and have never been arrested before. I went to work at 6 am as usual and by early afternoon, the police had searched my property and found the firearm. I pleaded guilty to possession of this weapon because I knew that really, I should have rung the person who dropped it off or called the police straight away. At the time I was genuinely afraid of repercussions because I was still living in the area.

I deeply regret my involvement in this criminality and I have learnt many lessons, I am a different person now.

I realise now that you can't really stay friends with people from that world, because it is too easy to be dragged into the mayhem and I have broken all ties with associates from my past. I am now a 30-year-old man with a young son and a long-term partner who is now my fiancé. After my release from prison, we are planning to marry and resettle in a totally different area.

♦

Being concerned in the supply of drugs - 6 years

I suffered serious kidney problems (renal failure) and was no longer able to work in a heavy load bearing environment which was what I had previously done. I became desperate to provide for my family and compromised my own values to do so. I don't blame anyone else; this was my fault; I never should have done it and I have learnt my lesson.

♦

Being concerned in the supply of Class A drugs, possession of Class B drugs, dangerous driving and driving without insurance - 5 years

My wife and I were desperate for a baby and due to complications, we had to have IVF, which is a very expensive treatment. I started to struggle for money and things became unaffordable. At the same time my mum, who was living with us, became ill with cancer. My wife and I reduced our working hours to help care for mum and take her to appointments. All of these challenges together made our financial position desperate. In a time of stress and personal weakness I got involved with the wrong people to try and earn more money.

♦

Conspiracy to supply class A drugs - 7 years

I was at a very low point in my life because my long-term relationship had broken down. I had to move out of my home and on top of all this, my specialist construction work finished. I became desperate and, in that desperation, I reached out for support to entirely the wrong people. I spoke to some past associates of mine and they offered me an opportunity to make money, in my vulnerable state I agreed to work with them. With hindsight, I wish that I had never got involved and that I had been stronger and stuck to legal employment.

This was my first ever offence and it will definitely be my last because I do not see myself as a criminal at all, this chapter of my life was completely out of character.

Whilst serving my sentence I have proven worthy of trust and worked in a number of support roles including that of visitor centre orderly. This was an important position in which I was able to prepare the visits hall and also make the distressing experience of visiting someone in prison a little easier for first time visitors.

I also used my positivity and compassionate nature to help several people in distress. I provided a calming influence to a man who was struggling to cope with the fallout of receiving a long prison sentence. I invested a lot of my own time with him and helped him to maintain stability, despite his world falling apart.

♦

Conspiracy to supply class A drugs - 13 years.

As a young man, I saw elders selling drugs and making money that way. I didn't know wrong from right. I was brought up in a bad environment and grew up around drugs. It was normalised, I didn't realise the harm because I was young. The area I lived in was a deprived area with a lot of poverty and little opportunity. As a young teenager, still at school, I was taken under the wing of elders who were established drug dealers. They told me how I could make money this way and I took them at face value. Everyone does make mistakes in life and I believe that what matters is whether we learn from our mistakes. I have definitely learnt and changed a lot, I am not saying I am perfect, there is always more room for positive change.

I have achieved Level 2 qualifications in Maths, English and IT. I have worked all the way through my prison sentence and achieved vocational qualifications as well. I have also completed many personal development courses and also a victim awareness programme which taught me a lot about the impact of drugs and crime on society. I am ashamed of coming to prison but I saved the life of two people who had been smoking NPS - a very powerful drug with unpredictable effects. The first had vomited and was unconsciously choking on it. I instinctively raised the alarm and placed him in the recovery position. The second was beginning to bite his tongue whilst in a psychotic state. I helped a young and inexperienced prison officer to clear his airways and keep him alive whilst waiting for the emergency medical team. I was highly praised for these interventions.

♦

Attempted murder - discretionary life sentence, minimum tariff 4 years, 6 months. 16 years served

My partner had kicked me out of my own home and put barriers in the way of me seeing my children. I was devastated and in a state of emotional distress. After a year of pain, I visited her to try to resolve the issue but we started to fight. The young man I was back then was desperate, angry and infuriated. I overreacted, struck out thoughtlessly and excessively. My victim was left with a broken arm, a small cut to the side of her eye and another to the side of her head. In mitigation the judge agreed that I was under tremendous emotional pressure, but I was convicted of attempted murder. In the 16 years since then, I have grown up a lot, I completed many personal development courses, most of them helped me in some way, but change was really from me wanting to become a better person.

◆

Conspiracy to rob - 19 years

As a youth I had been through the care system and had ended up homeless. I became a drug user and got in trouble with the law. Years later, after I matured and grew up, I was proud to have turned my life around. I had a stable relationship and I was successfully self-employed in my own removals business. Unfortunately, my past caught up with me and some very dangerous people who I had owed money to years before found me and demanded money. I was in fear for my life and also for my family. I turned to crime and got involved in this conspiracy with the hope of clearing my 'debt'. I know now that I should have turned to legal solutions for help, but at the time I was very single minded and couldn't see a way out of the problem. I do accept responsibility for what I did and I am truly sorry. I took part in an intensive victim awareness course which comprehensively taught me about crime and its effects on victims. I was highly praised in post completion reports for the work I put into the course, how I gave it 100% and also helped other inmates on the course.

I know that what I did was wrong and I do accept all responsibility myself, I am the only one to blame for the mess I got myself into. Coming to prison and leaving my family has been really bad for all of us; I will never do anything to put myself or my family in this position ever again.

◆

Being concerned in the supply of class A drugs - 42 months

I regret being involved in this crime which I did because I was behind on my rent and I was worried that we lose our home. I had been self-employed but I found myself out of work for an unusually long period. I didn't have the necessary qualifications to get a number of roles that I was aiming for and I turned to crime out of desperations.

I have no previous criminal record; this was my first time in prison. Since coming to prison I have gained the necessary qualifications that I was missing before and I know that I will be able to maintain a consistent flow of work in future.

Whilst in prison, I have worked consistently and continued to build on my CV. I have also completed a number of personal development courses which have helped me to gain additional skills and live a crime free life.

◆

ABH and two counts of burglary - 4 years' indeterminate sentence (IPP) 9 years served

I am a quiet and reserved person and from a young age I fell in with a bad crowd who led me to get involved in criminality. I developed a habit of drug use and fell into a spiral of crime to feed my habit. I deeply regret the harm I caused to other people through my earlier years of crime and I have been determined to turn my life around.

When I came to prison, I completed many personal development programmes (including getting it right and enhanced thinking skills) and I have grown and matured.

During my time in prison I sadly lost my mum to lung cancer at the young age of just 54; a harsh realisation for me was that I had missed so many years with her and that now at the age of 41 I still have a chance to live a normal, decent and positive life. I have fully detoxed from drugs and ended all drug use; I have a hatred for drugs now for the harm they did to me and the harm they drove me to do to other people.

◆

Murder - mandatory life sentence, indeterminate, minimum tariff 15 years

A man was threatening my brother's family. As the older brother, I felt a responsibility to protect him and I over-reacted. I ruthlessly hurt that man and he sadly died. I have regretted that day ever since. My crime was very out of character for me, I had never been violent before. I accepted responsibility by pleading guilty.

Whilst in prison I have always worked, or studied to improve myself and with formal training from the Samaritans, I have helped other people, whilst they were at their lowest points. I have also taught many prisoners to read via the Shannon Trust's "Toe by Toe" programme.

I do accept responsibility for what I did. I voluntarily completed an accredited Victim Awareness course. I gained certification in the Restorative Justice Process (reducing crime in society). The course, and my commitment to complete it, had a profound effect on me; I will never create victims again. I regret my crime and I have learnt many lessons. I am a different person now.

◆

Conspiracy to Commit Armed Robbery with Firearms - 6 years and 10 months' minimum imprisonment for public protection (IPP), indeterminate, 13 years served

I grew up in a very rough area of the West Midlands where drugs and crime were normalised. Even the police rarely entered our estate. People bragged about the money they were making illegally. I was in my late teens when I was taken under the wing two older men; you could say I was groomed; with hindsight it was a bit like that. I am not solely blaming them however; I should have known my own mind and kept out of trouble myself. I committed the crimes with them and I have to take responsibility. I accepted responsibility by pleading guilty.

I deeply regret that people were so badly affected by my actions; I know that I deserved to be punished and I have been determined to change and better myself. I completed several personal development and victim awareness courses and I also changed my thinking and behaviour totally.

I am particularly aware of the power of association and peer influences. I have developed something which I call 'jail smart' where I can assess someone's motives and intentions better than I ever used to before. This allows me to avoid negative influences and steer my own path in future.

◆

Violent disorder and manslaughter - 7 years

A group of drunk men attacked my friends and me without provocation when we were celebrating a birthday. One of the men stabbed two of my friends. I managed to take the knife off him but he continued to attack me. Caught up in the intensity of the moment I reacted instinctively and stabbed him back once. My friends and I called the emergency services; my injured friends made recoveries despite their stab wounds, but the attacker who I stabbed, died at the scene. The sentence length I received shows the significant mitigation put forward to the court. It is judged to have been manslaughter. This terrible incident only happened because I was attacked and acted in self-defence, albeit completely excessively and in a reckless moment of temper.

♦

Conspiracy to supply a firearm and class A drugs - 8 years and 4 months.

I was educated in high quality independent schools both in the UK and overseas but returned to the UK at short notice to finish off my GCSEs at a state school in a deprived area. The change in setting was a big shock to me and to be accepted I began to hang around with undesirable people from the age of 16. I allowed myself to gradually slip into crime from a young age. I didn't actually handle the firearm or the drugs but I made a number of introductions, which was where I went wrong, I should have refused to get involved at all. I did plead guilty straight away.

I have no further contact with my co-defendants or past associates and I want to build a healthy and normal, crime free life after my release.

♦

Conspiracy to Theft - 6 years and 6 months

I was a security driver making collections and deliveries in armoured vehicles. My co-driver knew a group of criminals and arranged for them to threaten my family. They would hurt them unless I co-operated with helping them to gain access to the money. I resisted and told them that I was going to report them to the police, but they made it clear that no matter what police involvement, members of my family would be at serious risk of harm. I had thought about leaving work but I was in a terrible dilemma and eventually I relented and did what they wanted because I have a wife and three sons and I genuinely feared for them. I stopped the vehicle and handed the money to the gang. I did not gain financially but still faced confiscation proceedings meaning that I lose my own personal assets.

I really regret my involvement in this conspiracy and I wish that I had told the police and my employer immediately instead of being weak and taking what I thought was the easy option.

Since coming to prison I have come off drugs and I have acquired many qualifications. I have a passion for personal fitness, I have excelled in this field and helped many people and this is where I believe my future lies. Now I know what I want to do with my life, I want to be a decent member of society, to contribute and to get married and have a family. I do regret my crimes and I intend to live a crime free life upon release.

◆

Conspiracy to Supply Class A Drugs - 6 years and 6 months

I had a good upbringing and despite living in a deprived area, I was doing well in school and even playing for local football teams to Academy level. Unfortunately, my dad was suddenly sent to prison. Having my dad taken away from me unexpectedly changed me because I had lost my male role model. I began to struggle and get in trouble at school and I 'took to the road'. I began associating with local youth and older men. I got into an environment and group that it is hard to get out of; I didn't feel like I could just leave once I was part of that life. My long-term girlfriend brought stability to my life and when she fell pregnant, I knew that I wanted to provide for my child. I did this the wrong way however; I dropped out of College and started selling drugs. It was shortly after this that I was arrested along with other co-conspirators and sent to prison. Coming to prison as a young man of 19 years old is scary, I had never been to jail before and it is an intimidating place. I witnessed a lot of violence, but I managed to stay out of trouble myself, knuckle down and gain extra qualifications. I also completed personal development programmes which helped me to learn about managing conflict, improve my communication skills and self-esteem and to plan for more positive, community-based living.

◆

Conspiracy to commit robbery and theft and also dangerous driving - 8 years

I deeply regret my offences which happened at a time in my life when I lacked focus and direction. I was 20 years old at the time. I met up with distant relatives who were engaged in criminal activity and I allowed myself to get involved in their schemes. I was on bail for 5 years while it was all being investigated and I never committed any further crimes but instead I grew up and matured a lot. I got married and moved an hour away to begin a fresh start in a new area. I also started a small business that was successful and allowed me to provide for my wife and the two young children that we became blessed with.

I am so sorry for my part in these crimes. I think how I would feel if I worked hard to achieve things only to have them stolen by people who only cared about money. I am angry and upset with myself for what I have done. I very much regret my crime and I have learnt many lessons, at 28 years old, I am a different person now. I have completed courses in prison and gained qualifications to help me to work legitimately again in future and I am determined to stay out of trouble; to watch my children grow up without coming back to prison.

♦

Armed Robbery - 14 years

I was a pub owner and landlord and my business was struggling. The economic climate became very challenging and the smoking ban devastated the pub industry such that from 2012 (when I was remanded), more than 2 pubs have been closing every week. I was being harassed by bailiffs and debt collectors. I was working as many hours as possible but couldn't get in front. I worried that we could lose both the pub and our family home. I wasn't brave enough to follow legal channels, go bankrupt and let it all go.

In my fear and desperation, I turned to crime. I was a fool, I got involved with old school criminals, they were thinking and acting like idiots, like they were in a movie. I let myself and my family down badly.

♦

GBH - Section 18 (wounding with intent) - 7 years and 6 months

I am a mature businessman specialising in traditional coach-building. Owning my own business and controlling my own time meant that I was able to spare time helping local charities. I decided to give one day a week to working for Citizen's Advice Bureau. I had been giving advice to a homeless man and I should never have got personally involved but I saw him walking in my village carrying some possessions. I naively allowed him to store his things in my garage until he got settled.

Unfortunately, sometime later, he burgled my house and I reported his crime to the police. I bumped into him a few months later and he pulled out a knife on me, angry that I had reported his crime. I managed to disarm him and, in my fear, I hurt him with his own knife. He did not get arrested for having the weapon or attacking me with the knife, but I did. I have never been in trouble before and I pleaded not guilty, not because I am not accepting responsibility but because I was acting in self-defence and out of fear of what would happen to me. The judge unusually accepted a majority verdict of 8 - 4 from the jury who had been rushed to make a decision or face coming back to court on Christmas Eve. My attacker has a long history of crime and using weapons and yet in this case the attacker perversely became the victim.

I do have an appeal in progress but the process takes a long time and I have been faced with spending years in prison awaiting the outcome.

♦

Burglary - 6 years

My brother was imprisoned for a serious offence when I was very young and my mum suffered a nervous breakdown. I was taken into care and remained in care homes from the ages of 9-16 years old. I got on well and learnt a lot in the care system, but as a teenager I started to hang around with people who were committing crime. I developed a drug habit in my early life and have struggled with this for many years. I regret causing trouble to so many people in my past and I have made a lot of changes in my life.

Whilst in prison, I worked full- time throughout my sentence and gained the habit of work as well as useful skills. I completed an 8-week intensive course called Thinking Skills Programme. I learnt so much on this course, particularly about making better choices. I was praised for completing the course and for my honest and positive contributions throughout.

I have been determined to stay clean of drugs. I sought help for my drug use and have now been drug free for almost 3 years. I have helped and supported many other recovering addicts. It does get easier; I look at how far I have come and I am always working to improve myself.

♦

Cultivation of Cannabis - 7 years

My first offence was for causing death by dangerous driving. I did not have a crash but I overtook three cars and a car came towards me at high speed. We didn't crash but the driver gesticulated at me as he went passed and crashed immediately afterwards. This was a tragic accident and I deeply regret being involved in the death of another person.

I served my prison sentence for this crime and after release I struggled to gain employment because of my criminal record and because I could no longer drive. I stupidly got involved with growing cannabis to earn money for myself.

Since this time, I have learnt that being upfront from the beginning and providing honest disclosure (such as this letter) is the best way to secure employment. I have worked hard to gain additional work-related skills and qualifications so that I can be more valuable to employers. I deeply regret my crimes and I would like the chance to make amends and contribute to society through work and by helping other people in mentoring and support roles.

♦

Conspiracy to evade duty - 5 years.

I was a professional property manager responsible for a number of properties both commercial and residential. I rented commercial premises to a man who passed all usual credit checks and his references proved valid. He brought tobacco into the country with the understanding that it would be leaving the country again and therefore would be ineligible for import duty. It later materialised that the tobacco was staying in this country and was therefore deliberate evasion. When HMRC investigated, I was arrested and so was my tenant. He left the country and didn't return. I was convicted as a member of a conspiracy. I had been naïve and had failed to do sufficient due diligence but even my legal team had not expected all the responsibility to fall on my shoulders and for me to go to prison.

♦

Fraud by false representation - 41 months

I had developed a gambling addiction which got a lot worse over time. I had taken the unacceptable action of taking out debts totalling £6,000 in my wife's name. We separated and we had to list out debts and liabilities because we were about to begin separate lives and my crime was discovered. I admitted my offence, apologised and pleaded guilty. I have sought help for my addiction and have now recovered, I no longer gamble. I am now sharing the lessons that I have learnt and working with an NHS Substance Misuse Provider Alliance. I am helping them to develop procedures and interventions to help other current and former gambling addicts.

♦

Being concerned in the supply of drugs and possession of a firearm - 5 years

I left the armed forces when my Father sadly died. I became depressed because I had been estranged from him for a couple of years before he died. I felt that I had lost some of the direction in my life and I started a drug habit. I began to associate with a bad group of people and got pulled deeper and deeper into this hidden life. My supplier had left a holdall in my house for safekeeping. I knew that the bag contained drugs but I didn't know it had a gun in there. We were under surveillance and the police arrested me. I had only been involved in this for a total of 3 days.

In a way I am glad that I was caught because this was not the life that I wanted for me or my family.

◆

Intent to supply class A drugs and possession of a bladed article - 3 years

I left School and College at age 18 having achieved a range of GCSEs and NVQ Diplomas. I was proud of myself and my parents were proud of me too. I entered the workplace and developed a good work ethic in a number of roles but unfortunately after committing to an agency, I found myself on a zero hours' contract and left with little or no work. I desperately wanted to work, I would have loved to start my own business but I didn't have capital and this time out of work meant I had no money at all. In a time of personal weakness, I looked at some other young people locally who seemed to have everything materially. I compared myself to them and thought I could do it too. I forgot that I come from a decent family and I was a good student, I just saw money and a way out of my challenges.

I have never been in trouble with the police before and certainly never been to prison so getting caught and being charged was a massive wake up call to me. To maintain my personal integrity and salvage any element of decency from my crime, I had to put my hands up and plead guilty. I did this because I wanted to accept full responsibility.

I know that a criminal life is not for me. This was a brief and completely out of character chapter in my life. I have gained new vocational qualifications and improved my employability so that I will never find myself without work again. I deeply regret my crime and I regret that I allowed myself and my life to get so off track.

◆

Conspiracy to supply class A and class B drugs - 10 years

I was a regular cannabis user myself and started using more and more to get the same effect. After a while I became dependant on it and I needed to get money to pay for it. I was working, I have always worked, but I wasn't earning enough money to feed my habit. One time a friend asked me to get some for them and I made a little bit of profit by doing this. Pretty soon, this became a habit that I sort of fell into.

I do now want to leave that life behind me and live a crime a free life. My daughter was 4 years old when I came to prison and she is 8 now. I have missed so much and I would walk any distance and do whatever it takes to make amends and to rebuild my relationship with her and other family members.

◆

Murder - mandatory life sentence, **indeterminate**, minimum tariff 12 years served 15

I suffered extreme abuse as a very young child and was removed from the family home. When I was 18 years old, I was still living with a kind lady who had been my foster mother in my teenage years. Her daughter was 11 years old and she came running into the house crying hysterically. She had been visiting a friend's house where she fell asleep and awoke to find a man sexually abusing her. I know with hindsight that I should have gone straight to the police and I would do this in future, but at the time I just was thinking of this young girl and of what had happened to me as a small child. I left straight away to confront this man and he just started laughing and mocking. With my own traumatic experiences in my mind, I couldn't tolerate this so we started fighting. In a fit of rage and emotional distress I went too far and killed him. I handed myself in, accepted responsibility and pleaded guilty. I had never done anything like this before; I am not a violent person.

I attended an intensive anger management course and whilst on this course I mentored many other people to progress and to understand their emotions better. I was praised by an eminent doctor for my contributions, both to my own rehabilitation, and to that of other people.

◆

Death by dangerous driving - 5 years and 3 months

I was involved in a terrible accident when a pedestrian ran in front of my car. I was going too fast at the time, rushing to get home and although I took avoiding action, the lady I hit sadly died. I have expressed my regret and remorse to the family affected by this terrible tragedy. I am truly sorry but I know that my words can do little to bring comfort after such a loss. I will never speed again.

I have never been to prison before and it was something I couldn't really prepare for. When I was first incarcerated, I saw lots of fights and drug use and it was very upsetting. I stayed away from all the problems and bad influences and came to a point of acceptance of my situation. The more I accepted personal responsibility, the more I was able to use my time positively to improve myself and my future prospects. I enrolled myself on to a number of courses and also helped to improve the prison visitors' centre.

◆

Being concerned in the supply of drugs - 4 years 6 months

I was brought to the UK and granted asylum when I was shot aged 5 years old in Iraq. I worked hard and built a life here. My younger Sister back home in Iraq developed cancer believed to be related to the Depleted Uranium munitions used there. I wanted to support her but medical care is chargeable there. Whilst working I sent her £1000 each month to fund her treatment. Now, my Sister is currently in remission. However, I had devastated my finances to pay for her treatment.

I thought I saw a way out of my struggles, to gain some easy money and get ahead. I self-medicated my fears and trauma from my past through drugs. I got involved with drug dealers as an extension of this. I knew it was wrong from the beginning but I didn't know where else to turn.

I let myself down badly as well as this country that cared for me. I am sorry.

◆

Murder - mandatory life sentence, indeterminate, minimum tariff 18 years

When I was 22 years old, I was imprisoned for Murder by joint-enterprise. This means that I wasn't the person who actually committed the crime but by being there I was considered to be an accomplice. In my early life I had been involved in gangs. My step father spent most of his life in prison and my mum was involved with drug dealers. I grew up depressed most of the time and with no direction. I struggled to find my identity and got involved in gang culture.

I have worked very hard while in prison to change myself and my outlook. I have spent seven and a half years in therapy analysing my previous behaviour, increasing my resilience, understanding empathy and developing my own self-awareness and emotional maturity. I have also completed many educational qualifications and I am in my third year of an Open University degree.

I also acted as a Restorative Justice Mentor and on one particular occasion I diffused an argument between two men who had been fighting. I helped them both to explain their feelings and to understand why things had escalated to a fight. At the end of the session they shook hands and moved on without further conflict. I regret my past; I have moved on completely and left my criminal lifestyle behind. I have matured and realised the impact of my actions on my victims.

I am optimistic about the future and feel confident that I have a lot to offer.

♦

Fraud and conspiracy to defraud - 6 years

I was contacted by a person who I had known from years before. I agreed to receive some money from a 'deal' for a commission or fee; I should never have agreed to do this and in effect turn a blind eye but with hindsight, I was attracted to the thought of extra money and I wanted to help this person. I should have been stronger and just said no. After a while I began to realise that there were other people involved (this is why I was charged with being involved in a 'conspiracy') and in fact this was a much bigger operation than I first thought.

I accepted responsibility by pleading guilty and I realised the massive impact that my crime would have on me and my family. When I came to prison, I took steps to use my professional skills and abilities to help other people. I became an Information, Advice and Guidance provider and helped and supported many desperate people to find practical solutions.

To support my own journey of change, I completed several personal development programmes which have taught me to consider my actions better, to be more assertive and confident when dealing with other people and to set more positive and achievable goals for the future.

♦

Robbery - 7 years Extended Determinate Sentence (EDS) (chance of parole at 2/3rd),

I have 6 older brothers who used to keep an eye out for me but we always played rough and tumble. When I left school, I stopped listening to my brothers but continued to be boisterous and want to fight. I began hanging around with a bunch of local troublemakers and very significantly I started to take drugs. This was a bad step for me to take and it marked a downward spiral. My crime happened after a particularly rowdy night out during which I had taken cocaine and drank alcohol and I became violent.

I deeply regret what I did and this was the turning point for me. I stopped drinking and taking drugs and cut those bad influences out of my life. I have always liked working and it is work that has kept me out of trouble in the past, so when I came to prison, I focussed on working hard and gaining extra skills and qualifications.

♦

Attempted murder - 22 years

I was 20 years old when I had an argument with a man who was a lot older than me. I sort of won the fight if you could call it that and I thought that was the end of it. A couple of days later however I was warned that he was coming back to kill me. I panicked and in fear of my life I got a weapon to arm myself. I went over the top and I am so sorry and shocked at myself for hurting this man. After my crime I wanted to show my remorse and that I accepted responsibility so I pleaded guilty.

I was scared of repercussions for my wife and our young daughter who was only 18 months old so we relocated 200 miles away. I wish that I had made this decision before the man came back to me, then he wouldn't have been hurt and I wouldn't have missed the most important years of my daughter's childhood.

I have used my time in prison to gain and education, work related skills and qualifications. I have achieved numeracy/maths, literacy/English and IT qualifications. I have also qualified as a Level 3 Health Trainer. I have been determined to turn my life around and build my future value to society; I have not let a single day of my imprisonment be wasted.

♦

Commercial robbery - 8 years

I was brought up in a deprived part of London and I did not know my Dad. Growing up I felt shut out from society and grew up "on the streets". I struggled for male role models and whilst I was still a child, I was taken under the wing of older men who made me think that crime was good. Once I was part of this group, I felt that I just couldn't leave and feared that I wouldn't fit in anywhere else.

I have broken all contact with these people and I am relocating to a totally different region where I can begin a life free of crime with my partner. We hope to start a family and I will work hard; I will do whatever is right and proper to be a good role model.

I am not that same street criminal now; I don't want to be him.

◆

Conspiracy to supply Class A drugs - 7 years

As a young teenager I was a football captain and was taking part in footballer trials for many major clubs, including Manchester City. I studied sports science in College and I had optimistic goals for the future.

Unfortunately, my life took a terrible turn when my Mum sadly died of cancer at the young age of just 46 years old. I was very close to my Mum and the loss hit me very hard. I didn't really talk to people about it, but turned to illegal drugs as an escape. With hindsight, I just couldn't accept the loss, it was just too big and I couldn't cope.

Within a short space of time I had found myself to be mentally and physically dependent on drugs and living my life in a circle of other drug users. I had always worked full time but even my work was affected and I was unable to afford my habit. I turned to selling drugs to fund my own use. Choosing drugs resulted in many lost opportunities in my life, including a chance to coach youth football in Australia and I have many regrets. Drug use and dealing has brought nothing but pain and loss to myself and to my family. I also understand the wider implications of dealing on society and how harm ripples out into our communities. I am very sorry for my involvement and I have been determined to change.

It has been a struggle but I have been drug-free for a number of years. I have completed a 'psychosocial workbook' in which I logged my determination to change, my goals for the future and additionally I studied urges, triggers and relapse prevention.

When I came to prison, I wanted to make a positive difference to other people. I know that many people have endured far greater challenges than I have. It was time for me to stop being so self-centred and feeling sorry for myself. I wanted to help other people in difficulty and distress.

I studied and achieved a formal Level 2 qualification in Information, Advice and Guidance and guided people in a mentoring role, to improve their family relationships and their functional skills.

I have started a BA (Hons) with the Open University as a further demonstration of my personal commitment to change and turn my back on both drugs and crime.

♦

Conspiracy to commit fraud by false representation, causing unnecessary suffering to an animal, failing to ensure the welfare of animals and keeping a pet shop without a licence - 4 years and 8 months + lifetime ban from keeping dogs.

Conspiracy means being involved in plotting and planning with other people to do illegal acts. I would like to share some background, not to justify what I did, but to explain a little. A family member had been successfully breeding and selling pedigree dogs for a number of years; the business appeared successful and I asked him how I could start a similar venture. I hadn't realised at first that he was so profitable because paperwork had been falsified and these were not really the pure breed dogs he was claiming. Additionally, the puppies were not home-bred but were in fact imported from overseas puppy farms and so their long-term health couldn't be guaranteed.

I had already invested and taken steps to commit to my new business and even though I discovered the origin of the dogs, I allowed myself get blinded by the earning potential and thought it was a victimless crime. I realise now that I behaved despicably. Defrauding people who were hoping to gain a family pet and also contributing to the wholesale almost intensive farming of such highly intelligent animals was something I should never have turned a blind eye to. As soon as the RSPCA became involved and highlighted conditions that puppies were kept in by our suppliers, I ceased my involvement totally. The dogs which we had looked after pre-sale were always looked after in our family home and were fed the best types of dog food (Royal Canine). All the puppies were checked by a vet and they were vaccinated by the same vet, nevertheless, some became ill. As soon as everyone involved in the conspiracy was charged and the matter went to court, I plead guilty at the earliest opportunity. As part of my guilty plea, I agreed to a lifetime ban from keeping dogs for life.

Causing serious injury by dangerous driving - 42 months

I was awaiting an urgent phone call relating to my uncle who was seriously ill in hospital after a stroke. I recklessly tried to answer my mobile phone whilst driving and in so doing took my eyes of the road and hit a cyclist. The cyclist was left with very bad injuries and will continue to suffer for many years solely because of my stupidity and selfishness. I am truly sorry.

Fraud by false representation, abuse of position and converting criminal property - 4 years

I was chair of trustees of a charity. I made the mistake of submitting inflated returns for gift-aid. My intention was to make as much money as possible for the charity at a time when it badly needed funds.

I know that what I did was wrong and that I should have had far greater oversight of the volunteer team before I signed off anything. I shouldn't have let myself get involved in recklessness or dishonesty.

Conspiracy to help asylum seekers to enter the UK - 4 years and 6 months

I was a shopkeeper, operating a local newsagent/ convenience shop. I had been doing well and had supported my family legally for 10 years. Unfortunately, however in a short space of time both a Tesco Express and a Poundland shop opened nearby. My takings literally halved almost overnight, yet my overheads stayed the same, or were set to increase like business rates. I didn't know what to do, I had put my life savings into the shop and still had financial obligations attached to it too. A distant relative introduced me to a way to make money by committing the crime which I pleaded guilty to.

I am ashamed of what I did; I should have faced up to my problems and stuck to legal solutions.

Possession of a firearm - 4 years

I did a really stupid thing - I bought a Torch Taser from Spain as a novelty and brought it into the UK. This is classed as a firearm and I got a 4-year prison sentence. These means 2 years in prison, 2 years on licence, 11 years before my conviction becomes spent, I lost my accountancy job and I have a lifetime ban from touching fireworks, which is an annual event in our house. I had never broken the law before and never will again. I gained nothing whatsoever from being in prison, it took a father away from his children. Worst of all, my Mum passed away shortly after I came to prison, my wife coordinated everything, but I had to attend the funeral handcuffed.

◆

Conspiracy to supply class A drugs - 9 years.

For a number of years, I had been caring for my wife who became disabled after a series of neck operations. The family finances were decimated by my inability to work and a lifetime of earning and saving had dwindled down to nothing. I took work as a mini-cab driver but could only work part time hours to fit around caring for my wife. I had a customer who booked me privately and gradually increased the amount of work he was giving me to include collecting his wife and children from various activities. After several months, he asked me to deliver parcels for him without him coming in the car himself. Looking back, I understand that I had allowed myself to be groomed into this role and to become dependent on his business. On one occasion he asked me to pick up an associate of his. I drove to the address and the man put a small suitcase in the car but didn't get in himself; he said he had to be somewhere else and gave me an address to deliver to. At this point I became very suspicious; I knew it must have been drugs but I stupidly took the case anyway. I didn't want to refuse because I really needed the money.

I deeply regret my involvement in this conspiracy, this was my first ever offence. The impact on my family by my imprisonment has been catastrophic. If only I had given more thought to the consequences of crime and criminality I never would have got involved. My wife struggles every day and just manages to get by with help from our adult daughter.

My father sadly passed away before I came to open conditions and although I was handcuffed, I am grateful that I was allowed to visit him in hospital on one occasion before he died. I have dealt with the tragedy and with my prison sentence as best that I can, particularly taking full responsibility myself; I am not blaming anyone else, I know that this sequence of events was my fault and I would always advise taxi drivers particularly, to never get blinded by the thought of money and carry parcels for anyone else. I do want to rebuild my life without crime and be a good role model to my children again.

Robbery - 3 years' minimum imprisonment for public protection (IPP), indeterminate, 8 years served

I really regret my offence which arose because I owed money to dangerous people who had made threats to me and my family (My son was a new born baby at the time). I became scared and desperate and acted impulsively to try to resolve everything.

♦

Armed Robbery - 14 years

When I was very young my dad went to prison and as I grew up, I learnt that that in my community in South London, crime was justified as a means to an end. I was raised in an environment with an 'us' and 'them' mentality. I looked up to some of the older boys who appeared to have plenty when others had little. The heroes round my way were into crime and I not only aspired to be like them, I wanted others to look up to me the way that they were looked up to. It is only with hindsight and the maturity of passing years that I realise how wrong those thoughts are and how dangerous such a lifestyle is. I had a chance to get out as a young man; I was a skilled centre-forward striker in the youth team for a South London Club, I wasted my opportunities through a lack of self-discipline and little family support. I try not to look back and think 'if only' but I know that I certainly have lessons to share with my own children and the youth that I help. When I came to prison, I was determined to change for the better. I have had the advantage of education being available in prisons and so with a huge amount of effort on my part, I graduated from intensive programmes called 'resolve' and Enhanced Thinking Skills (ETS) which covered so many helpful life skills like positive thinking, managing emotions, problem solving, improving communication and setting future goals. I am very sorry for my crimes and I am a completely different person now. I honestly do not believe that anyone could have created such a complete and utter turnaround in their life as I have.

♦

Fraud and money laundering - 5 years and 10 months

I had lived in Thailand for many years, working throughout my years there. I first worked as a diving instructor and then as an English language teacher in a private college. Unfortunately, I began to struggle financially when I wasn't able to work sufficient hours to sustain myself. I had an idea to set up an online business carrying out administration, checks and online searches. This started to take off and I put it in the hands of an associate I knew who I thought had a good understanding of SEO and managing online businesses. Unfortunately, he began to break rules and set up a whole suite of websites using my name and contact details. I turned a blind eye at first because he was making good money and I had got busy again with my teaching. After a while however his criminality became clear and I wanted to stop but I had got in too deep. It was at this time that Trading Standards and the Police in the UK contacted me and I agreed to return to the UK for investigation. My associate became my co-defendant and he disappeared without trace.

When it came to court, I accepted full responsibility and pleaded guilty. I was very sorry that people had lost money and been misled through my websites.

♦

Conspiracy to rob and conspiracy to commit commercial burglary - 14 years

I was the proprietor of my own building firm which was carrying out major home improvements such as loft conversions and extensions as well as smaller drain work, ground works and roofing. Unfortunately, my wife became unexpectedly ill over a long period of time and I tried to care for her whilst also continue to manage my company. I had taken on too much and overcommitted myself and my business. I began to suffer from exhaustion, depression and anxiety. I started taking pro-plus caffeine tablets and drinking energy drinks, before I knew it, I was suffering anxiety and panic attacks, but I didn't see the link. I was so tired that I sourced a drug called speed (amphetamine sulphate) and began taking this daily. I didn't speak to anyone but bottled up all my problems and hid my worries from the most important person, my wife, justifying my isolation by saying to myself that I didn't want to burden her. I suffered a serious bereavement when I lost my Aunt; she had been like a mother to me and I cross the line into more serious drug use and became a daily cocaine user. I felt that I needed to keep taking drugs just to function. I was falling deeper and deeper into their grip. I ended up in serious debt to the drug dealers and my business started to fail quite dramatically. It was in this period of self-inflicted pain and personal weakness that I agreed with criminals to commit these crimes.

When I was caught, it was almost like a weight had been lifted from my shoulders. I felt relief that I didn't have to live this double life anymore. I am so ashamed of my actions and how I acted at the time. I have completed drug rehabilitation and relapse prevention courses and I embraced them wholeheartedly, I then went on to mentor and coach other drug users into living a cleaner better life.

I have achieved a lot in the last few years through being proactive and determined to change for the better.

♦

Conspiracy to burgle commercial and domestic premises - 5 years

I also have previous convictions for petty crimes when I was a juvenile. I was brought up in a deprived area of Northamptonshire and when my mum remarried, I did not get on at all with my step dad. He was very strict with me bordering on intimidation and abuse. I stayed away from home as much as possible and fell in with a bad company. I started fending for myself on the streets and committing crime. It took me a long time to find myself and stabilise; I was committing offences for financial gain and I got trapped in a spiral of offending. My convictions meant that I was unable to get employment and once I was released from prison, I felt like I had to reoffend just to live.

I have gained a number of vocational skills and qualifications in prison and I am proud of my folder of achievements; this is bursting at the seams with the courses I have completed and the certificates I have gained. I hope that this time I can get out of prison into full-time employment. I have had periods in my life where I have been employed and these have always been the times where I was stable and crime free.

♦

Evasion of import duty on tobacco - 5 years and 9 months

In 1999 I fled Iraq as an asylum seeker when I was in my early twenties and my wife joined me later. I had witnessed terrible things in Iraq. I have been badly affected by the trauma and devastation and this does affect my ability to concentrate and gain formal qualifications. I do love learning but the menial jobs I had been working in were very low paid, intermittent and also, I wasn't supported to gain qualifications. My wife is a dentist and retrained in the UK before entering practise. I cared for our two children as a full-time parent at home but as they got older, I found it very difficult to join the workplace. I had a series of low paid part time jobs and I allowed myself to get too attracted to the thought of easy money.

I pleaded guilty to my crime of importing/ smuggling cigarettes and I am so very sorry for breaking the law; particularly because this country has treated me so very well.

This is my first ever offence and my very last; I have been absolutely devastated to be separated from my wife and children/ It has been very hard for all of us and they have paid a high price for my recklessness.

◆

Conspiracy to help asylum seekers to enter the UK - 6 years

I was refurbishing a property in France when I saw a family with young children sleeping in a skip at a supermarket. My heart went out to them and I made the illegal decision to take them in the back of my van to the UK. I was caught at the border. I regret that I broke the law; I have never been in trouble with the police before I did plead guilty in court. Such direct and illegal action is definitely not the way forward but I will stick to supporting legitimate charities and causes in future. I enjoy helping other people and so I used my time in prison to contribute to the community and support others. I particularly remember that I had a room-mate who had never learnt to read so over a period of several months I dedicated all my spare time to introduce him to the magic of reading. It is such a simple thing that we all take for granted but to him it was life changing. Knowing that he was able to read and respond to letters from his family has brought me some personal pride.

◆

Conspiracy to Supply Class A drugs - 6 years

I know exactly where I went wrong, I have learnt my lessons and I know that I won't break the law again.

It all started when I was training to gain my electrical qualifications but really struggling financially. I was desperate to get on the housing ladder but prices just seemed to be moving further and further away from me. In a moment of weakness, I found myself meeting with a young man of similar age who had plenty of money and seemed like he had freedom from financial pressures. I took my eye off the ball totally and moved from my career path as an electrician onto the path of crime. I did plead guilty to my crime and I am truly sorry for my involvement, this was my first ever time in prison. I caused a lot of embarrassment to my Mum and Dad; they were very unhappy about my behaviour and I definitely have a lot to make up to them. Before I came to prison, I completed my electrical qualifications, so that I would have a stable future.

It was a shock coming to prison and losing so many years of my life. I knew however that I had to get on with it, get through it and use the time wisely for self-improvement. I completed courses called 'Positive lifestyles' and 'Personal and Social development', I also learnt about the long-term effects of both crime and drug supply on families and on society. I do much regret my crime; I do believe that I have matured a lot and changed for the better.

◆

Conspiracy to destroy property and intent to obstruct a coroner - 7 years

I was associated with a very influential man who was in a lot of distress due to dramatic media publicity and I wanted to support him. My friend eventually committed suicide and I withheld a mobile phone from the coroner with the misguided and criminal intention of helping his family to avoid further scandal.

◆

Possession of an unlicensed firearm and going to a public place to endanger life - 10 years

My wife and I had separated and I had moved out of the family home some ten months earlier. Most of my property was still in the house and farm buildings. My father had left an old shotgun in one of our farm buildings as well as air rifles. When I arrived at the house, my wife's new partner began a struggle with me and produced the shotgun, as we fought the gun went off. Fortunately, no one was hurt and the gun fell in the mud. I hadn't shot the gun, but it is true that I should have licenced it. When it came to trial, I was initially charged with attempted murder and then when I wasn't convicted of that, the prosecution reduced the charge down to bringing the gun to the property. I pleaded not guilty because I hadn't brought the gun to the property. My ex-wife had made a number of previous allegations against, trying to get me in trouble with the police, all of which had proven without merit. The man who fought me had a previous criminal record for violent offences. Unfortunately, the judge wouldn't let these important points of evidence be admitted in the trial. A young witness said he saw a ginger haired man with the gun, which was the other man (who dyed his hair black when he was a witness in trial!). The man who fought me was not charged with anything.

Coming to prison and for such a long time was a huge shock. I handled it with as much positivity and resilience as I could muster; it has had a big impact on my daughters. My youngest daughter is receiving counselling; fortunately, the other two are older and support her as much as possible.

I have tried to use my time in prison as best I can, completing personal development courses and working throughout my sentence.

◆

Conspiracy to rob - 14 years

I am sorry for what I did, I turned to crime when my partner was pregnant and I didn't have a stable job. I was desperate to provide for my family and I panicked and basically said I would do anything to make money.

This was my first ever offence and I do accept responsibility for where I went wrong in my life. I have taken great steps to turn my life around and to change for the better. I have realised the impact of my actions on other people, something that I had stubbornly refused to consider or acknowledge previously.

I have proven worthy of trust and responsibility by leaving my prison, going to work and returning on time each day.

◆

Contravention of the Customs and Excise Management Act 1979 - 37 months

All of my life I have been an ornithologist and loved studying and photographing birds. Whilst living in South Africa I became increasingly concerned about the rampant habitat destruction and how birds were being threatened. I very carefully packaged 19 eggs and brought them to the UK. It is true that these had a monetary value but this was a secondary motivation for me, it wouldn't have been much more than the costs of my trip. Upon arrival in the UK I declared that I had the eggs by going through the red route (something to declare). The eggs were confiscated and I recommended that they be sent to a specialist breeding centre where they were incubated; only one perished and it was stated in my case that I had looked after them well and that they had had a better survival rate than would have occurred in the wild.

I was (perhaps naively) surprised to be prosecuted but I did accept full responsibility and pleaded guilty. I hadn't realised that I would go to prison but nevertheless I tried to use my time in prison as best I can to help other people and to contribute. I served as segregation orderly which is a position where I work alongside officers to help and support isolated prisoners who were very often in difficulty and distress. After my experiences in this role I volunteered to work as reception orderly and I was able to sit with people when they first come to prison and offered them guidance and support.

♦

Possession with intent to supply class A drugs - 2 years and 10 months

From a young age I started to hang around with older people. At the time they seemed like they had a life I wanted to copy. Spending time with people who make crime seem clever and normal actually warps your mind. I had quite a low self-esteem and got involved in drugs supply because I couldn't see any employer wanting to accept me and offer me a job.

I accepted responsibility by pleading guilty and I braced myself for the prison sentence. Coming to prison was hard to handle especially because the prison I was in was very volatile and violent but nevertheless it helped me to mature, to grow up and accept responsibility for my future.

I am proud of myself now because I have gained employment related qualifications and I have developed the habit of work. I have also made the positive decision to move away from my past problematic area and break ties with the people I used to know.

♦

Conspiracy to supply drugs and cultivation of cannabis - 7 years

I was a cannabis smoker and grew my own supply. I became a target of a robbery with violence. I was hurt so much by the robbers that I was in a coma for two days. I do know that I was associating with the wrong people and that the life I had chosen was not a healthy one.

I am looking forward to starting a completely new type of life, no crime, no drugs and with a stable job and structure instead of chaos. I have stopped smoking cannabis and also tobacco. Mentally and physically I am in good shape and ready to begin this new, positive chapter in my life. This new chapter will be one in which I am an involved and present father to my son and where I am a good husband to his mum, working legitimately and providing legally for my young family.

When I came to prison, I cleaned up my act straight away. I engaged in drug rehabilitation courses and also helped other people who were less academic than me to complete the written parts of the course. I also helped others who were going through withdrawal from drugs.

◆

Fraud - 5 years and 8 months

I deeply regret my offence which arose because I was unhappy in my work and felt unfairly treated by my employer. Additionally, I was living beyond my means and not budgeting properly. I got my finances in a mess. I stole some money and covered up what had done. In so doing my crime became fraud and not theft. I know that my behaviour was not acceptable; as soon as I was caught, I felt a great sense of relief. I took full responsibility and pleaded guilty immediately.

I have a lot to make up for and I am very focussed on giving back, I know that paying my debt to society is just the first part of it. I studied and gained an extra qualification so that I could serve as a Peer Mentor/ Classroom Assistant. I provided huge amounts of help to people in desperate need. In this role I also taught Maths, English, Relationships and Social Skills as well as an introduction to self-employment.

I am very sorry for what I did and I have made a number of apologies to the people concerned.

◆

Causing serious injury by dangerous driving - 20 months

I had an undiagnosed sleeping disorder known as Sleep Apnoea. This is a legitimate medical diagnosis which is progressive. I was unaware that I had it at the time of my accident and people are not generally tested, before it manifests.

Sleep Apnoea means that a sufferer will suddenly and uncontrollably fall asleep. These are known as "micro-sleeps" and this is what happened to me. I was driving on an 'A' road, I was not speeding or driving dangerously, until I suffered a micro sleep at the wheel. My car tragically drifted and struck a car travelling in the opposite direction. The driver is sadly paralysed through no fault of her own, I am truly sorry.

I pleaded guilty because I wanted to accept responsibility and to show to my victim that I was sorry, despite this terrible accident having been caused by a confirmed medical disorder. I know in my heart that this was an accident.

I cannot continue to let the guilt and pain affect me so much and I must move forwards in order to contribute to society as a decent and law-abiding citizen again upon release.

♦

GBH Section 18 - 5 years

I was out with some friends on a Friday evening in our local pub. It was a social evening we were not rowdy or drinking heavily. Unfortunately, a local man had been drinking and was harassing my friend's younger sister. He was touching her inappropriately and making lewd suggestions. Many of us kept asking him to leave her alone. I turned around engaged in conversation when suddenly she shouted out in distress. One thing that I cannot stand is predatory men and on the spur of the moment I went straight to him and assaulted him. I did this as a warning and instinctively. We left shortly after but I did ring the landlady to check that the man was okay and all had seemed fine at that time. A few days later on the Monday, I had put the incident behind me and was about to leave to collect my daughter from school when the police came and arrested me. I was remanded straight away, kept in prison until a court date was set. This took four and a half months and was a very difficult time in prison, not knowing what the future held and not being able to be there for my children.

I am a very family-orientated man and coming to prison was very difficult for me, I was in pieces. When I came to court, I pleaded guilty to a charge of S20 which means hurting someone but without the deliberate intent, because I really only wanted to warn the man and discourage him from assaulting the girl. I was convicted of the charge of S18 but the judge did sentence me on the lower end of the scale because of the background to the offence and because I provided many references from family members and respectable friends who hold responsible positions as teachers, social workers and charity coordinators.

All my referees said that this was completely out of character for me. With hindsight I know that I should have called the police and reported that man, there was CCTV in the pub and he would have been warned against continuing his harassment of the girl.

I acted impulsively and recklessly, I admit that and I am sorry for what I did.

◆

Conspiracy to defraud - 5 years

I have had a stable and illustrious career, primarily in the operational management of charities and third sector organisations. I was approached by a family member who wanted to leverage my experience and skills to set up a company. This person had not been so stable in his life and unbeknownst to me he merely wanted a vehicle for short-term profit, through fraudulent means. I was very naïve and reckless when I agreed to put my name to such a venture. This family member became a co-defendant, who also went to prison along with other people he had involved. I deeply regret that I allowed someone to trade dishonestly and that I did not retain oversight of everything in accordance with a director's obligations.

This was my first ever offence, I have never been in trouble with the police before. It was a shock coming to prison as a mature family man but I knew that I had to make the most of the time available. I have served other people in prison and learnt humility in a number of support roles, I have worked consistently throughout my sentence and also continued to study to improve myself.

◆

Four counts of fraud - 4 years

I experienced tremendous financial pressure after a business failed. I was working as many hours as possible in my job but couldn't seem to get in front and I saw a way to remove the financial problems. My crime was very out of character for me. I am actually a mature person with a strong work ethic and I am ashamed of the way I tried to cheat. I accept that the harm this caused to the victim and also my own family is appalling. I have subsequently completed many personal development and vocational courses and know that I will never reoffend.

◆

Conspiracy to supply class A drugs - 7 years and 6 months

I have always worked hard, primarily in construction. I was self-employed and I unfortunately found myself in a dry spell with very little work coming in. I got myself into debt and the debt got passed to some dangerous and undesirable people. I was given a week to pay the money or 'work it off'. I wanted to put this behind me so I made the illegal decision to take them up on their offer of working it off, which involved driving and delivering parcels for them. I deeply regret my decision to get involved in crime and I accepted responsibility by pleading guilty. Whilst in prison, I have always worked or studied to improve myself. I have gained extra academic and vocational and also completed a victim awareness course. I am sorry for my part in this conspiracy and I have learnt many lessons, I am a different person now. I will never commit crime again particularly because I am aware that I am missing so much time with my young son and because I have learnt so much about the awful degradation and suffering that drugs cause.

◆

Armed robbery -12 years

I was a very young teenager when I had my own daughter. I hadn't known my dad growing up and I didn't have a role model to follow; this meant that I felt a desperate pull to provide for my daughter but didn't know how to. I turned to the only male role models that I knew in my local area who were drug dealers. They got me involved in drug supply. I never considered the illegality of it because in the part of East London I was from, this type of criminality was considered normal. I became more involved in crime until inevitably I was taken away to prison.

Coming to prison has given me a lot of time for self-reflection as well as the opportunity to change my life for the better. I have worked hard and studied hard to achieve a number of formal qualifications and work-related skills.

I have also completed 24 months in therapy which helped me to understand my own drivers and triggers as well how to identify more positive role models and choose my friends and associates more carefully. I improved my relationship skills and self-worth and my desire to contribute and help other people. I also enrolled on a victim awareness programme and completed the modules to a high standard; giving lots of thought to empathy and the effects of crime on other people; something I am ashamed to say that I had chosen to ignore before. I completed a number of courses in prison including victim awareness and I also trained with a fantastic charity called the Shannon Trust. After completing this training, I was qualified to teach adults to read for the first time which is very rewarding to do.

◆

Conspiracy to supply Class A drugs - 11 years and 6 months

I completely admit that I was financially motivated and became greedy to earn more money. I pleaded guilty to my offence and I am sorry for what I did. I have always enjoyed business and business development. Unfortunately, I channelled my talents and interests in completely the wrong direction. I used to justify this by saying that I never force anyone to buy drugs and that I was no different from any other commodities broker. Unfortunately, the ultimate drug users are forced by their addictions to continue taking drugs and it does affect their lives in a bad way. I no longer want to be involved in such a dark trade that is responsible for ruining lives.

◆

Robbery, theft and fraud by false representation - 2 years and 6 months I am very sorry for my outrageous behaviour. I had developed a cocaine habit after I started hanging around with an undesirable group of people from the college I had attended. Drug use was glorified by the group and so I started taking drugs to fit in. My habit spiralled out of control to where I was addicted. I accepted responsibility by pleading guilty and admitting all of my crimes.

With strength of will, by attending a number of recognised programmes and by rediscovering my faith I broke my addiction. I now facilitate support groups to help other people on that journey of overcoming alcohol and substance misuse. Whilst in prison, I used the time to change my life and my attitude. I gained trade skills, numeracy and literacy qualifications and completed a range of personal development courses. When I came to prison, I was full of remorse and regret and I have been determined to change for the better. My baby daughter was born after I came away and my fiancé has struggled a lot on her own. I want to provide well for my young family on my release and I am doing everything I can to improve myself and my opportunities.

◆

Possession with intent to supply class A and B drugs - 4 years

I was made redundant from my permanent job and whilst I was in between work the benefit cap and universal credit came in. I am a father to three children and I was left with £384 to live for a month. I tried to explain my problems to the DWP but they seemed disinterested and unable to do anything to help. In a time of desperation, I panicked and turned to some associates I had known from years earlier and they gave me a chance to make some money. I really regret getting involved but I didn't know what else to do. With hindsight I should never have broken the law; I do regret my decision and how it has resulted in me being taken away from my family.

When I came to prison it was really a punishment for my partner and our children more than anything else, they are the ones who have suffered the most. I have suffered by worrying about them and not being able to support them through the ups and downs of life. Whilst in prison I have completed many courses that have helped me personally to gain transferrable skills that make me more valuable in any workplace and also specific vocational skills and qualifications.

◆

GBH, Section 18 - 5 years

I had stopped at a village pub to have a quiet drink and relax. I walked in and accidentally bumped into a man. He then kept following me around the pub and hassling me, even though I had apologised. I didn't know it at the time but this pub had a reputation for being rough and not liking outsiders. I turned and said to the man "are you going to beat me up, what are you going to do?" He said "Let's put it this way, you are going to get it when you leave!" I walked away from him three times but on the fourth time, I hit him. I am strong and regrettably I did hurt him so that he needed surgery. I was so very sorry, I handed myself in to the police the next day and I pleaded guilty in court. I have never been to prison before. I completed two lengthy personal development programmes in prison and gained 4 new qualifications in just 2 years. I am ready to re-enter society as a more rounded and mature person.

◆

Conspiracy to Supply Class A drugs - 10 years and 8 months

I am not in any way trying to justify what I did but I have found that understanding the reasons for my offences has been an important part of my personal journey and will always be an essential part of desistance so that I know what 'triggers' to avoid. I was expelled from school because I rebelled against learning. I loved sports but wasn't at all academic. As a young teenager, I started to hang around with other troublemaking young. I ended up in prison (Young Offenders Institution) at the age of 18. Unfortunately, this did not provide any rehabilitation but instead it exposed me to more anger, aggression and criminality. I felt outside of society and struggled to build a meaningful life. This time when I came to prison, I was ready to learn and change. I finally gained numeracy and literacy qualifications and also work-

Quotes - The BEST ADVICE I can give to someone coming to prison

related certificates. I am now a mature man of 33 years old and I realise that I must make better choices to not come back to prison. I know not to mix with bad company and to manage my time and money better. I have a much calmer outlook and a strong work ethic; I am ashamed of my past actions and I am determined to turn my life around.

If you found these reflections interesting and insightful, then I also recommend that you read my book entitled '**If criminals can change then so should society and our prisons**' which contains 100 more narratives.

"Make the days count - don't count the days." ED

"Don't serve your sentence, make your sentence serve you." RG

Quotes - The BEST ADVICE I can give to someone coming to prison

The following quotes were given by serving prisoners who had spent a wide range of time in prison from 1 - 19 years in a multitude of prisons and who were now in the final few months of their prison sentences. They were asked to give their best advice to someone who is coming to prison.

These are not necessarily the views of the author; a wide range of replies have been included for perspective and to help understand a wide range of thought processes.

"Stay calm." WL

"Set goals to achieve." LI

"Use the time constructively." KA

"Accept help when it is offered." AH

"Don't get involved in prison politics." SB

"Get as many qualifications as you can." LM

"Behave and relax, do your time calmly." KS

"Stay away from debt and drugs, totally." VY

"Don't borrow anything or get into debt." PF

"Remain focussed and never give up hope." JR

"Be yourself and don't change for anyone." EO

"Be patient and tolerant, keep a long fuse." DM

"Use the time to improve yourself, read and learn." OA

"Stay strong - do not let the injustices destroy you." SS

"Go to work or college everyday so the time goes quicker." JA

"Try to give your day to day life some structure and routine." CG

"Gain skills and improve your mind, while you have the time." HW

"Ask what courses are available and get booked on them asap." PC

"Take every opportunity to change and improve your prospects." CB

"Be patient and tolerant. Remain pro-active as much as possible." DM

"Keep yourself busy do as much as you can whilst you are inside." EG

"Stay out of trouble, don't get involved if it doesn't concern you." ZM

"Learn from mistakes, value what you have, prison's not worth it." TS

"Prison is hard on you and family, do anything you can to avoid it." VN

"Talk things through, talk about your feelings: don't bottle it all up." RN

"Don't despair, time flies, things are never as bad as they first seem." LF

"Get a prison job, no matter what, work it hard and the time will fly." NA

"Stay strong mentally, this bad time will pass. You will get through it." GE

"Stay alert, follow the establishment's rules and comply with regime." MY

"Be polite and respectful to other prisoners and also to prison officers." PF

"Behave, don't get involved in drugs or debt and keep your chin up, there is an end goal." JG

"Abide with the rules, get a job and focus on doing courses that will benefit you when you leave." HA

"Set goals, have things to aim for even if they are little things or a long way ahead in the future." CB

"Make the most of your time, try to achieve something and go out a better person when released." FR

"Be strong and keep your head up. See it as a test, a challenge that can either break you or make you." SV

"Be prepared take your clothes and belongings with you if there is a chance that you may be sent to prison." JP

"Learn from your mistakes and value what you have in the real world/ on the outside. Prison isn't worth it." GD

"Keep your chin up, keep your spirits up, prisoners have a saying - they can turn the locks, but they can't stop the clocks!" LR

"Don't get involved in anything shady, dodgy or illegal, just one slip up can set you back a long, long way, years if you are IPP or Lifer." NT

"Study and gain skills and certificates to help you when you leave prison; stay out of the madness that others will try to drag you into." LL

"Stay positive. Don't get involved in drugs, get a job or join a course that will help you gain qualifications and make the time go quicker." AS

"Listen to your Offender Supervisor/ OMU; they are the ones who can help you to progress, so follow their pathway and recommendations." PC

"Use your time wisely, do as many courses as possible and don't be inactive which leads to depression. Shake up and wake up, do something!" MG

"Own your sentence; it can be what you want it to be, use your time to better yourself, be polite and respectful to staff. Stay away from drugs." DB

"Spend time with the right people; association is a powerful force in prison and people are judged based on their affiliations. Find decent people who aren't running loud and stupid and don't get pulled into trouble." MB

"Do not get into debt for any reason. The idea of double-bubble means that borrowing anything whether it is food, tobacco or whatever will become a huge problem very quickly. Do without debt and do without the drama." RD

"Don't be afraid to ask for advice and support. You will be amazed how many mentors, insiders and orderlies give time to helping other prisoners. That is what they are there for, you won't owe them anything, just ask." LR

"Think of yourself, your progression and your family, people will try to use you to make their life easier or shift focus and blame away from them, don't let them. Take care of yourself and be selfish, I don't mean don't help, but not at your own expense and nothing illegal." RU

Chapter 6 - Institutionalisation and Recovery

"Don't smoke or take any prison drugs, they are terrible chemicals that aren't even designed for humans, there is a high risk of death or long-term mental anguish. They are not like drugs on the outside, not that they are much better but they are less likely to kill you stone dead." GD

"Educate and improve yourself. Do as much as you can that is available to progress your wellbeing, knowledge and qualifications, not just sentence related interventions and therapy programmes but also things that will put a roof over your head and provide for you so you stay legal." PH

Express your feelings and thoughts to other residents. Make friends and a problem shared is a problem halved. Alternatively call on Chaplaincy or listeners; just do not store it all up inside." TC

"I like the little things, a properly cooked English breakfast, my warehouse job, meeting a friend for a few quiet hours of backgammon. I take things slow and steady, one step at a time. I have learnt to be very patient with myself and others. I also know my limits; I am easily overwhelmed. Life outside is very fast, after 18 years behind the door, even cars and modern films move too quickly for me. People ask me if I get bored in my job and my life, I try to explain to them that boredom is a blessing because it means stability. I spent a large part of my life praying for boredom. I take things very slowly because I am not really a very confident person; or rather I am not overconfident anymore. I don't take anything for granted." SY

Institutionalisation, Habits and Comfort Zones

Institutionalisation can be explained in some very simple stages; it is not really as complicated as it sounds.

Our brain has developed to lay down neural pathways each time it experiences something new. Initially the path of neural pathways is like a mud track cut through a jungle.

As the path is used more and more frequently it widens, clears and strengthens; it becomes less of a path and more of a trench (ideas literally become entrenched).

Even something new and strange becomes a habit after a typical lunar cycle of around 28 days. The path becomes a motorway, a shortcut in the brain that is used frequently. These pathways are actually visible constructs under an electron microscope.

You may have heard of the NASA experiment which evidenced this further - trainee astronauts wore goggles that made them see the world upside down. Initially they were uncomfortable, they kept bumping into things, they couldn't eat or sleep properly and they were often physically sick.

After 28 - 30 days however, their brains all suddenly adapted, they became used to their new way of interacting with the world around them; the new previously uncomfortable environment became normal to them and they could see the world normally.

When the goggles were removed a week later, they became sick and disorientated again but not for a full month because their previous neural pathways were still in place and had not been deconstructed.

Bringing this back to Institutionalisation, we can see how brain function biologically explains how a person can become institutionalized i.e.

> **They are accustomed to a certain environment and are likely to experience fear and distress in a dissimilar environment.**

Initially when entering an institution for the first time, a new resident will be uncomfortable and fearful, it is unknown and disorientating.

Just like the goggles however they can adapt and after a while the uncomfortable becomes the new comfortable and familiar.

The earlier life would then become uncomfortable and unfamiliar and they will experience fear when returning to it.

The longer a person is in an institution, the demonstrably larger the neural pathways become with an eventual reduction of the original pathways.

"People leaving institutions, particularly after years, need a lot of support to adapt rather than to experience the sudden shock of forced change." PM

This is like gradual controlled decompression to avoid decompression sickness (aka the bends, which can be fatal) when surfacing after deep sea diving.

These vulnerable people need to build routines and gradually rebuild their lives. Sensory overload is just one problem they can experience as well as trying to adapt quickly to new surroundings or new technology.

> **"After a long time inside, a lot of people become as fearful of coming out of prison as they were of going in."**
> Gethin Jones, Founder - Unlocking Potential

The following three elements are all essential to assist reintegration of institutionalised people:

- Support from Family

- Stable Employment
- Long Term Accommodation

In the absence of two out of these three elements long term prisoners are statistically likely to return to prison.

If a released prisoner has two out of these three elements, they are statistically likely to succeed and not return to prison.

> "Significantly more help than is presently offered must be given to support the gradual reintegration of people released from prison, particularly those who have served long sentences." PM

Recovering from the Detrimental Effects of Closed Conditions and Improving Wellbeing

A criminology researcher conducted an interview with Phil Martin in March 2019 whilst he was still a serving prisoner at HMP Springhill, a D-Category, open prison.

This transcript has been amended slightly to improve readability.

Interviewer: Please introduce yourself and how long you have served in prison.

I'm Phil and I've been in the prison for 3 years and 4 months and I have 8 months left to go. So, I was sentenced to 8 years with 4 to serve altogether.

Interviewer: What does a good day in open prison look like?

HMP Springhill is a surprisingly inspiring place for a prison – it's not like any other prison, it's not even like other open prisons, people are given a lot more responsibility here and it is a beautiful, natural, healthy space.

It's a bit like living on a run-down caravan site but in a beautiful mature country park.

My day is slightly different from a lot of the other residents because one third of them are typically out on licence each day, out of a population of 330 about 110 go out every day to work or to visit family members at the weekend, that sort of thing.

I have chosen to spend my last 16 months on site at Springhill, rather than going out to outside work. I set up a careers department here; partially because I want to build my own career in the resettlement of ex-offenders.

My wife and I discussed it and we made a conscious decision to sacrifice around ten thousand pounds that I could have earned by working full-time, which we really don't have at the moment and we could really use but by doing this it's given me a huge amount of personal experience in dealing with helping people to progress and build careers and future lives.

At the same time as I say, I have been preparing for myself to run a recruitment business in this sector.

So, we made a conscious decision that I wouldn't go out to outside work, I would stay here – so I'm on camp all the time, apart from when I'm on my home leaves – I've just now hit the level where I qualify for 7 days a month home, that's two Saturday's and one five-day home leave each month. So, 7 days a month I'm home with my wife and children, which is wonderful.

But while I'm at Springhill, it's not a gloomy place, it's not an oppressive place, it's not depressive, even all of the residents here are generally optimistic; once they've got through their first few weeks, there's generally a great sense of positivity here.

It's partly because people are coming to the end of a long journey for them.

I would say they're probably going to be that much more content even if they were in closed conditions but it's also partly because of where we are. Not being shut away, not being locked up, able to go out and get some breathing space, get fresh air, see the birds, the squirrels, rabbits. Wherever you look there's something – at any time of day or night, there's something to make you smile.

There are flowers out there. You know I actually pick a few of the daffodils and I put them in my room, so I have an empty coffee jar, and I have got fresh flowers in my room. They probably wouldn't like me picking the flowers!

I've got a spider plant in my room, (which are my favourite type of plant), someone from 'Farms and Gardens' gave it to me a few months ago, and it's grown, and it's bloomed. This is a beautiful thing because having been shut away in a tiny room, the size of a disabled toilet, typically with a roommate, banged up for you know, locked up for 23-hours a day in some prisons. When I'm in bed I stroke my spider plant, this is a really therapeutic thing, and it sounds weird but I've missed all of that nature. My spider plant has got babies coming off of it, and I was telling my wife about it the other day and she was looking at me as if I was a bit weird but this is a big thing for me, that my plant is living and doing so well.

You can't really put into words what it's like to be shut away and have nothing but concrete outside your room, and not even fresh air – you've only got vents. You can't even breathe proper fresh air, and you're in that tiny space for a huge amount of time, and it's really, really, painful and damaging to people, to people's wellbeing.

I would consider myself a very resilient person, very stable, I've been with my wife for 24 years, I met her on my 22nd birthday, we have 5 daughters together, and we're still as close as we've ever been.

But it was really hard and closed conditions put a tremendous strain on our marriage because you're unlocked for a very short period of time, maybe an hour or half an hour, and in that time, people have to choose to have a shower or phone home or get food – what should you prioritise?

Those regimes are gruelling for people and they do traumatise.

Not every prison is like that, but typically in remand prisons where you have a very transient population; the populations aren't very settled.

People don't really know each other and they don't look out for each other. They are angry and distressed and you can see it when they're banged-up for long periods of time.

They come out of their rooms angry and they hit each other; if they've got china cups, they hit each other over the head with china cups. There's violence and people take drugs in those sorts of environments because that's a holiday to them; it's their sort of escape for a few days or for a few hours.

At Springhill they don't need a holiday because it's a bit like we're on holiday. They haven't got their cares and worries so much, of course you don't have the joys either.

Your food is taken care of, even if it's not the best food; your bills are taken care of, to a minimal level. So, it's almost like, one can see this place as almost a poor version of a rubbish holiday camp or something.

That's why people walk around here much more optimistically.

You see this very physical transition when people first come to Springhill.

When they come from closed conditions most have a clearly identifiable 'prisoner walk' where they move with their heads down, slouched and hunched - That's how they've been walking for years – not interacting, not looking at other people, because they don't want to be moaned or shouted at by another prisoner 'what are you looking at?' They are trying to be invisible and not get involved in any problems. People in prison have this terribly depressed walk which manifests in all of their physical movements.

When they come to Springhill they still have that walk for a few days, and they get a bit shell-shocked, because it's like 'oh my God', 'I'm not banged up' because institutionalization is a real thing and it doesn't take long to be institutionalized – you can be institutionalised after a matter of months but you get over it quickly, whereas when you've been institutionalized for years it takes a longer time to get over it and become normal or normalized again.

Within the first few weeks typically people gradually start walking a little bit taller, they smile hesitantly, and for me, I felt like I was able to be myself again, which is quite hard to do in certain closed conditions, to be yourself.

I think I managed and coped with my prison sentence quite well.

I'm a gentle man, you know, I'm not fierce or rough or tough like a lot of people. I was surprised in prison by how much I was able to actually be myself; I didn't have to put on an image at all.

I'm soft and I like to help people but in prison I actually found that I could really be myself. I didn't get into prison debt; I don't smoke and don't take drugs - so I didn't need to get into debt over anything. I didn't experience the violence and the degradation that so many people end up going through.

We all get through our prison sentence in our own way.

I got through my prison sentence by helping people. Things like relationship challenges, legal paperwork, mentoring on courses, with progression through the prison system and with planning their future lives.

I love speaking, I love motivation and business, this sort of thing outside, so I would help them with all of these and use all of my skills.

Basically, I was able to help a lot of people, maybe they've got literacy challenges or, like I say, relationship difficulties, so before I knew it people were sort of like keeping an eye out for me in the background anyway, so I didn't really have problems like some people would have,

But coming to Springhill was like a whole new world, the first week I was here (pause, emotional) sorry, (pause) yes, it's totally different and what people need really.

Interviewer: What were your first impressions when you got here?

I just loved it. I just loved being out.

I think it's really unhealthy locking people away like animals; or it's worse than animals because you wouldn't be allowed to lock animals in a tiny space without anything.

You wouldn't make animals eat their food next to the toilet or on the toilet, and even a lot of the best of closed prisons don't have enough tables and places for people to sit and eat their dinner. Coming here one of the biggest things for me was being able to sit with other human beings and eat my dinner.

I think closed conditions are so damaging to people, it's really, really, damaging and traumatising.

I'm very resilient and I'm absolutely fine, I just express my emotions in a different way, but for most men who don't feel that they can cry or express themselves, they have to be tough all the time, they don't have a support network – how they deal with it, it comes out in other ways.

Yeah, and I don't believe, I don't believe that humanity has to be earned, I don't believe that compassion has to be earned, I believe that compassion is what people freely give to other people and I believe that humanity is something that every human being is entitled to – it's not something that you either earn or you don't earn and you don't deserve it because you broke a rule, or you broke a law, or you hurt someone, or whatever you did, you are still entitled to be shown compassion.

People in closed prisons are not being shown compassion.

At Springhill they are shown a bit more compassion; just being acknowledged that you are a human being that has a value is what matters as much as the open space.

In closed conditions people are treated like they are lower than low, even those people who've had an accident like a car crash.

I have got to know loads of people in prison who have had an accident – they didn't deliberately set out to kill someone or hurt someone, it was an accident. Maybe they were at fault, yes, the jury's decided they were at fault but still, should they be degraded and damaged and hurt?

Should they be treated the way they're being treated when they had a moment of thoughtlessness or stupidity; an accident?

Maybe they were texting, or turning the radio up, or shouting at the kids – we've all done it but their accident unfortunately had serious consequences, whereas maybe for the other ones of us it didn't have such consequences.

Our prison system in this country is only doing one thing and that thing is making people worse.

> *Interviewer: How do you see that play out in closed conditions in comparison to here? How do you see that affecting the way that people are?*

Well it's obvious every single day, because in closed conditions when people are unlocked; like being let out of their cages, they are panicked and deeply stressed.

When they're on the phone to their partners or their wives they're shouting and hollering, arguing because they probably know they can't speak to that person again for another day or two, so they're just trying to have some relevance in that person's life.

When I was in closed conditions, most of the time I was in reasonable regimes, I was able to ring up once or twice a day but sometimes they'd shout "bang up!" and I've said goodnight to only two of my younger daughters and not the third one.

Other times, I've had arguments with my wife and we've not had time to get through to the other side of the argument, the resolving and pleasant bits, the 'good night, I love you' and all this sort of stuff.

So, you get locked up again, into a tiny space, with unresolved issues churning round and round in your head and too much thinking time.

People in prison tend to overthink things – they spend far too much time thinking, thinking, thinking, without being actually able to do anything or resolve anything.

Very often the partners and the relationships cannot handle this and don't like the changes in the person; it becomes far too much and they break up; I would say that probably most relationships do break up.

I've known a lot that have made it through and thank God my wife and I are stable and steady and we've made it through but that's not because we didn't have a lot of arguments the whole way through – we did.

It's to my wife's credit, more than anything else that she stayed focussed and steadfast, she kept her eye on the end goal of being back together.

The prison system recognises that there are 7 pathways to resettlement; the three primary ones are *employment*, *housing* and *family-ties/ relationships* then *addiction* and less essential perhaps, *mental and physical health*, *thinking* and *budgeting*.

Keeping people locked up is degrading those critical relationships through attrition.

With very small amounts of time available on the phones and with oppressive visits - my wife would have to drive two hours each way to visit me, for a visit which, if we're lucky, might last an hour and a half.

Now, when you've got children there and you've got your wife and your only allowed to cuddle briefly at the beginning and again at the end of the visit that's really difficult, because all you can do in that time is say 'right what are the tasks we need to talk about?' and one becomes very task-orientated – 'what jobs do we need to do, what problems do we need to fix?'

Rather than sitting down and talking about the future and our relationship and how a normal couple would be – you can't have a normal relationship and you can't be an effective parent.

So, you asked kind of how it manifests, well it manifests in damaged and destroyed relationships, and that then makes people even angrier.

They're angry when they come out of their cell, they shout at their wives, then they punch someone and break their jaw, because they feel like they've got no hope because their relationships are failing, and then they end up getting longer time on their sentence, or they get sent down to the Seg or they have closed visits and these kind of punishments which make, everything even worse.

There's hardly anything that makes things better.

Now, when I first came to prison my wife and I struggled; I didn't treat her well, I was arguing with her a lot on the phones and we couldn't adapt quickly enough to this terrible shock, so we were arguing.

At HMP Woodhill they did something called a *'father & child'* visit, like a family visit and it was at that family visit that we were allowed to sit down together.

I think it was 3 or 4 hours, and we sat down on the floor and we were playing, the floors filthy and dirty but none of that mattered, we were playing with farm animals with the children and we were able to sit and cuddle.

We sat and cuddled basically for two hours, just sitting next to each other and then all the arguments stopped and we'd sorted ourselves out until the next visit a couple of months later, the next family visit, and that kind of contact – that made things better.

Sadly, those incentives or interventions are very rare, most things in prison are designed to wreck the relationship, destroy that person's life altogether.

There is no hope and very little support for that person to start planning for a future life.

They might say 'oh you need to do Maths and English' or 'you need to go in that class', but then the regimes are locked up so they don't get to go to classes all the time.

No one actually acknowledges that prison destroys a person's life.

You lose your house or your flat, you do, because you can't go to prison and keep a long-term tenancy agreement or keep a mortgage going, you know it's almost impossible to do.

You're gonna lose your housing, you're probably going to lose your relationship, you're probably going to damage other relationships with family members, you're going to lose your job – 75% of men come into prison employed, 2 years after release from prison 50% of them are still unemployed.

So, we have more than 500,000 men outside of prison, released, still unemployed because of their criminal records, but we've got 800,000 job vacancies in this country, it's ridiculous – right now we've got more jobs than people and we've got half a million people unemployed because of their criminal record!

At the same time the prison service is saying "yes well, we need to cut, well we'll cut the National Careers Service".

What a ridiculous thing to do, because all you're doing at every single step is taking away a person's hope, and when you take away their hope you've got nothing left.

It's not a coincidence that since the year 2010, so 9 years ago, self-harm and suicide in prisons have doubled.

Now let's try and think – What has caused this DOUBLING? What is this an unintended consequence of? It's not difficult to realise that what's caused it...

Destroying peoples' lives, removing all hope and then not helping them to rebuild a life of any meaning.

People will say "oh well they destroyed their own life - they deserve it".

People; the media and the public, can think what they like about prisoners, they can despise them – despise us, hate us, say "they deserve it", "they're lower than the low", "lock 'em up and throw away the key".

You can think all that as much as you like but it all boils down to a simple question –

Do you want these people to be more or less likely to commit crime in the future; do we want more or less victims of crime?

That's it!

If you want them to be less likely to commit crime in future, less likely to create more victims, then you need to help them to have humanity, a future.

Show them how to have a normal, fulfilling life.

If you don't do that, they will commit crime again.

Norwich, right now HMP Norwich is releasing 46% of people homeless - with tents. How can a prison in this country, in 2019 be saying "well, we're going to give you a tent, good luck mate!" but then say; "we don't want to see you back here". That's nonsense, what can you do – would you live in a tent? They're not giving them a chance.

So, we're dehumanising them, turning them into animals, making them violent or victims of violence, or making them shut themselves in their room, taking drugs to drown out the hell that they're in.

Then we're wondering why these people are coming out being damaged and unable to interact and behave like normal people.

Now this is the problem we've got in England at the moment, because The Sun newspaper and the politicians promote the idea of "lock them away, throw away the key".

The truth is that prison sentences have got longer, substantially longer in the last twenty years. People are spending a lot more time in prison, but it's temporary.

Everyone that is in prison is still in prison temporarily.

There are only 70 people out of 82,600 who are in prison for life, natural life, seven zero.

So, in other words there are around 82,500 people who are going to be released back into society at some point and we can either have them more feral or more domesticated.

The power to change and choose is not in their hands.

Power to change is not in the hands of the prisoner at all, because their life, their responsibility, their decisions have all been taken away from them. The power to domesticate that person is in the hand of the prison service and the people involved.

Open spaces go a long way to normalising someone's mental health, and helping them cope better, helping them to breathe a sigh of relief. When I came here it was like a massive weight had come off my shoulders, I was able to breathe – normal air, not stinky, stagnant prison air (which you can smell when you go into a prison), not air through a vent, but air.

Feeling the sun on my face, which you don't get in closed conditions; well if you're lucky you get half an hour in the exercise yard, even in the C Cats, half an hour or an hour in the exercise yard, you know, and you'll be lucky if you get the sun. The rest of the time you'll try and look out, try and catch a bit of sun while you're in the cell, and it's not healthy, it's really, really bad.

So, you asked what it was like when I came here. When I came here, I was walking around and I was picking up acorns, feathers, leaves and bark and I was looking at the rabbits, and I made a card.

I'd gone through my prison sentence making lots of cards for my girls, my daughters, out of all sorts of things – papers and pens, getting hold of whatever I could.

After a few days at Springhill I made a card for them saying that this is where I was, with all these pieces of nature stuck on it, (voice trembles) and everyone deserves that, it doesn't, matter what their past is and what they've done.

If we believe in humanity, then they deserve to have some of the natural world, even if it's just having a plant in their room. You know, like I've got a plant in my room, or years ago people used to be able to keep budgies or canaries, why can't they do that anymore. Even the worst, most vile criminal, was allowed to keep a pet bird, and show that he can learn to care for something, develop a bit of empathy.

A lot of these people, 24% of people in prison, have come through the care system and the care system does a lot of things but it actually doesn't care.

I've met many people that typically get abandoned at the age of 16, one lad who was moved 7 times between the ages of 15 and 17 and even experienced homelessness.

Now, if you're going to be moved 7 times as a teenager, and you're going to be homeless at that age, it's almost inevitable – you could certainly put money on it and get good odds that this person is going to come to prison at some point.

If 24% of people in prison come through the care system that says that's there's something wrong with the care system, actually it's a feeder school, it's a feeder school for prisons.

Another feeder school for prisons is people leaving the armed forces, and a similar percentage of people leaving the armed forces are in prison within four years of discharge.

So, we have people who are coming through the care system who are traumatised, because they were traumatised as children to end up in care, so they've seen poverty, abuse, or neglect. Then we've got people traumatised leaving our armed forces who come into prison.

Between those two groups that is more than 50% of the prison population, who are already traumatised.

If you traumatise someone who is already traumatised, do you think that we will be able to make them better or worse?

Will they be more or less likely to commit crime by traumatising them further?

If we actually say:

"Right, we understand that the first part of your life has been characterised by hell – a life that's hardly worth living, you've experienced agony, pain, death, misery, you've witnessed things that no human being should ever see, not even in a movie – you'd certainly fast-forward it if it was on TV; you wouldn't want to see it, and yet you've lived it, <u>so we're just going to make things worse and traumatise you even further</u>".

Or could we say:

"Actually, we understand that you've been through hell. I can't begin to imagine what it must have been like for you. It is apparent that the things you have gone through have affected you and you have made some really bad decisions, things you regret and things that you recognise have cause harm to other people.

We'd like to help you, we're going to give you counselling and a bit of Cognitive Behaviour Therapy, we're going to help you to be able to leave the past in the past, we're going to help you to rebuild and build some of those things that you were missing – you never learnt the emotional building block of empathy, we're going to help you discover that. You never learnt what it was like to have a stable education, we're going to help you learn that and support you – we're not going to force you to do it, we understand that you feel uncomfortable and anxious in classroom settings, so we'll work a bit one on one, take it at your own pace.

We understand that you've not had a stable job yet, so what we'll do is we've got these companies that would like to help train you and give you different opportunities and maybe hold your hand along the way into full-time employment.

We also understand that you've had so much upheaval that you don't know what it's like to have a stable roof over your head and that you still wake up having nightmares in the middle of the night, so it's not going to be a mansion but we're at least going to give you a room, where you can settle and be stable."

Then what we're doing is we're <u>repairing</u>; we're not making people who are already damaged, worse.

You know the open spaces and normal environment is one part of a bigger picture of showing that these people still have value. We are not executing them anymore, 100 years ago we would execute these people, or we'd exile them to Australia or we'd send them off to fight in our overseas wars.

We chose not to do that; we chose a path of a civilised society.

If we've chosen a path of being a civilised society and we're not going to end that life, then the idea of 'lock them up and throw away the key' can't happen anymore because all we're doing is, we're letting them self-execute.

We've got people tying ligatures around their neck because officers have treated them really badly. One deaf lad I looked after, the officers didn't understand his meal was wrong at the servery, he's 19 years old this lad, his meal was wrong, he's saying "my meal's wrong can I get my right meal that I ordered?" (You order the meals a few days before).

They're telling him "STOP SHOUTING STOP SHOUTING", he says "I'm not shouting, this is how I talk". He's deaf, he can't speak properly right, next thing I know (I'm on the next landing), alarms have gone off, three officers manhandled him to the floor, he's shouting now! "GET OFF ME, GET OFF ME".

At around one forty-five in the morning he ties a ligature around his neck, hangs himself. Thank God he didn't die but if it wasn't for chaplaincy taking care of him the next few days, he would have still done it.

If it wasn't for a friend of mine who was a mentor, like myself, who mentored him in the class and started helping him with maths and English and gave him time and attention.

It's not just helping him with maths and English, it's basically saying 'I give a sxxt about you, I care about you and I don't want you to die'.

That's what mentoring is, it doesn't really matter what the subject is, it's just saying that there is at least one person in this world who cares – please don't kill yourself.

So, last I heard he hadn't killed himself but where's the compassion for this lad? Where is the help for disabled people in prisons?

There's a massive care crisis in prisons, people in wheelchairs being locked up in closed conditions.

What they don't realise, and what the media don't care to tell the truth about is, is that closed prison conditions are permanently damaging people's metal health.

Closed conditions are the nearest thing to a warzone that we have in this country.

There is nothing to justify keeping most of these people locked away.

Only a small percentage of people in prison are there because of crimes against a person, so that's violence or sexual harm.

That means the majority of people, going from official figures are NOT in prison for crimes against a person, they're not violence or sexual harm; that means that they do not pose such a high risk to other people.

Why on earth can't we have dozens of Springhill like establishments for this huge majority of the population who aren't violent or don't pose a massive risk of harm.

Put the massive fences all around, at a distance so these people aren't going to be able to escape because the fences and the barbed wire are all still there, they've got all the prison officers and everything.

Why can't we have the trees? Why can't we have the fresh air? Why can't we try and be normal human beings? Why can't we sit around a table with people we're having a conversation with, like normal human beings?

Why do we have to be banged-up within 10 minutes of getting our food, sit on the toilet to eat it, in a room with someone else we've never met before and who may well be one of the violent ones and yet we're locked up with him for the next 18 hours or however long it is until we're let out again.

This natural environment normalises people, jobs normalise people, housing normalises people.

If you want criminals or people who've made mistakes or come to prison for whatever reason, to not commit crime again, we need to normalise them.

Nature normalises people, it helps them with their mental health and their physical wellbeing.

There is a therapeutic, evidential therapeutic benefit to spending time in the fresh air and around nature, and around spending time with other human beings in a normal environment. You can't put a price on nature, and people's wellbeing and mental health and it's really that important.

> *Interviewer: What is Springhill doing right? Are there things it could be doing better? What do you see working?*

In the last quarter, 73% of men were released from Springhill into full-time employment. There is no other prison in the country, which I know of, that comes anywhere close to that figure. The nearest ones that I know of are half of that figure. To have just 27% of men released from Springhill without full-time employment is a massive achievement. Some of those men were retired or disabled and others might be going into their own business.

I mentioned in one of the book chapters that I've handed to you that we should be trying to emulate this across the prison estate.

On top of this, the establishment has just received the Enabling Environment award, and I spoke a bit at an event to help to secure the award. It is the only men's prison to have achieved the award from the Royal Institute of Psychiatrists in full across all of the criteria.

Springhill is an environment that from the very beginning focuses on progression and the future, rather than the past.

The Ministry of Justice say that people do not get sent to prison to be punished but that it is the deprivation of liberty, being taken away from your family and everyday life that is the punishment.

Unfortunately, that is not how prisons work in this country.

Prisons and prison officers have a strong, ingrained culture of punishing the individual for their crime, and punishing the families that come to visit the individual.

They fill the families with shame, they treat them with disdain, they are rude, insulting, in some cases physically abusive to them, there are many, many stories that you'll read in my books of families that have experienced extreme humiliation.

The Prison's Minister got it absolutely right recently when he said that it's ludicrous to assume that the wave of drugs in our prisons are smuggled in bras and nappies, it's crazy.

The drugs in prisons come from the staff; a small number of staff who make a lot of money doing it, and once they've done it a few times they have to keep doing it because they're blackmailed and they get used to the extra money.

One or two people may get small amounts of drugs from a visitor but in closed conditions it would be almost impossible to do, very, very difficult to do.

If we're focusing on rehabilitation, then the families need to be a key part of that.

Visits at Springhill are wonderful. The first time I had a visit here shortly after arriving, it was literally a breath of fresh air, you can walk around the visits, you can go up and get your own food, you're not glued to the chair and you can sit and cuddle your children.

I remember my daughter was eleven years old and she was very upset about something that had happened at school and she sat on my lap at HMP Stocken. A big officer came up, deliberately stood over us to intimidate, telling her that she has to get down and sit on the chair opposite – she was just eleven years old, crying, she's not going to see me for another two weeks, they got let in late, we've only got an hour and a quarter of what is meant to be a two-hour visit and my daughter can't sit on her dad's lap; she's already devastated that he's not there at home.

My middle daughter who is a teenager cannot today talk about closed conditions without welling up and becoming anxious, despite visiting me more than 50 times, those places had a huge impact on her. It was just awful.

Yet here we're allowed to sit together as a family, walk around in the fresh air, spend time together, and we get the full two hours, it's lovely. I don't need visits here anymore because I get to go home, but during the first three months when you have, like, a settling-in period, (they call it a lay-down period here, but settling-in period is probably more appropriate), then those visits are wonderful, because again it's just bringing back normality and, that's what people in prison need, is a sense of normality.

They've made a mistake, they're being punished, they're paying the price but they're going to have a normal life, they deserve a normal life the same as other people do, they deserve a chance of forgiveness.

Unfortunately, after prison, society doesn't forgive, you know, as we've seen from the half a million people with criminal records, there are a lot of barriers put in the way of people resettling.

There are housing problems on release, there are employment problems on release, discrimination on release, there's societal search engine discrimination, there's social media shaming, there's all these things that don't stop, and in the age of the internet it's a hundred times worse.

We're mean to have right-to-be forgotten laws, where you can ask Google to de-index old news results but most of the time Google refuses, saying it's still in the public interest, and they don't have the money to get a solicitor to remove that.

We are talking about people who have climbed a massive mountain to get through their prison sentence, without cutting themselves up terribly, without being too badly scarred by it, and they still face a massive mountain on release as well to try and live a normal life – and we want them to live a normal life because we want them to not commit crime again.

Whether we like them or not is not relevant, not relevant at all.

We want them to be able to fit into society, and you know, the self-harming is one sign of how hard it is for people to cope.

I was told yesterday by an Offender Supervisor that HMP Woodhill currently has over 70 people of an ACCT, which is an Assessment of Care in Custody. There's only seven hundred and something prisoners in Woodhill so that's almost 10% of people self-harming or at risk of suicide, and, you know, that's a terrible statistic. That points to the regime being too severe because people aren't getting out of their cells.

When I was at Woodhill, I was Segregation orderly for 3 months and I saw a lot of shocking things; the most extreme forms of self-harm and manifestations of mental illness. The Seg officers are exceptional, they show care and compassion; the Chaplains also come in every day, and they do things for probably the least deserving people, and that's where you can really see humanity, and I just really took my hat off to them so much.

But the regime is tough; just before I left Woodhill the regime was tightening up, so much so that bang-up was at 5:30pm, so if people have gone to their industries or gone to education, they come back at 5 or 5:15pm and they're locked up straight away as soon as they get food. That means they can't even phone home, and it's not that they don't have time to phone home, it's if you pick up the phone they're shouting "GET OFF THE PHONE", "GET OFF THE PHONE". So, you can't phone your children when they get home from school, you can't phone your wife and ask her how she coped today.

My wife developed anorexia when I came to prison, she's 45 years old. We've been together, like I say, for 24 years, when I came away, we'd been together 21 and a bit years, and we had this incredible marriage where we've never really been apart, we've raised our girls and worked together.

For a lady of 45 years old to become anorexic shows the tremendous bereavement feelings that she was experiencing, where she just lost her appetite. It wasn't that she wanted to lose weight, she'd been exercising, she's very healthy, she'd been doing that for 10 years, but it was just that she, she said 'I can't eat, I don't feel like eating, I just can't eat'.

We would have to, my girls and me, would have to coax her to eat things, and gradually it's getting better now, because I'm coming home more, she's eating more, but, you know, she plummeted through her dress sizes to now where she's smaller now than she was when I met her, and she was slim when I met her aged 21.

It is really important to be able to offer support to family members struggling at home. Just to phone and say, 'hi, how's your day been?' you know, and just even have 5 or 10 minutes is really important. Yet to have an officer scream at you 'GET OFF THE PHONE'.

I even had an officer who took a disliking to me, it happens, personality clashes - no particular reason. I was saying goodnight to my family at 5 o'clock in the evening and as soon as he shouted bang-up, he made a bee-line straight for me and pressed the phone down, in the middle of a conversation to my wife.

Now I can't phone her back until, if I'm lucky, the following morning at half past eight. If they unlock quickly enough, you can get a few minutes at Woodhill before you go to work. So, if I'm quick enough I can speak to her in the morning but knowing that she's gone at 5pm and I can't speak to her until 8:30am, now that plays havoc with someone's mental health.

I haven't really had mental health problems but I know that I was feeling emotional turmoil and distress and wrecked.

For the first time in my life I could understand why some people cut themselves badly and why others decide to take their own lives.

I've never been able to understand it before, but when you're not only locked away but it is considered acceptable for other human beings to submit you to mental torture and *deliberately* traumatise to cause pain.

That is wicked, and it all points to this institutional aggression, and feeling that we have to punish these people. That is not what their job is, not to punish.

There are no officers here like that, they might be busy and things might be inconvenient, 'no I can't help you with that application' 'no I can't help with inquiry right now' they might be too busy, but no one here is interested in traumatising people or hurting them, or making them worse, or making their families suffer like they are in other prisons.

There are a lot of officers in closed conditions who take great pleasure in hurting people, mentally or physically. I think that closed conditions are damaging for the officers as well, the fear and unpredictability must affect them too.

There were two parts to my prison sentence. I was sentenced and I did just under 6 months in prison then had HDC tag. 8 weeks' home and 5 of these weeks were a court trial because I'd pleaded guilty to the first charges of running a business while bankrupt, and there was a trial for the rest, fraud and fraudulent trading which I had pleaded not guilty too; I will never agree that there was deliberate intent in my case.

Anyway, I was found guilty and I ended up coming back in which I hadn't expected to come back in, so I'd had 8 weeks at home and I was devastated to come back to prison with a seven-year sentence to serve three and a half. This made it even worse for my wife and children, and when I went back in, I was very upset for us all.

On the induction wing in any prison is where it's worst, because you have no purposeful activity and you're almost constantly. Every prison has an induction wing where it's pretty much 23 and a ½ hour a day lock up, with a stranger, with a toilet, with a vent, and that's really hard to handle.

And once in while they unlock the door – thank God someone's unlocking the door! For two minutes, and it was a psychologist or a psychiatrist peep his head in.

Psychiatric nurse "oh hi, I'm just checking if you're depressed or not".

I said "sorry?"

Psychiatric nurse "I'm just checking if you're depressed or not",

Me: "Actually it's an entirely natural reaction for someone to be depressed when they're locked away for this amount of time, away from their family, with no one to talk to, no help, no support, nothing, are you saying you want me to be depressed? of course I'm depressed! But I'm not depressed so that I need to be taking prescription medication

Psychiatric nurse "Oh well, that's fine then",

Me: "So you're offering me anti-depressant medication?"

Psychiatric nurse "Well only if you need it",

Me: "Well I don't think I need it but of course I'm depressed. I can't get any lower than this. You know I know what it's like to be beaten by a drunken father growing up. Things were pretty tough for me growing up, but I've never been as miserable, and as sad and as gutted as I am right now, so yes, I'm depressed and I think that's a perfectly normal reaction, don't you?

Psychiatric nurse (laughing) "Well yes ok then",

Me: "So can I come out now?

Psychiatric nurse "no" and then locked the door.

Me: "Thanks very much! Great"

That was it until the next day, when they would see if I am more or less depressed. So, it was really bad.

> Interviewer: When you have people here who might have come from closed conditions, or be going back and forth, what do you think means that the behaviour doesn't cross back over?

Well, we haven't really talked about the effect of closed conditions on the prison officers, because it's extremely disruptive and degrading to them as well.

Where they have to lock up human beings, (in some cases very decent human beings who have just made a mistake), this is distressing for them too.

When we look at the people on the news and in the media, that's just a tiny percentage, most estimates say that just 1% - 5% of crimes and prison sentences make news, so like I say, most people in prison aren't the terrible murderers, rapists, stabbings etc.

> Interviewer: You see the worst of the worst and that's it

Exactly, but officers are in the position, unfortunately, where everyone is treated the same, the regime is the same for everybody.

It's not nice for them to have no time, to be overworked, you ask them a question and they've got no time to deal with anything, and just banging up, and they see awful things.

I've seen a little bit of violence probably a dozen incidents but they've probably seen many dozens, fifty, I don't know, and it must have an effect on them as well.

We're going to have some of the prison officers, like some security guards, like some police officers, who probably love a little bit of aggression and violence and things, most prison officers probably don't but what they do know is, a place like that it only takes a little spark to create a massive upheaval.

Bedford rioted only two months ago, and it didn't even make the news again, Bedford rioted, as you know, a little over a year ago, they have rats running around in people's cells, they have people waking up with rats on them in Bedford prison today.

There are cockroaches everywhere but the rats are the worst, and Bedford is in a terrible state, if there's violence the prison officers just lock the wing, they don't even come on the wing they let it fizzle out before they'll come on.

That violence might be to an innocent, they won't like this phrase, member of the public – we're all still members of the public.

People in prison deserve the same protections as someone outside, really, and yet they're not getting it.

Normal, everyday people are subject to violence and assault, and harm, and fear, and the prison officers see this, they're scared, they're seeing horrible violence.

Our prisons are experiencing record levels of prisoner on staff violence. Ladies being really badly hurt, men being smashed round their heads, you know.

I know of many incidences personally and things certainly haven't got any better since then.

There you're in a state of fear and the only way people can deal with that kind of fear is to become more controlling, so they are forced to come down heavy and keep the regime tight, and to not accept any backchat, do you see what I mean?

Either way, the damaging environment is damaging to the officers as well, and it can only make them behave worse as a kind of self-protection and control mechanism.

Here we don't have that, because the officers are walking around in a nice therapeutic environment, "good morning, good morning, hello, how are you?"

You know, and it's better for them as well, it's a normal environment for them.

Prison is not a normal environment. Somehow, we built loads of those kinds of closed condition establishments and they house 80 odd thousand people.

Really those environments should only be reserved for the worst, maybe that small percentage of violent people with weird desires and obsessions, who hurt other people.

If it's true that according to the Ministry of Justice that the majority of people aren't in prison for crimes against a person, well then why are we locking them up and caging them up as if they are dangerous animals that should never be released?

We're locking them up worse than lions, as if they're dangerous when they are not and we're putting them in with dangerous people.

That is not good for them or for the prison officers either. That's why there's a massive difference between the staff in open conditions and the staff in closed conditions; you know there's some staff who are lazy and some staff who are rude, you're going to get that in any work environment, and there's some staff you'll have a personality clash, but you'll get that with any work environment.

In the main the prison officers, the governors, the support staff, have all pointed this prison towards the Enabling Environment award. That was a massive achievement, and that's because they care about progression, and they care about helping people, they believe that people should leave Springhill better off than when they arrive.

If we emulate that concept across the whole prison estate, the idea that people leave prison better off than when they arrive, then those people would be demonstrably less likely to commit crime because they are leaving a better person mentally, emotionally and physically than when they arrived and are better equipped to thrive in society.

If we make them worse, then we increase the likelihood of them committing crime, and it's as simple as that for me.

If we want them to be human beings, we treat them like human beings. If we want them to become animals, we treat them like animals.

Interviewer: Something I've heard is that sometimes people get to open conditions and they just can't deal with it, it's almost too much freedom, so they'll abscond or they'll ask to be sent back to closed conditions, what do you think it is about you, that means that it didn't happen to you, that means you're able to be here and enjoy it and appreciate it?

Drug addiction is a big thing unfortunately and although addiction is treatable and people can recover there's always going to be the temptation for some people to take drugs.

Some who've turned to drugs whilst in closed conditions have that addiction or that psychological need for it. Most of the absconds that I, and I've done quite a lot of research and writing on this subject, most of the absconds that I know of from Springhill are primarily due to drug debts, rather than a failing to adapt to the open conditions.

Here, you can get hold of cannabis, whereas in closed conditions cannabis is easier to drug test for so there isn't any in the closed estate, they use NPS which is SPICE new psychoactive substances, which is hundreds of times worse than cannabis.

Interviewer: Yes, it's a big crisis at the moment isn't it?

Yes, people drop down dead from it; it causes a lot of problems. I saw a really fun Rastafarian man came into Woodhill, I was reception orderly at the time there, and err, he was dancing and happy and he said "oh, I've only got a short sentence" and we had a little laugh and a joke and he went off and he died the next day – he'd smoked spice.

Interviewer: Oh my God

Yeah, because Rastafarians generally smoke cannabis as part of their culture, so he's just lit up and it wasn't cannabis, it was spice from someone else and he dropped down dead. Literally 24 hours after I met him – it's a terrible, terrible, drug.

It is very prevalent in closed prisons, I have seen a young man smoke it once and he ended up in the Seg with psychosis, his mind had gone. The Governors made the unusual decision to let his family visit him directly in the SEG because his case was so extreme and doctors thought that there was a chance that his family could help. To the best of my knowledge he never did emerge from his psychosis.

But here they do smoke cannabis, which is certainly less harmful and more predictable perhaps than these modern chemical concoctions.

Occasionally you walk around and smell it here, they do test for cannabis and I wouldn't say that it's a huge problem here. Nevertheless, it is a gateway drug and people do sometimes turn to stronger drugs.

There was one old fella I knew and I'd helped him get work, at a car wreckage yard and he really loved it and was thriving but unfortunately, well he'd been inside for, 15 or 16 years and he was very skeletal because he was a drug user, and he was about my age but looked about 65 or something, really, really thin. Unfortunately, he was using heroin, where he'd been earning money, he'd been using it for heroin.

I don't think there's much class A drug usage here at all, but he very, very responsibly went to the officers and said, "I've got myself fucked, I'm addicted again, take me back to closed conditions, that's the only way I'll detox".

He knew that he couldn't stop on his own and that he'd always give in to temptation.

Being a parole sentenced prisoner – an indeterminate sentenced prisoner without a fixed release date, means that he's voluntarily gone back to closed so he can come back to open conditions again, probably in two years' time, do perhaps a year or two in open conditions and if he manages to get through, he'll probably get his parole again.

If he hadn't taken drugs, he would have got his parole because he'd been out working full-time and successfully completing ROTLs.

He realised that he's been taking drugs that he would fail a drug test and would probably get sent back to closed conditions. So, by leaving voluntarily he was taking responsibility, that doesn't always happen, people do sometimes abscond because of drug debts.

There are a number of reasons why people abscond from open conditions. One of the main ones is not to be blamed on the receiving open prison at all but is more to do with flaws in the categorisation process from the sending establishment.

If someone absconds within the first 2-4 weeks of arriving here, I don't believe that Springhill can accept responsibility for that because they haven't had the person long enough to influence him in any way but the people who should take responsibility for that are the sending prisons who have re-categorized this person wrongly. Categorisation from C to D-cat is a risk management process and there's a lot of work involved in that and clearly that person wasn't suitable at that time and presented more of a risk than was documented and considered.

Absconding 3 to 6 months after arriving is Springhill's fault; that's where we need to look at what we could have done differently, what did that person need support in?

There has been a couple of cases I've pointed out in writing to the Governors here where Springhill did fail people.

To help counteract that I've produced a guide entitled 'what to expect at HMP Springhill'. This will hopefully be issued to all the feeder prisons so that people learnt important things before they arrive.

When they come here, they share a room, whereas in a lot of closed conditions if there's long term prisoners they don't share, so it's a shock for some people, but I explain that you'll be sharing a room but you're not locked up so you can get out of that room at any time. There's a curfew at 10 o'clock where you have to stay on the huts but you can still sit in the association room, which is like a little lounge, watch telly or they can cook light meals in the kitchen.

Interviewer: You can still move around a bit?

Yes, it's like student halls of residence, you know, you've got a shared kitchen, shared lounge, so even if they don't want to share, they're only in their room to sleep really. You know, other things in the what to expect guide, if they haven't got their numeracy and literacy levels they'll have to engage with education.

What else they've got to expect is that they'll have to do their settling in period, they don't just come here and get ROTL's, release on temporary license, straight away.

So, I felt that it's important that people know this before they come here, so that actually they can turn around and say, 'oh no, I actually don't want to go to Springhill, I'll try a different D-Cat'.

We're doing a lot of work to reduce or stop absconding but still, if there's a family crisis, or someone finds out that their best friend is sleeping with their partner, some people will just go off on one, and they'll just go.

Unless you put fences around the grounds - and personally I don't see a problem with having a fence at a distance around the grounds, I don't know why it doesn't have it.

Unless you do that, there is always going to be a tiny element of absconding from open conditions. And that is part of the trust as well. Indeterminate sentenced prisoners who are lifers or IPPs, these sorts of people who have a parole release, so their release isn't on a set date, it's determined by if they have lowered their risk sufficiently to be trusted in the community.

When those type of prisoners come to open conditions it's literally to be "tested in open conditions" for a year or two years before their potential parole date and release. Some people if they're being tested will, naturally, fail that test and they don't cope in open conditions for whatever reason.

I would prefer to see dedicated open conditions for people who are being tested in open conditions – for indeterminate sentenced people. Lifers and long-term prisoners, people who have done 12 - 15 years have a very different set of experiences from mine; when I arrived here, I had completed about two years and two months in closed conditions.

My experience is very different, you know institutionalization is a real thing and it gets deeper and deeper, deeper and deeper entrenched, you'll find almost every single lifer or long term sentenced prisoner – more than 10 years – has OCD and severe obsessions. To the point where their ketchup will be in that spot and their mayonnaise will be in that spot. Everything has to be a certain way because they lived in a tiny little space with no control over their life; the prison system manufactures these kinds of mental outcomes in people.

It becomes - "the only thing that I can control is where I put my ketchup and mayonnaise, the only thing I can control is how I lay my clothes out for the next day".

Long term institutionalized prisoners do have very ingrained, deeply rooted thought processes which are different from the general population of shorter-term prisoners.

> Interviewer: So, it would be better for them and more supportive to have a place that was more engineered to deal with their specific needs?

Yes, exactly, I would prefer to see a dedicated lifer's prison. There would be so much more we could help. HMP Grendon is a great example of a prison that is designed and built for the demographic of the population – it works really well and it has a huge success rate.

Mixing everybody together in the prison population doesn't have the same success rate because the stronger prey on the weak. I don't mean that in a derogatory way, the softer and weaker people sometimes suffer more which affects their mental health, they then begin to self-harm and the whole thing spirals out of control.

Grendon as a therapeutic community is fantastic at healing past hurt and most importantly at preventing the creation of future victims through reducing reoffending.

The only reason that there is only one such dedicated prison in this country is because it is expensive to operate. The concept works, the figures should not be ignored. I don't have access to all the information necessary but I think the concept of prisons specifically built for certain demographics should be investigated and explored further.

We should have more of this kind of establishment for lower risk prisoners even when they have longer to serve. My vision is for an open C cat, so an open C cat like this for lower risk prisoners who still have 4 or 5 years to go but with employment academies, workshops, local employers joined on to the prison, helping people to gain vocational skills and qualifications that lead into real employment. With fences all the way around so they still can't escape, you know, they might be able to hide somewhere within the prison and give officers the run around but the minute their behaviour goes downhill or they fail drug tests they're back in closed conditions much like here, but that would reduce the traumatising effects of the prison sentence and it would allow people to build those building blocks of a future life better.

Interviewer: you've talked a lot about the senses, so the smell of being in closed conditions, being able to see the views here, but one of the things that certainly struck me about here is the sound – it's so quiet and you know you can hear the birds

Oh absolutely.

Interviewer: What do you think about that kind of peacefulness?

You're absolutely right. Thank you for mentioning that because prison wings are very, very loud. In most closed prisons, there are 80 -100 people on each wing and the sound just reverberates round, so if I was on the phone to my wife and children, I had to put my finger in my ear to hear them, and I could hardly hear them.

It was so loud that the volume must be above any legal decibel limits and any time there's 'association'/unlock time, the volume was unbelievable – it would hurt my ears, it's really, really unbearable and again it all contributes to this detrimental effect that it has on someone.

But yes, here, you're absolutely right, I didn't even realise it before until you just said it, but you're right it's a really peaceful place. I always sleep with the window open a little bit. At home, (we live in a little village), I'm woken up by the birds singing and here I'm woken up by the birds singing and I love that.

And the smells (takes a deep breath) I take a deep breath, so I walked around here the back way where there's a willow tree, I walk round the country way like that and I take a deep breath because the air smells so beautiful, it's like me being at home, because it's the countryside again, so yeah, it's really lovely.

Sensory wise you just feel healthier, and happier, able to cope with things better. When you are in shock or in distress, any little thing can become a big problem.

It's a very stark comparison comparing closed condition to open conditions. Even if we compare open conditions to home for a lot of people in prison, in some ways this is a better environment than where they've come from. It is a chance to sit back and reflect, you know there's lots of benches around, lots of quiet spaces around, you see a lot of people reading books and things, it's a reflective place, it's time out of the busy-ness of society.

Some people come here and they've only got a short sentence to do, they might only have got a year, a year and a half, maybe doing half of that, so they might only have spent a week or a month in closed conditions, um, and they'll come here. For those people it's probably quite a healthy timeout from their chaotic lives outside, or whatever they were doing, a chance to reflect and reset goals for the future in a decent environment.

> *Interviewer: so, some of the spaces which I think are some of the nicest ones, like the woodland area and the Buddha grove, and things like that, they're quite restricted in terms of how and when people can access them. Do you think that that's a good thing, that there's a purpose for that or ...?*

I don't know, I'm guessing there's security reasons when they can't see people very well when it's dark and that's probably why they're restricted. But it's still a beautiful environment and compared to where all of us have come from it's fantastic. If they need to make a few little rules for whatever their security reasons are that they have knowledge of that I don't have, then that's fine.

> *Interviewer: It's worth it?*

Yes, definitely, Springhill is a very inspiring place, if I wasn't a serving prisoner (and part of my plan is actually this), then I'd be more than happy to come and work here and interact and help the men here because the whole attitude is one of positivity and progression.

It is what you make it – you're always going to get people who moan "oh I'm upset because I missed my ROTL date, they're late with the paperwork", "oh this didn't happen" or "why have I got to do maths?", "why have I got to do English?" there's always going to be people who focus on problems instead of solutions but I do believe in counting our blessings and I think Springhill is a massive blessing.

Compared to closed prisons, it's incredible. I had my first grandson last year...

> *Interviewer: Oh wow!*

That was in June and to be able to go out - I was given an open license; to be able to go out within a day of him being born, it's amazing. They didn't have to do that, it's quite complicated to do an open license so you can go any day in the next seven days, you know they could have said 'no you're going out on that Saturday and that's the day', but they said that's fine you can go, and when the baby was born I had the paperwork signed and my wife picked me up the next day - they do go out of their way to help you here where they can.

> *Interviewer: It's that compassion you were talking about; that recognition that people's lives change and things happen*

Yes, exactly, and where's the harm? Where was the harm in doing that sort of thing for me?

There wasn't any harm, it could only help me and they recognised that, and it's something, I know that I always will be grateful for that (emotional).

Prison is terrible, it really doesn't help people, but it could.

I've been more than twenty years in business. I've employed a lot of people and I've done a lot of speaking. I know how to help people and I care deeply about helping people.

In 2005, long before I came to prison, long before I ever thought I could or would come to prison, I spoke at a parole hearing on the basis that employment would help this person to resettle, and he got released. He was a two-strike lifer and that means at the time it was two violent incidents in your life and you got a life sentence.

One happened when he was very young and one happened in a period of emotional distress, anyway he got out and since 2005 - 14 years later he never reoffended.

So, I do care, I do believe that people can change.

But I believe that people need help and support to change.

I think that's where a decent environment like Springhill encourages people to change for the better and that's really important.

It is also abundantly clear that society and the individual people in our society have a real opportunity to help and support people to change for the better, to reduce reoffending and to create fewer victims.

GLOSSARY

We can do this by reducing the damage done by imprisonment, by providing practical help and support (both before and after release), acceptance back into our communities and the chance of forgiveness.

"Such very clear explanations for once; thank you very much this has been a great help." SN

"This book helped me greatly, I realised that I am not the only one going through some of these challenges. It helped me to put things into perspective and come to a point of acceptance. Thanks, and well done." CM

Important Reminder	The author has used his best endeavours as a layperson to ensure that all information is correct and current in the UK at the time of printing. Laws, rules and processes may be different in Scotland. This book is for general guidance only, the content should not be relied upon in isolation and nothing within the book constitutes legal, financial or medical advice. Personal advice should be sought from qualified third parties. No liability is accepted at law for the outcome of any decisions made whilst relying on the content of this book.

Glossary – This helpful guide simply explains the processes, terminology and legal language that people experience from when they first enter the justice system to when they gain employment after release. If you would like any terminology or processes added to this glossary or if you have any resettlement related questions, please contact the author.

A

Aggravating Factor - Something that worsens

Aggravating factors are considerations that increase the severity of a crime and the sentence given. Examples include continuing to commit crime whilst on **bail**, abuse of a position of trust, substantial and deliberate pre-planning, exploitation of vulnerable victims, intimidation of witnesses etc. These are the opposite of **mitigating** factors.

Application Letter (AL) – A letter which introduces your **CV** and your Personal **Disclosure** Statement. AL is also known as an introduction or covering letter.

Appeal - Application to reconsider a sentence or overturn a conviction

An appeal can be made by any **convicted** person who feels they have grounds for the conviction to be overturned or for the sentence to be reduced. The **prosecution** can also appeal sentence lengths under the 'unduly lenient scheme'.

The first stage of an appeal goes to a single judge; it can be funded by legal aid (for eligible appellants) and there is no risk of a **loss of time order**. If the single judge feels that the appeal has:

a) Merit - the appeal can be renewed to a panel of three judges, legal aid would continue and there is no risk of a **loss of time order**.

b) No merit - the appeal can still be renewed but legal aid stops and there is a risk of loss of time. This risk increases substantially if a warning box is ticked on the single judge's decision notice. In these cases, the loss of time order could be for the entire amount of time served from when the appeal is first refused, up to when the renewed appeal is heard. If the box is not ticked then there is still a risk of loss of time, but it is a lesser risk and usually a smaller loss of time of 28-56 days.

In summary, there is no risk of extra time with the first stage of an appeal but renewing an appeal after refusal by the single judge, carries a real risk of extra time in prison.

B

Bail - A type of licence

Bail allows people who have been accused of crimes (and who present as low risk of harm to the public) to continue to reside at their homes in the following circumstances:

- Whilst the crime is being investigated.
- Between **charging** and **conviction.**
- Between conviction and **sentencing.**

and occasionally:

- Between **sentencing** and imprisonment.
- Whilst an **appeal** is waiting to be heard.

Burden of Proof and Standard of Proof

The burden of proof means who is responsible for proving something. In a criminal trial the burden of proof falls to the **Prosecution** to prove guilt; theoretically, it does not fall to the **Defence** to prove innocence.

The standard (level of proof) is different for criminal and civil trials:

- Criminal trials must meet a standard of proof known as 'beyond all reasonable doubt'; technically, the jury must be 99% sure before they can convict.

- Civil trials must meet a much lower standard of proof known as 'balance of probabilities'. The judge only needs to be surer than not, meaning 51% sure before they can rule in favour of one party.

C

Categorisation - Risk level and accommodating individuals appropriately

The categories in the UK prison estate range from higher security categories AA (Maximum Security), A and B, and C cat and the lowest security D cat (resettlement prisons) - known as open conditions.

CCRC - Criminal Cases Review Commission

The Criminal Cases Review Commission investigates possible miscarriages of justice they are the last-ditch body for **appeals** against conviction and /or sentence.

The CCRC will only investigate cases where an appeal has failed and where there is new evidence or argument that has not previously been seen or heard by the court, or by the court of appeal.

The CCRC refer a very small percentage of cases for appeal but if they do then the applicant is not at risk of any extra time being added to their sentence (**loss of time order**).

Unlike the normal appeal process, when the CCRC are successful in overturning a conviction, compensation can be claimed by the wrongly imprisoned person. The equivalent body in Scotland is the SCCRC.

Charging - Formally accused of an offence

The police have decided that there is enough evidence to refer the case to the **CPS** for a charging decision and the CPS have subsequently given the police permission to formally charge (accuse) a person with the crime.

A date will be set for Magistrates Court who will either hear the case or refer the matter to the Crown Court if it is deemed serious.

Circa - Approximately

Used in job adverts to mean 'in the region of' e.g. 'Salary circa £24,000 pa' means that the salary will be around £24,000 a year depending on the applicant's skills, experience, qualifications and ability to negotiate.

Concurrent - At the same time (the opposite of consecutive)

Frequently when a person is convicted, they will have committed multiple offences or committed the same offence multiple times. If the crime is similar, or if it forms part of the same overall criminality within the same timeframe, then the multiple sentences will usually run concurrently.

e.g. someone who committed two crimes with a sentence of 2 years for each crime, concurrently, would receive a 2-year total prison sentence.

Confiscation Order - An amount of money which a defendant must pay after a POCA confiscation hearing

When a Confiscation Order (See **POCA**) is generated, a defendant generally has 3 months to pay the full amount of the order or to apply to extend based on legitimate reasons e.g. sale of the house not completed yet.

Where a defendant deliberately does not pay, a default prison sentence is issued. There is a scale of sentences based on how much is unpaid but put simply, the prison sentence is usually similar in length to the original prison sentence issued by the criminal court.

Even after the serving of a default prison sentence, confiscation orders remain due and enforceable for life; the debt cannot be extinguished until it is paid.

Consecutive - **Following on from (the opposite of concurrent)**
Frequently when a person is convicted, they will have committed multiple offences or committed the same offence multiple times.

If the crimes are serious or very different from each other, then the multiple sentences will be usually run consecutively. e.g. someone sentenced to 2 years for each of 2 crimes, consecutively, would receive a 4-year total sentence.

Conviction - **An offence has been admitted or proven in court**
Conviction is the point at which someone is now guilty of an offence; they may have pleaded guilty but at guilty they were found guilty by a jury or they may have pleaded guilty without a trial.

CPS - **Crown Prosecution Service (aka The Crown)**

The organisation which conducts most criminal prosecutions in the UK. The CPS regularly review charging decisions and court proceedings to ensure that the prosecution has a reasonable chance of success and is in the public interest.

N.B. this does not mean that the public are interested in it but rather means that a prosecution would be of benefit to society.

CRC - **Community Rehabilitation Company**

Privatised probation monitoring the lowest risk and shortest sentenced prisoners when they begin their supervision in the community.

CRC delivers 'through the gate' services for **MOJ** including delivery of resettlement courses, (such as 'Getting it Right' and 'Thinking Skills Programme') and provide resettlement support such as making referrals to housing charities and councils. Most CRC contracts are ending in 2020 due to poor outcomes.

CRL - **Childcare Resettlement Leave**

A form of **ROTL** where a prisoner is allowed to leave the prison for a set period of time to look after their child or children. CRL is subject to risk assessments and passing **FLED**.

Only for those parents who are the sole carer for a child or vulnerable adult are eligible. These criteria are very hard to meet because someone else will obviously be looking after the child in the place of a parent, when a parent goes to prison.

It is for this reason that CRL is exceptionally rare.

CSU - Care and Separation Unit

CSU is a recent rebranding of Segregation unit to reflect a move towards compassion and rehabilitation. See **SEG**.

CV - also known as résumé - Curriculum Vitae

A formal document which provides an overview of your personal strengths, qualifications and employment experience.

D

DBIS - Department for Business, Insolvency and Skills

A department of Government that often undertakes criminal prosecutions for business offences. Sometimes they act on behalf of, or alongside, the Insolvency Service or Trading Standards.

DBS - Disclosure and Barring Service

Maintain a database of criminal convictions and related intelligence and provides access to approved organisations for DBS checks.

Defence - Acting for accused and convicted people

The defence team are tasked with protecting their client and serving the client's best interests, they do this by:

- Advising and supporting their client/ defendant.
- Persuading them to plead guilty and in so doing, benefit from a reduced sentence.
- Identifying weaknesses in the prosecution's evidence and casting doubt on their assumptions, assertions and arguments.
- In the case of conviction, arguing for a lesser punishment by explaining mitigating factors and relevant historic cases.

Determinate - Prison sentence with an end date

Also known as a 'straight sentence'. A determinate sentence has a fixed end date. The prisoner is released at their **ERD** and unless they are recalled, will stay on licence in the community until their **LED**.

Disclosure - Revealing a criminal conviction

Disclosure of criminal convictions is usually requested by employers, insurance companies, financial institutions and before travelling to most other countries. Full disclosure includes all unspent convictions, sentence lengths and background circumstances and is usually done on a Personal Disclosure Statement (PDS).

Discretionary - There is a choice

A discretionary life sentence means that it was the judge's choice to hand out a life sentence - this is the opposite of **mandatory**.

E

EDS - Extended Determinate Sentence

A prison sentence used where the risk to the public is higher than normal and rehabilitation is unpredictable; almost as a middle ground between **determinate** and **indeterminate**. With EDS the prisoner is not released at the halfway point (as is usually the case) but instead serves 2/3 of the sentence and only then becomes eligible for **parole** (consideration for release). EDS prisoners have extended supervision, under **licence** in the community which are set at the time of sentencing, typically being 1 or 2 years after the full sentence end.

ERD - Earliest Release Date

The date when 50% of a standard **determinate** custodial sentence has been served. At this point (or the day preceding it, in the case of weekend and bank holiday) the prisoner will be released to serve the remaining time on licence in the community, unless recalled for a breach of licence conditions or charged with a new offence.

F

FLED - Facility Licence Eligibility Date

The date when a prisoner has served 50% of their custodial period or when they have 2 years left to serve, whichever date is the latter. A prisoner becomes eligible to apply for **ROTL** for resettlement purposes (family ties, interviews, work, driving lessons etc.). **SPL** is not dependent on FLED having been passed although these will usually be escorted by prison staff prior to FLED.

G, H

HDC - Home Detention Curfew

A home monitoring system that allows the lowest risk determinate sentenced prisoners to be released earlier that their **ERD** to an approved address (usually home) and subject to a curfew (usually 7pm-7am). The prisoner can serve up to a maximum of 4.5 months on HDC but in the case of weekend and bank holidays will be released the day after. Under current rules, HDC is only available to those prisoners who are sentenced to less than 4 years imprisonment.

I

Indeterminate - Undecided/not fixed

A sentence which does not have a fixed end date (**IPP** or life). **Parole** must be granted before an indeterminate sentenced prisoner can be released and they will be subject to **licence conditions**.

IPP - Imprisonment for Public Protection

A controversial and now abolished type of Indeterminate prison sentence. The sentence came with a minimum tariff and a minimum of ten years' supervision under licence upon release. Despite its abolition, thousands of people are still serving IPP sentences in prison and many years over their tariffs. Recent changes to the **Parole** test have seen more prisoners being released or re-**categorised** to D Category to be "tested in open conditions".

J, K, L

LED - Licence Expiry Date

The date when a released prisoner is no longer monitored by probation and is informally considered to have become an "ex-offender".

Licence Conditions - **Restrictions and Requirements for the second half of a determinate sentence or for indeterminate sentence prisoners who are granted parole.**

Prisoners are released under licensed supervision by The Probation Service (or CRC for the lowest risk prisoners) in the community. There are three purposes of supervision which are to:

1. Help resettlement.
2. Protect the public.
3. Prevent re-offending.

The standard licence conditions (simplified) are:

1. Be of good behaviour.
2. Only carry out pre-approved work.
3. Allow probation to visit as required.
4. Keep in touch with probation as required.
5. Reside permanently at a pre-approved address.
6. Not travel outside of the UK without permission.
7. Not to touch or use fireworks or any objects containing gun powder.

Additional licence conditions may be imposed to reduce risk but to be lawful, each condition must be proportionate, reasonable and necessary to achieve the three purposes of supervision.

Such additional licence conditions may include, but are not limited to, exclusion zones, curfews, drug testing, non-association with named individuals, courses to complete and additional reporting.

Sometimes courts and police impose additional conditions which run for a timescale which is separate from the licence duration (see **SCPO**).

Loss of Time Order - **Penalty for unmeritworthy appeals**

A loss of time order can be made for any **appeal** which is renewed to the panel of three appeal judges after rejection by the first judge and which is deemed to have no merit.

A loss of time order can be for the entire amount of time served, from when the appeal is first refused, up to when the renewed appeal is heard, to no longer count towards the sentence.

Such a penalty is rare however and is reserved for the most frivolous of appeals, the loss of time order is usually in the region of 1 - 2 months.

M

Mandatory - No Choice (the opposite of discretionary)

There is no choice. A mandatory life sentence means that the judge had no choice but to hand out a life sentence.

MAPPA - Multi Agency Public Protection Arrangement

MAPPA is the name given to police, prison service and probation (the "responsible authorities") who work together to assess and manage the most serious offenders who pose a high risk of harm to the public. Cooperation is required from other agencies as well including housing, health, social services and education services.

All agencies contribute to the creation of a personalised risk management plan for each individual offender. MAPPA offenders are categorised from 1 to 3 with **1 being the highest** and 3 lowest risk. The multi-agency management is then tiered from Level 1 to Level 3 with 1 (reversely) being the lowest and **3 being the highest** level of monitoring and management.

Mitigating Factors (Mitigation) - Something that lessens

Mitigating factors are considerations that reduce the severity of a crime and the sentence that will be given. Mitigation covers a wide range of possible circumstances and may include repaying money taken by fraud, references provided by respected people, poor mental/ emotional state, medical aid given to a victim, previous good character etc. These are the opposite of **aggravating** factors.

MOJ - Ministry of Justice

The Government department responsible for the management of the court system, prisons, prisoners and ex-offenders.

N

NVQ - National Vocational Qualification

Widely recognised qualifications related to employment and careers e.g. Bricklaying, Catering, Customer Service or Childcare.

O

OASys - Offender Assessment System

OASys is a substantial and detailed record which is designed to help with sentence planning and manage, and reduce the risk of reoffending. OASys contains a wealth of historic, current and future information such as housing, family, education, employment, finances, associates, mental and physical health, lifestyle, drug and alcohol misuse, attitudes, thinking, emotional management, courses completed, background and reasons for offences, and may also include verified and unverified information from court records, police intelligence and other agencies. This information is invaluable when identifying 'criminogenic needs' i.e. those areas which are problematic for the offender and which are likely to trigger re-offending, e.g. someone who has:

- Challenges gaining employment due to a lack of functional skills may be required to attend Maths and English classes.
- Problems with their family ties will be able to complete a course on personal and family relationships as part of their sentence plan.
- An identified problem with past criminal associates may have an additional **licence** condition on release banning them from associating with known criminals.

OASys generates risk scores, as percentage predictors for re-offending and serious harm.

OASys is respected worldwide but it is only as accurate as the information placed into it by people; much of which is based on opinions rather than evidence and it is for this reason that many question its accuracy and impartiality.
Prisoners and ex-offenders can get a copy of their OASys by sending a **SAR** to Data Protection Compliance, MOJ, 16 NDC, Burton Road, Branston, Burton Upon Trent, Staffordshire. DE14 3EG

OMU - Offender Management Unit

The OMU is the department within prison which is responsible for sentence planning. The majority of prisoners are allocated an Offender Supervisor (OS) within OMU and an Offender Manager (OM) from outside Probation. The OS and OM liaise with offenders, police and prison staff to create and update **OASys** and a sentence plan.

Parole - The board which considers whether a prisoner should be released or re-categorised

Parole means consideration for release from prison, under supervision in the community. The Parole board will only consider releasing **indeterminate** sentenced prisoners (around 5% of prison population) when they are satisfied that their risk has been reduced enough that they can be managed in the community. An alternative to release, or precursor to release, is for the prisoner to be re-**categorised** to D-category to be "tested in open conditions".

"**Overall, the serious rate of re-offending is less than 1%, which suggests that the Parole board makes the best decisions it can.**" Dean Kingham, Head of Prison Law and Crime, Swain and Co Solicitors

POCA - Proceeds of Crime Act

Civil proceedings aimed at removing the benefit of criminal conduct. The Act is "deliberately draconian" (with far reaching extreme consequences for criminals, families and associates) apparently to serve as a deterrent rather than punish further.

A benefit figure is arrived at by adding conviction amounts to unexplained income over 6 years, civil claims and adjusting the total for inflation. The benefit figure is based on turnover not retained profit, hence why it is almost always substantially more (by many multiples) than the real amount by which the criminal benefitted. Once a benefit figure is established, investigation into assets and past transactions will uncover tainted gifts, sales at undervalue, realisable and hidden assets.

A **confiscation order** will be generated for the amount of the realisable assets together with any assets or money deemed to be hidden. POCA trials are based on balance of probabilities (see **Burden of Proof** and **Standard of Proof**).

Proprietary - ownership

Owned by the worker typically self-employment as a sole trader.

Pro Rata - In the ratio

Used when advertising part-time jobs to show the equivalent annual salary. A 20hrs per week part-time salary of £24,000pa pro rata means that the salary you receive will be £12,000 each year (because 20hrs per week is half of the usual 40hrs per week)

Prosecution - Acting on behalf of a prosecuting authority (usually CPS) against the accused and convicted

The prosecution team are primarily focussed on:

- Providing enough evidence of a person's guilt and presenting it in a compelling way such that it encourages an accused person to plead guilty.
- Proving and/or convincing jury members of an accused person's guilt.
- Arguing for the harshest punishment after **conviction**, explaining aggravating factors and relevant historic cases.

Q, R

RDR - Resettlement Day Release

A form of **ROTL** where a prisoner can leave the prison for a set period of time to undertake resettlement activities e.g. to rebuild family ties, attend employment or university. Subject to passing **FLED** and risk assessments, eligibility (not entitlement, nor guaranteed) for RDR for family ties purposes is generally a maximum of 1 RDR every fourteen days. RDR for other purposeful activities e.g. attending employment or driving lessons does not affect the allowance for family ties.

Recidivism - Re-offending

Returning to patterns of past behaviour; usually used in the context of "reducing recidivism".

Recall - Being returned back to prison

Returning a prisoner, who has been released on **licence,** back to prison. Any person on licence can be recalled by probation for a range of reasons including, but not limited to:

- A perceived increase in their risk.
- An allegation made by a third party.
- They have been **charged** with a new offence.
- They are in breach of any **licence conditions.**

No court process is required for recall decisions.

Remand - Imprisonment before trial (the opposite of bail)

Remand is supposedly reserved for people accused of the most serious crimes, who pose a flight risk or who face overwhelming evidence of guilt of a crime that would definitely result in imprisonment. Many thousands of people are remanded into prison and kept for long periods of time before they have been found guilty of any crime. Many are released from prison after being found not guilty and they receive no compensation, little or no resettlement support and do not even qualify for the £46 discharge grant because they are not considered to have been serving a prison sentence.

Right to be Forgotten - Legal entitlement to request an end to linking to historic online content

Under Right to be Forgotten you can request that search engines no longer link to historic articles and web pages which feature you if the content is out of date and/or no long relevant. Many search engines will argue against de-indexing stating that listings are still in the public interest or that subjects are still being discussed.

ROR - Resettlement Overnight Release

A form of **ROTL** where a prisoner is allowed to stay overnight at their home, approved premises (hostel) or resettlement address. Subject to passing **FLED** and risk assessments, eligibility (not entitlement, nor guaranteed) is generally 1 ROR every 28 days.

The first ROR is generally 2 nights/ 3 days, the second ROR is generally 3 nights/ 4 days, the third and subsequent ROR's are 4 nights/ 5 days.

ROTL - Release on Temporary Licence

Permission to leave the prison temporarily under certain conditions (available after **FLED**).

All ROTL is at the Governor's discretion and is subject to police and probation checks. ROTL may be **CRL, RDR, ROR** or **SPL**.

S

SAR - Subject Access Request

A letter requesting a copy of all personal information held on you under the General Data Protection Regulations (GDPR's). No fee is payable for the provision of this information unless a request is repeated or excessive. Here is a template - an example of the wording to use:

Dear Sir/ Madam,

I am writing this letter to you as a Subject Access Request. My date of birth is _____ and I enclose evidence of my identification.

Enclose copy of driving licence, birth certificate or passport, (serving prisoners writing to MOJ, will not need id.)

I am the subject and owner of substantial amounts of data that you hold and I formally request ALL such information. In line with the revised GDPRs I understand that the timescale for fulfilment is now one calendar month and that there is no longer a fee to be paid.

I believe that this satisfies the requirements of the GDPRs; should you require additional confirmation of my identification or if you require a template form to be completed, please advise immediately by return. Thank you in advance for your kind attention,

Yours faithfully,

SCPO - Serious Crime Prevention Order

Designed to prevent or disrupt future crime, these orders are effectively personalised laws which place requirements or restrictions on ex-offenders after release from prison. Restrictions may include only having one mobile phone, one bank account, one vehicle (and to provide full details to the police), not to conduct certain types of transactions, not to carry more than £100 in cash, not to access certain websites etc.

SCPO's run separately from **licence** conditions and can continue after a licence has finished.

Suspected breaches can result in **recall** and proven breaches can result in up to 5 years in prison, based on the low, civil, rather than criminal, **burden of proof**.

SED - Sentence Expiry Date - Usually called **LED** (Licence expiry date)

SEG - Segregation Unit aka Care and Separation unit (CSU) or 'The Block.'

Single cells in a higher security part of each prison where each prisoner is subject to intense monitoring and a restricted regime.

People are sent to the Seg for many reasons, sometimes for their own protection, for control or behavioural issues or prior to being **'swagged'**. Prisoners who are the hardest to manage, who have been violent, unpredictable or involved in drug supply in the prison can be managed better in segregation where officers are able to wear body protection and follow specialist safety protocols. Generally, prisoners in the Seg get daily access to phone calls, showers, exercise and library books. Conduct and the need for segregation is regularly reviewed.

Sentencing - Deciding on the punishment

The process that a judge works through to decide the most appropriate level of punishment. There are sentencing guidelines for each offence and for the brackets (levels) of culpability.

Previous cases are researched for guidance, known as 'authority' to help with sentencing.

Consideration is given to **aggravating factors** put forwards by the prosecution and **mitigating factors** put forwards by the defence, to finally arrive at the sentence.

There is a lot of discretion in sentencing and many sentences are successfully **appealed** where they are considered to be "manifestly excessive" (too long) or unduly lenient (too short).

Spent Convictions - No longer disclosable

Convictions resulting in prison sentences of 4 years and less become spent after a certain period under The Rehabilitation of Offenders Act unless they overlap with further convictions in which case, they do not become spent until and unless the later ones do.

Spent convictions do not need to be disclosed but they may still show on Disclosure and Barring Service (**DBS**) checks. If this is the case, you may prefer to still disclose and explain your side of the story upfront.

Original news and commentary may remain accessible online and links to these may still show in search engine listings. The **Right to be Forgotten** can be used to de-index listings unless they are still deemed to be in the public interest.

SPL - Special Purpose Licence

A form of **ROTL** which can be applied for at any time during a prison sentence, purposes include attending medical appointments or funerals of close family members.

Suspended Sentence - Delayed subject to certain conditions

A prison sentence that is not served unless the convicted person commits another crime during the period of the suspended sentence.

If another sentence is ordered, then the new sentence will usually run **consecutively** to the triggered/ activated suspended sentence.

Suspended sentences count the same as normal prison sentences for **disclosure** purposes i.e. they have the same rehabilitation period before they become "spent".

Swagged - aka Ghosted/ Shipped out - Suddenly transferred between prisons

Involuntary transfers to different prisons due to security concerns or overcrowding.

These are different to resettlement or re-**categorisation** transfers which are usually nearer to home and for which the prisoner will have some limited input in the decisions. They are also different to pre-planned transfers for progression purposes e.g. to complete courses which are unavailable in the current prison.

Tariff - Minimum sentence

The minimum amount of time that **indeterminate** sentenced prisoners must spend in prison before they become eligible for **parole**.

Quotes, Memory-aids and Acronyms

"Phil Martin has a unique way of explaining things and when he talks, people listen, you can hear a pin drop."
HMP Custodial Manager

It is my intention that these quotations are clear and concise and that they ease understanding.

They may be republished and shared, subject to you attributing them to:

'Phil Martin, Author - 'The people in prison and their potential'.

I hope you have enjoyed this book and found it insightful, thank you for buying it; I hope you found it interesting enough to warrant buying further books in the series!

The meaning of life is to create meaning in your life.

Forgiveness and reconciliation are possible in an enlightened society.

The most progressive attitude to have is to treat every day as a school day.

You cannot RESTORE rational thought, until you REMOVE emotional distress.

It is possible to turn Devastation and Despair into Optimism and Opportunity.

Your CV is probably the most important personal document that you will ever create.

Leave any feelings of shame or anger in the past; these will not help you in the future.

As ex-offenders, we can either: be the statistics or beat the statistics and build a better life.

Remind yourself of this simple acronym POW! - which stands for Planning Overcomes Worry.

The biggest distance you will ever have to travel is to turn around and face a different direction.

The concept of Rehabilitative Culture can only work if we believe that everyone's life is of value.

Rehabilitation and reconciliation must replace retribution, if we are going to reduce reoffending.

We can either: see the opportunity or seize the opportunity to help people to change for the better.

I believe that helping people to change for the better is one of the most worthwhile things you can ever do.

Revenge and Retribution are not justice; Remorse, Responsibility, Rehabilitation and Reconciliation are justice.

Whether we like those people in prison or not is not relevant to whether we should help them, not relevant at all.

Rehabilitation is a process that only happens when it is supported by people, organisations and communities and by society as a whole.

The ultimate goal of Rehabilitative Culture is for people to be personally improved by the prison experience, to be better citizens when they leave.

Our country should feel desperately ashamed at how we still spit people out unwanted and virtually unsupported after giving their all, in military service.

A deficiency in skills with people is responsible, long-term, for more social isolation, depression and poverty than any external circumstances will ever be.

Significantly more help must be given to support the gradual reintegration of people released from prison, particularly those who have served long sentences.

The purpose of prison should be intuitively aimed at release day - a day when a successfully rehabilitated citizen is returned to an accepting community.

Rehabilitative Culture is not complicated; it simply needs to support all of the 7 pathways of resettlement and point towards them in every way possible.

Surely prison should be a last resort? Imprisonment is palliative; it merely manages and masks the symptoms of crime, whereas rehabilitation provides the cure.

Our prison system in this country is only doing one thing and that thing is making people worse. Prison is terrible, it really does not help people, BUT IT COULD.

It is those people who have lived experience of the Criminal Justice System who know the most effective ways to rehabilitate criminals and resettle ex-offenders.

Having a job is a massive risk reducer. Unemployment is a proven trigger that increases the likelihood of relapse for both problematic drug use and also crime.

The judgmental days full of hatred for criminals and their families must be relegated to the past if we are to end the cycles of Anger, Bitterness, Crime and Destruction.

The Justice System needs very long term thinking but frustratingly, few people of influence think or care, more than one electoral cycle or one cabinet reshuffle ahead.

If all the 5 R's of change - Remorse, Reasons, Responsibility, Rehabilitation and Reconciliation, are adopted by an individual, then change can be as permanent as if it was set in concrete.

In order to reduce the likelihood of re-offending, our prisons need to be places of healing, not places where people are traumatised and released with poorer mental health or new mental illness.

Most people in prison want to change but they need help and support to do it. Those who are chained by habit cannot usually break those chains on their own; people need help and support to change.

Nowadays, with the help of modern technology, virtually all criminals will get caught, without question. It is just a matter of time. Not if, but when. Forensic Footprints and Digital DNA are everywhere.

I define a Rehabilitative Culture as one which encourages and supports positive change and personal growth at every opportunity, and which empowers people to enjoy law-abiding, productive and fulfilling lives.

Rehabilitation manifests in reduced reoffending rates and the creation of fewer victims. If we are committed to rehabilitation, then we need to capture detailed information. We cannot improve what we do not measure.

Having a job normalises people and their lives. Normalisation is exactly what we want to happen to ex-offenders so that they can become productive and fulfilled members of society who want to, and do, follow rules and remain crime free.

ABC - Attitude, Behaviour, Consequences. Attitudes and Behaviour create Consequences. Those same Consequences then re-affect Attitude and Behaviour. The cycle spirals for better or worse until or unless, we consciously change our habitual ways of thinking and behaving.

It is a fallacy that our prisons house the very worst people in society. In fact, our prisons are full of Damaged, Disadvantaged and Disillusioned people - some of the most vulnerable in society. These 'D's are kept alongside a small minority of the worst people we hear so much about.

In order for them not to contribute to a worsening re-offending rate, modern prisons must become centres for rehabilitation and positive change. Prisons should heal people and help them to gain pride and self-worth, to feel that they can contribute and thrive, unique and valuable as they are.

Prison is a temporary home for all but the 75 prisoners serving natural life terms; the other 82,600 will all one day become eligible for release. The simple question is: "Do we want these people to be more or less likely to re-offend; more or less likely to create victims of crime, after their release?"

"Don't let it change you" is not good advice. Life's experiences and lessons are meant to change you, we are meant to be learning and growing all the time. You must let the storms of life change you. Just bear in mind that like a pebble in the sea, those same storms can either GRIND YOU DOWN or POLISH YOU UP.

Traumatic events in our lives can act like a ball and chain, keeping us stuck and holding us back, long after the events themselves have finished. Difficult life experiences leave many of us with low self-esteem, little confidence, guilt and fear. BUT no matter what has happened in your past, you can have a fulfilling future.

Compassion is not something that is earned by the recipient; it is something that is freely given by the giver. Humanity is not earned; it is something that all human beings must be shown, lest we lose our own humanity.
C.H.A.R.I.T.Y. could stand for Compassion and Humanity for All, Regardless of Imprisonment or Trouble Yesterday.

Few people acknowledge that prison destroys a person's life. If we do not help, support and empower them to build a new positive crime-free life on solid foundations, then they will inevitably be released into chaos, confusion and crime. We need to stop abandoning people on release day with no hope and nothing else to lose.

It is possible to maintain our financial health in the same amount of time it takes to care for your dental health. Our financial health can improve in the same way that our oral hygiene, our wellbeing and confidence improve, by carrying out a simple process for a few minutes each day. Therefore, I call daily cash-flow management and planning - The Toothbrush Method.

Daily Diplomacy™; literally developing good skills with people does not mean that you need to change who you are as a person. You just need to become consciously aware of the dynamics of human interactions, to learn a few simple shortcuts and strategies, and make a sincere effort with other people. This is like pouring oil on the gears and cogs of life, making everything run easier and more smoothly.

I am convinced that we could do a far better job than we do at present, of raising children in the care system to feel that they have an identity, that they can contribute to society and that they are valued. It is essential that we put steps in place to reduce the institutionalisation and abdication of responsibility that children in care experience, so that as young adults they do not develop the subconscious yearning to return to an institutional life i.e. prison.

I believe that housing should be treated as an essential utility - I would ask why people in our country are protected from having their water supply disconnected (they cannot legally be left without running water) yet they can have their housing disconnected and be left without a roof over their heads? Perhaps this is an oversimplification but why the difference in policies? What help is running water with no home? Surely a modest home and protection from the elements is a basic human right - as essential a utility as water?

Many members of our society determinately hang on the outdated assumption that all prisoners are evil, wicked and cruel, a sub-species of humanity that is beyond any hope of reformation. They believe that the people in prison deserve neither compassion nor support and at best should be shunned or met with disinterest. Before grouping all prisoners together however we should consider that the majority of people in our prisons are not there for crimes against a person (including violence, sexual harm and robbery) Source: House of Commons, Prison Population July 2019. When we look deeper into the circumstances and the minority of those perpetrators who have committed crimes against a person, most would still not merit the label 'evil'.

We have now entered an era where someone can make a mistake, break the law and be punished. Then pay the price that those who are most qualified to decide (the judges), have said they must pay. Despite having served their time however, they and their family still suffer for their crime for decades because the internet never forgets. You may ask, "Aren't you curious, wouldn't you like to know about someone?" and I agree; that is why we have DBS checks, so that when it is absolutely necessary to know, we will know. When it is not absolutely necessary, we should not know. We should not have the opportunity to pre-judge someone based on their past. Whatever happened to someone paying their debt to society? There must be a time by which one sided media reports are archived and third-party keyboard warriors are silenced, so that people can at least have a chance to build a life and contribute to society.

Memory Aids and Acronyms

6 Steps to take before attending a job interview — P.R.O.P.E.R.
(From: How to Get a Great Job When You Have a Criminal Record)

| Plan | Research | Organise | Prepare | Enquire | Rehearse |

The 5 Primary ELEMENTS of EMPLOYABILITY — Q.U.E.S.T.
(From: How to Get a Great Job When You Have a Criminal Record)

| Qualifications | Understanding | Experience | Specialist Skills | Transferable Skills |

The Purpose of Prison — S.C.R.A.P.P.E.D.
(From: If Criminals Can Change Then So Should Society)

| Safety | Change | Remand | Assistance | Punishment | Profit | Example | Deterrent |

The New Purpose of Prison / Essential Elements of Ex-Offending — A.T.R.E.H.A.B.
(From: If Criminals Can Change Then So Should Society)

| Addiction | Thinking | Relationships | Employment | Health | Accommodation | Budgeting |

The People in Prison — D.A.M.A.G.E.D.
(From: The People in Prison and Their Potential)

| Desperation | Addiction | Mental illness | Accident | Greed | Evil | Disillusioned |

10 areas of Disillusionment Predicting Prison — T.H.E.N.P.O.L.I.C.E.
(From: The People in Prison and Their Potential)

| Trauma | Homelessness | Education | Nothing (to lose) | Parenting |
| Opportunity | Law | Inequality | Care | Enlisted |

The Vital Role of Faith and Pastoral Care in Prison — F.A.I.T.H.C.A.R.E.
(From: The People in Prison and Their Potential)

| Fellowship | Acceptance | Inspiration | Teaching | Help |
| Community | Accountability | Rehabilitation | Empathy |

6 Primary Drivers for Personal Development in Prison
(From: The People in Prison and Their Potential)

I.M. P.A.S.T. I.T

Intervention	Mentors	Pain	Age
Self-Image	Time	Incentives	Training

The 7 Primary Transferable Skills
(From: How to Get a Great Job When You Have a Criminal Record)

IT skills	Functional skills	Work ethic	Organisational skills
Skills with people (interpersonal skills)		Problem solving skills	Mind-set management

The A B C D staircase of job progression
(From: How to Get a Great Job When You Have a Criminal Record)

Dream Job
Career Job
Better Job
Any Job

NB: This ABCD is widely used and was not originated by the author

The 5 R's of Change

R1	Remorse	I am sorry for what I did, and I do regret my crime(s).
R2	Reasons	I understand the background circumstances and my personal buttons/ triggers well enough that I can explain to others.
R3	Responsibility	I admit that it is my fault and I am not passing the blame.
R4	Rehabilitation	I will not do it again; I have learnt lessons and changed.
R5	Reconciliation	I want to make up for what I did wrong and contribute.

20 ways that people change for the better in prison
(From: The People in Prison and Their Potential)

1. Tolerance	2. Future goals	3. Personal fitness	4. Caring for others
5. Appreciation of family	6. Personal development	7. Overcoming addictions	
8. Personal responsibility	9. Emotional intelligence	10. Counselling and therapy	
11. Contribution and community		12. Functional skills education	
13. Higher/ further education		14. Leadership and mentoring	
15. Charity awareness and fundraising		16. Work ethic, skills and experience	
17. Work (vocational) qualifications		18. Understanding wider impact of crime	
19. Understanding criminal urges and triggers		20. Sharing lessons learnt to discourage crime	

The ABC of Creating a Rehabilitative Culture
(From: If Criminals Can Change Then So Should Society)

A	**Allocate** time, money and resources.
B	**Believe** that change is possible.
C	**Care** and show compassion, allow yourself to feel empathy.
D	**Decide** "I am here to change lives".
E	**Examples** to follow.
F	**Find** their motivation.
G	**Give** people opportunities to grow and develop.
H	**Help** prisoners and practically support them.
I	**Individualise** your approaches.
J	**Journey** with prisoners.
K	**Knowledge** is important and should be shared with others.
L	**Look** for good, praise and encourage.
M	**Make** the effort. RC is hard work and a difficult process.
N	**Never** give up on anyone.
O	**Organise**.
P	**Pathways** to resettlement are ready to be followed.
Q	**Question** everything.
R	**Relationships** are to be valued.
S	**Sustainably** implement each new policy.
T	**Test** prisoners.
U	**Underutilised** is the prison population.
V	**Victims** should be involved.
W	**Windows** of opportunity are what we have.
X	**X-Offenders**. Okay it should be spelt ex-offenders, but the point is the same!
Y	**You** have the power.
Z	**Zero** deaths in custody, zero self-harming and zero re-offending are the only acceptable figures; anything else needs investigating and understanding.

Today I have a CHOICE. My choice is to be...   **C.H.O.I.C.E.**
(From: 'Your Positive Life After Prison (or any other apocalypse)'

Confident	Happy	Optimistic	Inspiring	Caring	Enthusiastic

Books by the Author

"With the right resources and the right motivation, it is not that difficult to help most prisoners to prepare for release and to live crime free lives after release. People need somewhere to live (home), something constructive to do (job), something to eat and wear (basic needs met), health care and a support network of crime free family and/or friends."

CK, HMP Senior Officer - 22 years' service

The author has produced the **Prison Pathways** series of books with the sincere desire to reduce re-offending and improve outcomes for society.

An easy-to-follow and proven system which helps ex-offenders secure meaningful employment that provides structure and stability in their lives.

120,000 words, 360 pages generously printed in an easy to use A4 workbook.

£14.97   ISBN: 9781 696 100 205

e-book also available via Amazon

"This book will be a huge asset to those that are taking that very difficult step to move away from a life of crime, which becomes an addictive and powerful vortex."

Tariq Usmani MBE

"It is no exaggeration to call this book a masterpiece. Phil Martin's step by step guide should be in every prison library and every job centre. If the MOJ gave a copy of this book to everyone leaving prison the costs saved by preventing reoffending would be significant."

Trevor Chrich, SSAFA

Benefit from the author's experience of employing ex-offenders and of establishing and running a careers department for serving prisoners. In this invaluable book you will discover:

- Full guidance on improving employability.
- The legal framework for disclosure and employment.
- How to prepare for interviews and then interview well.
- How to maintain employment and manage your money.
- How to be self-employed or operate your own business, legally and profitably.
- How to use the 'CV Builder' system to easily create a clear and professional CV.
- Using 'Grant Builder' to secure grants for education, training and employment.
- How to use 'Application Builder' to successfully apply for jobs on and off-line.
- How to use the 'Disclosure Builder' system to turn a negative criminal record into a positive Personal Disclosure Statement that inspires.
- More than 500 easy to use templates (including the skills and experience gained from 100 prison jobs and 200 conventional jobs) to copy and amend to suit.

Includes free support for people in prison to draft their employment documents and an invitation to register with Ex-seed™ the specialist recruitment network for ex-offenders.

Preface by the Rt. Hon. Lord Wilson,
Justice of the Supreme Court of the United Kingdom

A unique work which reveals insights into a wide range of Criminal Justice issues, stimulates discussion on the real purpose of prison and explains how prison could absolutely reduce reoffending, leading to the creation of fewer victims of crime.

90,000 words, 250 pages
£9.97   ISBN: 9781 696 356 565
e-book also available via Amazon

"I am full of admiration for your work on If Criminals Can Change and I wish you every success for its publication." Stephen Fry, Actor, Author, Presenter and ex-offender

"I would be more than happy to be quoted in your excellent book. Very best wishes." Diane Curry OBE, CEO POPS Charity

"So few people seem to understand the appalling state of our prisons or the amazing work - despite those conditions - that is still undertaken in prison. I congratulate you on managing to both research and write such a book whilst still in prison." Jon Snow, Presenter, Channel 4 News

As you read through this ground-breaking work, you will discover:

- The problems with the current prison system and how to solve them.
- How prison could find a new purpose as an effective tool for rehabilitation.
- The challenges faced by people in prison when trying to change for the better.
- The crisis facing our overwhelmed prison system and the tragic consequences.
- More than 200 real accounts from people who broke the law and lessons they learned.
- The flaws within our Criminal Justice System that contains institutional barriers to rehabilitation and which unfortunately encourage crime.
- Why many people who want to change struggle to remain crime free after release from prison and how positive change could be better supported.
- The ABC of Creating a Rehabilitative Culture, a simple manual for how prisons could create a culture that encourages and supports rehabilitation.
- Author's commentary based on questions asked and focussing on how, with a set of progressive changes, our prisons system could really work well for society.

**Foreword by His Honour John Samuels QC,
President, Prisoners' Education Trust**

An uplifting book which reveals the potential of prison to help people change for the better

90,000 words,

240 pages

£9.97

ISBN: 9781 696 356 886

e-book also available via Amazon

"The book that stopped me resigning from the prison service. I was reminded why I originally chose this career - to help that one person, to change one life each day." MF

"The most well-articulated, easiest to understand and best presented argument for prison reform in my lifetime" RL

"By 2019 I had become so fed up with warehousing people - locking them up and only moving them around so that they don't hurt each other (or themselves). Working in a resettlement prison in open conditions is my dream job because now I can actually make a difference and help people to turn their lives around."

HMP Governor 28 years' experience

Coming Soon...

A light hearted and easy to follow book, containing strategies which help people who are emerging from personal crises, to live happy and productive lives.

Includes the author's personal story as well as numerous inspiring accounts of people who have built lives of meaning and purpose after imprisonment.

Have you ever felt like your life was over? Even in our darkest times we can be reminded that there is still a purpose to our life and that one snapshot in time does not reflect an entire life.

Not everyone in society believes in revenge and karma, many instead believe in forgiveness and redemption. Labels do not need to define you. There is more to you than your mistakes and you still have more to give.

We all have that chance of a new life, a new chapter in our lives, with the past firmly in the past we can move forwards with positivity and hope, a new feeling of gratitude and appreciation for each day and wanting to make a contribution. Your life still has value and purpose and this book will help you find yours.

About the Author

Phil Martin is a family orientated businessman and the founder of Ex-seed™ - the recruitment network dedicated to placing ex-offenders into employment.

Phil is a widely consulted authority on the rehabilitation of prisoners and resettlement of ex-offenders.

'The ABC of Creating a Rehabilitative Culture' (from his book entitled *'If Criminals Can Change Then So Should Society'*) has now been repurposed by HMPPS Rehabilitative Culture Team to form part of a national training programme for prison officers.

In May 2019 Phil met with then Justice Secretary, David Gauke, to discuss the employment of serving and released prisoners, rehabilitation within prisons and effective resettlement after release; particularly focussing on ways to reduce reoffending and create fewer victims of crime.

He is a memorable public speaker and is frequently invited to talk at rehabilitative culture conferences, third sector events and award ceremonies. He has changed lives and inspired audiences at a range of prisons including HMP's Brixton, Coldingley, Lincoln, Springhill, Stafford, Stocken and Woodhill.

Phil is also in demand at business conferences and workshops where he speaks about strategy, mind-set, motivation and change. He has shared insights at several hundred property investment events, networking groups and self-improvement seminars. He offers business consultancy and personal mentoring, by referral only, to a small number of clients each year, both individually and in group training settings.

Phil is known for simplifying complicated subjects, sharing practical tips, for inspiring people to break through comfort zones and create turning points in their lives.

In 2025, by merging his earlier expertise in the property sector with his lived experience of the needs of ex-offenders, Phil intends to begin purpose-building and nationally providing supported housing and temporary homes for ex-offenders and homeless people.

Phil is a devoted family man with a wife, their five daughters and two grandsons.

Feedback, comments and questions are welcomed. These can be submitted by email to info@philmartin.co.uk or post to Philip Martin t/as Ex-seed™ 5 Crabtree Dive, Northampton NN3 5DR.

"It was great to meet you Phil, what you are doing is truly inspiring!" HMP Governor

"Phil Martin is very inspiring and caring about people and wants to help make positive changes in people's lives." Serving Prisoner

"The talk you delivered on faith provision and pastoral care in prisons was the highlight of this regional event."
Prison Chaplaincy Development Manager

"When Phil delivered his talk called 'Your New Chapter' he was like a breath of fresh air to the residents and staff in attendance." HMP Regional Education Manager

"Phil Martin has a unique way of explaining things and when he talks, people listen, you can hear a pin drop." HMP Custodial Manager

"Your workshop called 'Your Problem-Solving Action Plan' was excellently written Phil, you kept all the men engaged and involved and filled them with confidence and positivity. Well done a good day was had by everyone!" Prison College Tutor

"Phil Martin delivered two talks about Rehab Culture, change and self-worth at our annual award ceremony at HMP Stafford. He was truly inspiring to the residents, the staff and honoured guests. Well done Phil - you smashed it!" HMP Governor

"I was in prison, stuck with no release date. Phil was a company director at the time, he spoke at my parole hearing and helped me to get out of prison straight into a full-time job; I have been out for 14 years since then and have not reoffended." MJ, a former prisoner

"Mr Martin gave an outstanding motivational speech to a packed auditorium at HMP Stocken. He was asked at the last minute and multiple groups joined the session along with numerous members of staff. He did not bat an eye-lid and inspired us all." HMP College Manager

"Thank you very much for participating in the interview for Prison Service Journal. It was a great experience to hear you talking with such insight and sensitivity. I believe that it will be well received when published and will help to promote rehabilitative cultures." HMP Governor

"You have played an important role in supporting the work of HMP Springhill towards Enabling Environment Accreditation, building the culture required to sustain this and demonstrating our shared commitment. The assessment day was a really inspiring session to be involved in. I offer you my personal thanks for your contribution." HMP Governor

"I really love the guide to creating a rehabilitative culture you've created. This is brilliantly and imaginatively presented, using the alphabet, with entries from A to Z and in your usual accessible style. I have distributed this to the National Rehabilitative Culture Team to be used as a resource for staff induction. I am so grateful to you for your work on this document and really appreciate your generosity with your talents." HMP Governor

"Philip Martin spoke at HMP Brixton about rehabilitation. The event was attended by representatives from 5 London jails including Governors and Operational Staff. His presentation was excellent and his content inspirational; he spoke about his experiences of rehabilitative culture and how staff can have had a big impact on the people in their care. He also produced quality hand-outs for all of the attendees to take away. Overall, the day was a big success." HMP Custodial Manager

Thank you for purchasing and reading this book, please be kind enough to leave a review, which will be really appreciated.

You can also tweet @philmartinuk or contact me via www.PhilMartin.co.uk

Printed in Great Britain
by Amazon